SATHER CLASSICAL LECTURES

VOLUME FOURTEEN

1938

PLATONISM
ANCIENT AND MODERN

PLATONISM

Ancient and Modern

BY

PAUL SHOREY

UNIVERSITY OF CALIFORNIA PRESS
BERKELEY, CALIFORNIA
1938

UNIVERSITY OF CALIFORNIA PRESS
BERKELEY, CALIFORNIA

———————

CAMBRIDGE UNIVERSITY PRESS
LONDON, ENGLAND

PRINTED IN THE UNITED STATES OF AMERICA

PREFACE

PAUL SHOREY was three times Sather Professor of Classical Literature in the University of California: in 1916-1917, in 1918-1919, and again in 1928-1929. On the last occasion he gave eight lectures on the history of Platonism.

Before 1921 it was not the custom to publish the Sather Classical Lectures, but in that year a series of annual volumes was begun. At the time of Professor Shorey's death, April 24, 1934, the manuscript of his lectures on the history of Platonism was not ready for the press: the text of the seven lectures which make up the present volume was reasonably complete and there were memoranda for the footnotes, but the introductory lecture "What Is Platonism?" could not have been made ready for print by any other than the author. The task of preparing the manuscript and seeing it through the press was entrusted to Dr. Procope S. Costas, of Whitman College, a former pupil of Professor Shorey and for several years his research assistant, who was thoroughly acquainted with the material actually on hand and with the plans for its revision and completion. Dr. Costas' unremitting effort, his meticulous accuracy, and his learning have made it possible to offer a text which will be instantly recognized as authentic by those who are familiar with Professor Shorey's views and with his characteristic style and methods of exposition. The Editors wish to acknowledge their great indebtedness to Dr. Costas, and also to thank the Editor of the University of California Press, Mr. Harold A. Small, for the great help he has given in a difficult task.

Had Professor Shorey lived to complete the work of revision, he would undoubtedly have made additional changes in order to accommodate the text to the medium of print. As the text stands, it is truly the spoken word, and it is incomplete in that it needs the voice, the personality, the nice inflections, the careful phrasing, the abundant vitality of Shorey. This incompleteness all will regret; but all will be glad—especially all Platonists—that what we have here has been preserved. Καὶ γὰρ τὸ μεμνῆσθαι Σωκράτους καὶ αὐτὸν λέγοντα καὶ ἄλλου ἀκούοντα ἔμοιγε ἀεὶ πάντων ἥδιστον.

THE EDITORS

BERKELEY, CALIFORNIA
APRIL 24, 1938

CONTENTS

The supposed portrait of Plato decorating the title page of this volume is taken from H. A. J. Munro's Horatii Opera (London, 1869) illustrated by C. W. King. The original is part of a representation of the busts of Socrates and Plato, engraved on a sardonyx of the great Paris collection. The engraved head is about one-half the size of the present reproduction.

CHAPTER I

PLATO AND ANTIQUITY

THE IMPACT of Plato on his own time and on the *fin-de-siècle* Athens of the fourth century is hard to estimate from lack of evidence. One late writer says that little attention was paid him during his lifetime, but this can hardly be true. Neither Plato nor Shakespeare could loom as large to contemporaries as they do to us through the mists of time. For, to change the figure, the comet has grown a luminous tail. His defense of Socrates, the moral eloquence of the *Gorgias* and the *Phaedo*, the philosophy of love and beauty in the *Symposium*, the daring social speculations of the *Republic*, must have stirred thoughtful minds and actually did move Isocrates to feeble emulation, as Wordsworth's success with the poetry of nature moved Byron's rivalry. If we knew the life of the fourth century and the age that followed more intimately, we should perceive further traces of the effects of Plato's educational and social ideas as set forth in the *Republic* and the *Laws*. These ideas have much to do with the organization of the Athenian ephebic schools[1] known to us in many later inscriptions and in a series of portrait statues of Athenian superintendents of education which show that even Greeks could not make objects of aesthetic contemplation out of superintendents of education.

Aristophanes' *Ladies in Parliament* may or may not have been a satire on the Platonic emancipation of women.[2] But there are enough references in the fragments of the middle comedy[3] to Plato and his school to show that he had, in American parlance, made the front page. Plato was a rather magnificent and dignified personage, and his pupils were often young men of wealth and high birth. In spite of this, or perhaps because of this, the Academy seems to have re-

[1] Superior figures refer to notes which will be found on pp. 239-240.

ceived more attention from the "yellow press" than the school
of Isocrates. The "yellow press" was the middle comedy,
which herein was a worthy successor of the old comedy that
had scareheaded the teaching of Socrates. A few specimens
would show that there is nothing original in the modern
newspaper's conception of what goes on in a university
classroom. In his later years Plato became much interested
in the theory of scientific classification and definition. From
Plato's highly specialized work are derived the logic of Aristotle and the entire terminology of science and philosophy.
That again is another story. But here is the *Athenian Examiner's* report of a lecture on the subject at the Platonic university:

What's Plato doing now? Come tip us
A word about the wise Speusippus
And the exploits of Menedemus
In olive groves of Academus.
What problem and what quest engages
The minds of those Platonic sages?
I'm well informed, for t'other day
It happened that I passed that way
And entering in to hear a lecture
Saw marvels there beyond conjecture.
The lads of the Academy
Were studying natural history
By dialectic to determine
The species of all beasts and vermin,
And every shrub and vegetable
As logically as they were able.
And the first problem of the number
Was to define a big cucumber.
For a long time no word was said
But every lad with bended head
Stood lost in deepest concentration
Of logical excogitation.
Then one, the quickest of the class,
Spoke up: "It is a kind of grass."

The next said "Vine" and number three
Affirmed it was a sort of tree,
While the fourth cried, "Professor Plato,
It's an elongated, green potato."
At this with loud and rude guffaw
A medical student cried, "Ah, bah!
Who ever heard such senseless drivel!"
The which, methinks, was scarcely civil.
But those nice boys were not offended,
And Plato courteously pretended
He had not heard the rude remark
And bade the boys resume their work
Of logical dichotomy
Of bird and beast and fish and tree.
And so I left him still presiding
Over defining and dividing.

> Epicrates *frg.* 11 (Kock, *Com. gr. Fr.* II pp. 287-288;
> Meineke III pp. 370-371)

The names mentioned in Plato's own writings are mainly those of his boyhood and the preceding generation.[4] He satirizes many tendencies in the thought of his contemporaries, but usually without naming them. We need not consider the too ingenious theory that contemporaries are masked and meant by the earlier names. Plato's satirical vein was the theme of much comment in antiquity, and perhaps the chief source of that tradition of anti-Platonism of which the history has been written in a German and in a Chicago doctor's dissertation[5] and to which, without dwelling on the detail, I shall occasionally allude. This tone of superiority and satire still gives offense to some modern readers, as for example to Mr. John Jay Chapman, who says that Plato's fault is that he writes as if thought were a game and he knew the rules of the game.[6] My answer to that would be that Plato does know the rules as no other writer has ever known them, and that though he sometimes jests and toys with ideas, he knows how to be nobly serious on all the serious issues of life and thought.

Plato's references to the four leading contemporaries in Greek literature are few. Xenophon does not mention Plato, but obviously took many suggestions for his *Memorabilia of Socrates* from the minor Socratic dialogues.[7] Plato mentions Xenophon but once. Xenophon wrote a long and dull book on the education of Cyrus, and Plato somewhere (*Laws* 694 C) dryly remarks that Cyrus has the worst education on record. This has given rise to a German dissertation on the quarrel between Xenophon and Plato.[8] Nothing has escaped the German professor's quest for subjects for doctor's dissertations. There is a monograph, which I have read, on Aristophanes' fit of hiccups in Plato's *Banquet*.[9]

The orator Lysias and his family are pleasantly mentioned in the introduction to the *Republic* (328 B). The *Phaedrus* begins with a playful account of the walk of Socrates and Phaedrus, an enthusiastic admirer of Lysias, by the banks of the Ilissus, just outside of Athens, and Phaedrus' description of an essay of Lysias which he had been studying with the author all that morning. Its theme, in modern terminology, was the heart-to-heart-talk problem whether it is better to marry with or without passionate love. The · essay is read aloud. Socrates extemporizes a match for it on the same level and then, in repentance, a higher and more poetic gospel of love resembling that in the *Symposium*. The three speeches are then made the subject of a broad discussion of rhetoric and the art of writing in relation to life, logic, and philosophy. Socrates censures Lysias' speech as composed of commonplaces and possessing so little necessary sequence of thought that it would read just as well backwards as forwards, like the famous inscription on the tomb of Midas,[10] which he quotes:

> I am a maiden of brass, I lie on the tomb of Midas;
> While the breezes blow and the waters flow and the
>   tall trees grow,
> I say unto all that pass, Here lies buried Midas.
> I am a maiden of brass, I lie on the tomb of Midas.

Diog. Laert. 1. 89 (attributed to Cleobulus)

The dialogue closes with a recommendation to Lysias to study philosophy like his brother.

One of the most eminent of Plato's contemporaries was the orator or publicist Isocrates, who for some fifty years conducted a rival school to Plato's so-called Academy,[11] and who has left us two volumes of excellent but commonplace Attic prose composed of orations, essays, or, as we might style them, magazine articles on political, social, ethical, and educational questions of the day. The writings of two such contemporaries naturally contain allusions to each other. Philologians have spent or wasted not a little ingenuity in the endeavor to construct an exact chronology of these seeming cross references. It cannot be done. But it is possible to state more clearly than is customary their essential significance. Isocrates was evidently emulous and a little jealous and envious of Plato.He tries in his own tamer fashion to emulate the moral fervor of the *Gorgias,* and he apparently copies some of the motives and ideas of the *Republic.* But he persists in employing Plato's word philosophy for his own ideal of education and culture. He maliciously or ignorantly confounds Platonic dialectic and metaphysic with the eristic logic-chopping and verbal fencing of the sophists. He ironically disclaims all pretensions to the metaphysical certainty that was the aim of Platonic dialectic, and he contrasts his own practical education in the writing of Greek, in the acquisition of a good Greek style and the serious discussion of contemporary politics and life, with the Platonic discipline in mathematics and dialectics, which he damns with the faint praise that it does no harm and may keep the boys out of mischief. Plato, on the other hand, cannot but be aware of his own crushing intellectual superiority and sometimes adopts a tone of condescension which must have been very irritating. His one mention of Isocrates by name is complimentary. At the end of the *Phaedrus* (278 E-279 A), Socrates sends by Phaedrus a message to Isocrates. There is a kind of philosophy in the man which if he will continue to cultivate it will make other contemporary rhetoricians or orators seem children in comparison with him. At the end of the *Euthydemus* (304 E), however, there is reference to Isocrates no less explicit, though not by name, in a tone of condescension, not to say disparagement. The passage is also worth noting because it brings out a point in Plato's own thought which is often overlooked. Some scholars deny this, but the parody of Isocrates' style is unmistakable.[12]

Plato's relations with Dionysius and Sicily have been exhaustively treated by various scholars.[13] The list of his students and their achievements in literature and politics have been studied by specialists. They include Dion, who liberated Sicily from the tyranny of Dionysius; Heracleides Ponticus, a versatile and encyclopedic writer, often quoted by Cicero; Eudoxus, the founder of the science of astronomy and the first historian of the science; Speusippus; Xenocrates; Philip of Opus, who, according to Diogenes Laertius and Suidas, edited the *Laws* and wrote the *Epinomis*; and Aristotle.[14]

Aristotle studied with Plato twenty years.[15] His writings show that he must have carried in his head or in notebooks an exhaustive index of the Platonic dialogues. There are few sentences and almost no pages of Aristotle that can be fully understood without reference to the specific passages of Plato of which he was thinking as he wrote. And as no medieval Aristotelian could know Plato, and few modern Aristotelians have the patience to know him intimately, Aristotelians as a class only half understand their author.

Aristotle mentions Plato explicitly most often when he dissents. Perhaps because he had an overdose of Platonism in his twenty years' discipleship, he seems to prefer to dissent. He cannot let the doctrine of ideas alone. In one of his earlier lost works (*frg*. 8 Rose) he is reported as saying that though some critics might think him contentious he found it impossible to sympathize with that doctrine. In his *Ethics* he goes out of his way, as he often does, to attack it with the remark that it hurts him dreadfully to do so but that truth is dearer even than a friend. From this passage is derived the saying, "Socrates is dear, Plato is dear, but truth is dearer still."[16] In his *Metaphysics* his impatience overcomes him, and he exclaims with more vigor than philosophic dignity: "As for the eternal Platonic ideas, they are just piffle and hot air."[17] Elsewhere he delights in rehabilitating the sophists and pre-Socratics in answer to Plato's criticism of them. In the *Gorgias* Plato satirizes one Polus, who talked of experience somewhat as Professor John Dewey does. Plato makes Polus begin a paragraph: "O Socrates, there are many sciences among mankind, from experience experientially derived" (448 C). Aristotle observes: "Science or knowledge is the outcome of many experiences as Polus says, and rightly says" (*Met.* 981 a 4-5). In the *Meno* (71 E) Meno not understanding Socrates' demand for a definition of virtue gives an enumeration instead of a definition and says there are many virtues, the virtue of a man, a governor, a woman, a child, and so forth, and Socrates ironically compliments him on his generosity in presenting him with a whole swarm of virtues when he asked for only one. Aristotle picks up an implied definition of Plato elsewhere and comments: "It will be better to enumerate the virtues than to define them in that way" (*Pol.* 1260 a 20-27). In spite of this captiousness, Aristotle was really devoted to his teacher, and even wrote a poem about him, which is somewhat as if Herbert Spencer had written a poem in praise of John Stuart Mill.[18]

Aristotle's criticism of Plato has been passionately impugned as unfair, and as earnestly defended. The temperamental differences between the two men and the divergences in their thought due to Aristotle's special studies in biology have been frequently discussed. The aphorism that every man is born either a Platonist or an Aristotelian[19] is broadly true, yet not for the reasons usually alleged in its support. It is not true that Plato is a dreamer and Aristotle a student of fact and reality. It is not true that Aristotle is a reasoner and Plato a mystic and enthusiast. It is true that Plato is a reasoner, an artist, a poet, a mathematician, and a symbolist, while Aristotle is a logician, a biologist, a classifier, and an encyclopedist. And with these generalizations I must dismiss a topic the further discussion of which would plunge us at once into an infinity of technical detail.

After the immediate influence of Plato and Aristotle was spent, we find no great speculative movement before the time of the commentators on Aristotle and the rise of Neo-Platonism two hundred years after Christ. This, of course, is my opinion, and is a flat contradiction of Professor Murray's statement that Stoicism is "the greatest system of organized thought which the mind of man had built up for itself in the Greco-Roman world before the coming of Christianity."[20] The history of philosophy in the interim is the story of the four or five schools which every schoolboy used to know, before the substitution of James Whitcomb Riley and Carl Sandburg for Milton in our teaching of English literature, from Milton's description in *Paradise Regained* IV 272-280:

> To sage philosophy next lend thine ear,
> From heaven descended to the low-roof'd house
> Of Socrates; see there his tenement
> Whom well inspir'd the oracle pronounc'd
> Wisest of men; from whose mouth issu'd forth
> Mellifluous streams that water'd all the schools
> Of Academics old and new, with those
> Surnam'd Peripatetics, and the sect
> Epicurean, and the Stoic severe.

I must refer the reader to special monographs, histories of education, and encyclopedias, for the external history of these schools, their endowments, their conjectured organization as religious foundations, their patronage by the Roman emperors, who endowed chairs in them,[21] the more or less continuous succession of their superintendents or scholarchs, their studies and the life of their pupils, and the imposing continuity of the Platonic Academy in particular, which after nearly eight centuries was closed by order of the emperor.[22] We shall be sufficiently occupied with the relation of Plato's thought to these schools and to the culture of those eight centuries.

The relation of Plato to the skeptical school need not detain us long. Pyrrho, who gave his name to that school, wrote nothing, and the literature of the school, if it may be called a school, is now represented by the volume of the physician Sextus Empiricus who lived about two hundred years after Christ. It is an immense repertory of all possible skeptical arguments, ancient or modern, good or bad. It quotes everything in Plato and in all the philosophic literature of antiquity that could possibly be given a skeptical twist, and its influence probably on the Middle Ages and certainly on the Renaissance is far greater than the current histories of philosophy recognize.[23] But for ancient culture as a whole the chief representatives of philosophic skepticism were the successors of Plato in the so-called Middle and New Academy, who elaborated the arguments for skepticism in controversy with the dogmatists of the Stoic school. This misled an eminent scholar into saying in his account of Zeno, the founder of Stoicism, that "the Sceptical school of philosophy, largely helped by Plato, had lately been active in denying the possibility of human knowledge and throwing doubt on the very existence of reality."[24] Cicero professed himself a disciple of this new skeptical Academy which he thought was not untrue to the spirit of Plato. He limited

his skepticism, however, to the hypotheses of physical science and the ultimates of metaphysics. He drew the line at
the Constitution of the United States and the Ten Com-
mandments. This philosophy, expounded in Cicero's *Aca-
demica*, exercised a still greater influence on subsequent
European thought than the obscure and ponderous treatise
of Sextus Empiricus. Written in fluent, easy Latin, it was
accessible to all educated men for many centuries. Even in
the Middle Ages, *academicus*, I think, is quite as likely to
mean skeptic as to mean Platonist. It means that, I believe,
when Abélard professes himself an *academicus*, and the
learned medievalist Reginald Poole is therefore probably
mistaken in quoting the passage to prove that Abélard regarded himself as a Platonist.

    With this historical perspective in mind, we need only re-
call and enumerate the chief skeptical elements in Plato's
own writings. First, and most obviously, there is the Socratic profession of ignorance, and the fact that the minor
dialogues, including also such masterpieces as the *Protagoras*,
the *Theaetetus*, and the first book of the *Republic* reach no
positive conclusion, and end with this expression of complete bafflement on the part of the leader of the discussion.
Grote and John Stuart Mill, indeed, regard this negative
and critical aspect of the Platonic writings as their most
valuable teaching and a still needed warning against over-
hasty dogmatism. Then, there is the fact that Plato himself
has no metaphysical system; from which, and from his satire
of the pre-Socratic and contemporary systems, it may be
plausibly inferred that he viewed all system-building skep-
tically.[25] This was certainly his attitude towards all pseudo
sciences such as the science of mythology, of which Socrates says when asked by Phaedrus if he believes in the legend
of Boreas and Orithyia, "It would be nothing strange if like
our wise men I disbelieved it," and then, rationalizing it,
"I might say that the blast of the North Wind hurled her

down from the rocks when she was playing with Pharmaceia, and that so it came to pass that she was said to have been carried off by the enamored Boreas. Now I, Phaedrus, think these speculations most delightful, but they are the affair of a laborious man and one not altogether fortunate in that he will thereupon have to psychoanalyze and rationalize the whole tribe of Gorgons and Hydras and Chimaeras dire and other monstrous tales. And if in his skepticism he shall try to force a plausible interpretation on all of them this rustic wisdom of his will demand no little leisure. And I have no leisure, for I have never yet been able to fulfill the Delphic injunction and know myself. And it seems to me an absurdity, while still ignorant of this, to inquire into unconcerning things. So I dismiss them, and, believing what is customary about them, I investigate and study not these things, but myself, trying to discover whether in my true nature I am a more complicated and a more befogged and fume-filled beast than any typhon huge ending in smoky twine, or whether I am a gentler and simpler creature participant of a diviner destiny and liberated from the fumes of illusion and passion."[26]

What we now call the real sciences were in Plato's day little more than conjectures, and he treats them as such throughout his one work on science, the *Timaeus*. Again, Plato's very fairness of mind and literary cleverness could be used as an argument to prove him a skeptic. As I have already pointed out, he states the case of the doctrine that he repudiates so plausibly as to disconcert his own adherents. Notable examples are the utilitarian or hedonistic argument of Socrates in the *Protagoras*, which was adopted by Epicurus, and which Grote and Mill regard as an admirable and conclusive analysis;[27] the exposition of the philosophy of flux in the *Theaetetus* (166-168), which modern pragmatists still innocently attribute to Plato himself; and the restatement at the opening of the second book of the

Republic of the case against morals which Mill says is a "monument to the fairness of Plato's mind." This played a great part in the historical development of the skepticism of the Academy. The Academician Carneades, visiting Rome as ambassador of Athens in the year 156-5 B.C., lectured one day in defense of justice to the approval of Cato the censor, and the next day, to his disgust, took the other side.[28] Hence Cicero sometimes repeats that the practice of arguing both sides of a thesis was genuinely Platonic.

A refined skepticism might even draw an argument from the two-sided personality of the Platonic Socrates, who is all things to all men, and at one time speaks and acts on an ideal plane and at another apparently, if perhaps ironically, adapts himself to his company and talks like a man of the world. Then there is an important point which nearly all the histories of philosophy persistently overlook. The attentive reader who looks below the surface will find that Plato usually limits his dogmatic affirmation to one or two elementary principles of logic or morals. He concludes nearly all his subtlest speculations, his myths, and his symbolisms with some such formula as this: "The rest I would not positively affirm; of this only I am sure." And that of which he is sure proves to be only some indispensable presupposition of elementary logic or ethics.[29]

Even in religion Plato's attitude sometimes seems equivocal. "Does Matthew Arnold believe in God?" someone asked Frederic Harrison. "No, but he keeps one in his backyard to sick on people he doesn't like," he answered. That drastic way of putting it would be an even grosser exaggeration for Plato than for Matthew Arnold. Plato usually speaks even of the popular religion with unction, being unwilling to disturb the faith of simple souls. He is, as we shall repeatedly note in this history, the chief and best source of ethical and natural religion throughout European literature. He is unsparing in his satire of pert, confident, and dogmatic atheism and materialism. And yet, when, like Matthew Arnold, he turns his satire from atheists to fundamentalists, he cuts very deep and goes farther perhaps in the direction of skepticism than he intends. Two notable passages will suffice for illustration. The first is his ironical recitation of the thirty-nine articles in the *Timaeus*. After his description of the eternal divinities of nature, Timaeus continues: "The story of the generations of the other divinities exceeds our competence; we must believe what the men of former times have told us about them. They were offsprings of the gods, as they themselves said, and, of course, must have known all about their own ancestors. We cannot withhold faith from these children of the gods, though they speak without proofs either probable or exact. We must obey the law that pronounces their testimony valid in family matters. Let us, then, following them, declare the generations of the gods to have been as follows: of Earth and Heaven were born Oceanus and Tethys, from these Phorcys, Cronus and Rhea, and their companions; and from Cronus and Rhea Zeus and Hera and all their brethren and descendants" (40 E ff.).

An interesting chapter could be made of the interpretation of this single passage. It would enumerate the interpreters, from the Christian Fathers to the philologians of twentieth-century Germany, who have or have not perceived the irony of these words; who have praised Plato for his submission of reason to faith, or reproached him for this cowardly conformity to superstitions which he knew to be false.

The other passage cuts deeper still and recalls Matthew Arnold's phrase about "the magnified non-natural man." In the *Phaedrus*, after describing the mortal animal man, compact of soul and body, Socrates adds, "but the immortal animal we conceive on no rational principle but imagine and feign what we have neither seen nor adequately grasped in thought, god, an immortal animal having soul and body conjoined in one and grown together for all time" (246 C-D).

The best example of the skeptical interpretation of Plato is Montaigne's longest essay, the "Apology for Raymond of Sebonde," which is an apology in the sense in which I have recently apologized for evolution. About a hundred years before Montaigne, Raymond of Sebonde wrote in Latin the first book explicitly entitled *Natural Theology*. It is not natural theology in the proper sense, the natural theology of the tenth book of Plato's *Laws*, of the Stoics, of Leibnitz' *Theodicy* and Pope's *Essay on Man*, limited to the essentials of God, freedom, immortality, and Providence or the justification of the ways of God to man. Sebonde tries to establish or defend by natural reason all the specific dogmas and sacraments of the Catholic Church. He does not quote Plato or any other authority. Montaigne translated this treatise at his father's request, and relieved his mind by his so-called apology, which not only quotes Plato twenty or thirty times, but numerous other classical authors besides, especially the Latin poets. Miss Grace Norton's introduction to this essay in the recent Harvard Press edition of Montaigne innocently assumes Montaigne's perfect good faith and the sincerity of his apology.[30] If that was Montaigne's meaning, it must be taken as an argument of despair, such as some critics find in the philosophy of Cardinal Newman. Since we cannot know anything, we might as well believe everything. However that may be, the essay is one of the most powerful statements in literature of the philosophy of skepticism and relativity, confirmed by the insufficiency of our minds and senses for the attainment of truth, our kinship with the animals, the varieties of opinion and custom, and the vanity of dogmatizing. Our present concern is that Montaigne, like the ancient skeptics and academicians, claimed the support of Plato, and for much the same reasons as those I have already indicated. I quote

a typical passage. "Socrates, the conductor of his dial-
ogisms," Montaigne says, "is eternally upon questions and
stirring up disputes, never determining, never satisfying."[31]

The different philosophic sects are said to have taken their
origin from Plato. As I take it, no teaching was ever wab-
bling and unassertive if it was not his. I think Plato preferred the dialogue form for philosophy in order to place
more becomingly the diversity and variations of his own
fancies in different mouths. I cannot easily convince myself
that Epicurus, Plato, and Pythagoras expected us to accept
as current coin their atoms, their ideas, and their numbers.

The relation of Epicurus to Plato is mainly that of opposition, an opposition of temperament, cultural ideals, and
philosophic doctrine. The chief extant texts of Epicurean
doctrine, outside of the discussions of Cicero, are the philosophic letters and sayings of Epicurus preserved in the tenth
book of Diogenes Laertius and the wonderful poem *On the
Nature of Things* by the Roman Epicurean, Lucretius. It marks
the comprehensiveness of Plato's thought that two or three
of the fundamental doctrines of the Epicurean philosophy
are dramatically stated for rejection and refutation in the
Platonic dialogues more effectively than Epicurus himself
can state them. They are the exposition in the *Protagoras* of
the theory that pleasure is the only intelligible good, and
wisdom and virtue consist in a shrewd measuring of pleasures against pains, and the theory set forth in the beginning of the second book of the *Republic* that justice and
right are based solely on convention and originate in a social contract, to anticipate the terminology of Rousseau.
Epicurus and modern Epicureans never improved the statement of these doctrines in Plato (cf. *supra* p. 11). To this
might be added the more obscure yet distinctly implied exposition and criticism of atomism in the *Timaeus* and the
Parmenides, the reflections on the origins of civilization in
the *Protagoras* and the *Laws*, and a few minor parallels in

thought or expression collected by me in a paper which I wrote a number of years ago.[32] Such detail is less interesting than the broad fact of the opposition between Platonism and Epicureanism that runs through the history of philosophy and literature from Cicero's friend Atticus to the seventeenth-century Frenchman Saint-Évremond, and from Saint-Évremond to the theory, if not the practice, of Walter Savage Landor.

The Platonist and the Epicurean are antithetic types in temperament, taste, and opinion. To the Platonist the Epicurean is an uncultured, dogmatic sensualist, a talking delegate of materialistic science, ignorant of mathematics and true science. To the Epicurean the Platonist is an idealistic dreamer and mystic who, when not himself superstitious, fosters superstition in others, an eloquent sophist, a scholastic cumbered with learning that is either useless culture or idle refinements of logic and transcendental mathematics. Plato had assimilated all the culture of his age, as Pater and Emerson often repeat, and men like Cicero, Plutarch, Lucian (though not philosophically a Platonist), the emperor Julian, Schleiermacher, Cousin, Mill, Martineau, Arnold, and Jowett are in respect of culture typical Platonists. Epicurus said that cultural education contributes nothing to life. He would have approved Herbert Spencer's bracketing of the servant girl, the plowboy, the grocer, in their ignorance of the true nature of the universe, with the average classical scholar or man of letters,[33] and would have agreed with Spencer and Lévy-Bruhl that in a rightly proportioned education as well as in adult life, literature should be assigned less space than it now has. Cicero and Plutarch are perpetually satirizing the lack of culture in the Epicureans, though Cicero qualifies his satire with a compliment to the learning of his friend Atticus, which he regards as a happy inconsistency with Atticus' professed philosophy.

Plato combated and disapproved the materialism of the

PLATO AND ANTIQUITY 17

pre-Socratic philosophers and ridiculed their dogmatic professions of certainty about the final nature of the universe. Epicurus accepted as ultimate truth, and not merely as a working hypothesis of physics and chemistry, the atomic system of Democritus, explained the soul in material terms as confidently as any behaviorist of today, and dictated to his students a compendium of scientific doctrine which they were to memorize as the final truth. But while the followers of Epicurus have always accused Plato and the Platonists of hostility to science, as a matter of fact, Plato was perhaps the first director of scientific research and organizer of systematic education in science,[34] and himself contributed to the progress of mathematics and astronomy.[35] Epicurus affirmed that the only value of science was to free the mind from superstition, which included religion, and, like many materialistic psychologists and neurologists teaching in our universities today, he thought any explanation of the phenomena of mind and the universe adequate that got rid of a possible design in the universe or of a soul in man. The consequence was that the Epicurean school, while constantly talking about its scientific attitude, contributed nothing to scientific discovery, and the magnificent poem of Lucretius, which even Huxley and Tyndall and Osler consider as the truest expression of the spirit and poetry of science, is disfigured by an ignorance of astronomy which a well-trained schoolboy in Athens or Rome, though not, I fear, in Chicago or Oxford, could have corrected.

All this is brought out in the polemics against Epicurus of the widely read and cultivated Platonists, Cicero and Plutarch. Another point on which they dwell is the contrast between the political and social activities of Plato and the Platonists and the supine selfish quietism of the Epicureans and even of the Stoics, who professed that the sage should take no part in politics. Plato, it is true, celebrated the life of pure thought as the highest, and the goal of Neo-Pla-

tonism was reunion with the One,"the flight of the alone to
the alone." But every reader of Plato is aware of his passion
for social, political, educational, and moral reform, and
throughout antiquity, as Cicero observes, the Platonists
and Aristotelians were more active in these ways than the
Epicureans or Stoics. Cicero himself is a conspicuous example of the Platonist in this regard, as his friend Atticus
is the perfect illustration of a type of Epicurean that recurs
throughout history.

I have mentioned Saint-Évremond, who is perhaps too
obscure to detain us, though a recent essay of Richard Al-
dington finds him very interesting.[36] A typical more modern
Epicurean, in theory if not in practice, is Walter Savage
Landor. He is typical at any rate in his enthusiasm for the
atomic philosophy and the personality of Epicurus, and his
hostility to Plato. In his dialogue between Epicurus, Leon-
tion, and Ternissa we have much rather silly philandering
of the elderly Epicurus with his girl pupils in the manner of
Landor himself, and of Goethe and Ruskin in their feebler
moments. In the more lucid intervals Epicurus is made to
utter sage maxims on true happiness and wisdom and to
speak condescendingly of Plato's fancies, affectations, and
pretenses. In the dialogue between Diogenes the Cynic and
Plato, Landor, who did not own a text of Plato, collects all
the foolish or captious objections that occurred to him in
his hasty perusal of the dialogues at the Magliabecchian
Library. Many of them are complete misunderstandings of
Plato's text. Others turn on the literal acceptance of the
science of the *Timaeus*, a favorite trick of modern assailants
of Plato, or on the assumption that the legislation of Plato's
Republic and *Laws* is designed to be put in operation in
modern England. "Plato," he says, "would make for ever
all the citizens what we punish with death a single one for
being once. He is a man of hasty fancy and indistinct reflection: more different from Socrates than the most violent of

his adversaries."[37] Landor's place, then, is in a footnote to a dissertation on anti-Platonism.

There is no such thing as an impartial and objective interpretation of Stoicism. The historian either likes or dislikes the Stoic pedantry, the pseudoscientific terminology, the overelaboration of logic, rhetoric, and grammar by hairsplitting distinctions and superfluous definitions, the oversystematization of the imperfect science of the ancients to give the appearance of consistency, the abuse of allegory and fantastic etymology, the combination of materialistic pantheism with accommodations to popular theology, the jumble of incongruous and hastily collected erudition, the reiteration of moral commonplace, the straining for moral impressiveness by hyperbole, the setting up of impractically rigid ideals only to whittle them away by a casuistry of compromise and the interpretation of their terms in a Pickwickian sense. From this description it will perhaps be inferred that I am more of a Platonist than a Stoic.

Stoicism, in fact, even more than Aristotelianism, is an episode in the history of Platonism. For four or five hundred years Stoicism was the dominant philosophy and ethical religion of the educated in Greco-Roman civilization. The history of the successive chiefs of the Stoic school, the development of its system and terminology, and the various phases of its doctrine, have been the theme of an enormous philological literature. Of much of this literature such a book as A. Schmekel's *Die Philosophie der mittleren Stoa* may serve as a type. You may divine its character from the fact that the middle Stoa means the lost authors between the founders of Stoicism, Zeno, Cleanthes, and Chrysippus, and the later Stoics, Seneca, Epictetus, and Marcus Aurelius, the only Stoic writers of whose writings we have any real knowledge. The scholastic history of Stoicism, then, is a linking of conjecture to conjecture and a pyramiding of hypothesis on hypothesis.

Fortunately, the essential inner history and meaning of Stoicism is a simpler matter. It is mainly its relation to Platonism—(1) the borrowing and sometimes the spoiling of Platonic and Aristotelian ideas, definitions, terms, and distinctions, for the original construction of the Stoic edifice; (2) the gradual and steady infusion and softening of the rigid pedantic Stoic system by the literary and ethical spirit of Platonism, due to the fact that everybody, and especially the fine minds, kept on reading Plato; and (3), as a result, the fact that the only Stoics that are known to or interest the modern reader, Seneca, Epictetus, and Marcus Aurelius, are nearly as much Platonists as Stoics.

No genuine appreciator of Plato can take Stoicism quite seriously. Cicero was greatly impressed by the ingenuity of the system and its moral austerity, but he speaks his real mind when he makes his Academician say that Zeno originated nothing, except the innovations of terminology in which he clothed ideas borrowed from Plato and Aristotle (*De fin.* III 2.5). Similar has been the feeling of nearly all sensitive literary and Platonic critics, from Plutarch to Santayana, who somewhere says that nothing in ancient philosophy after Plato and Aristotle is really of any significance. There is nothing in Stoicism to interest such minds except the overrated hymn of Cleanthes and the Platonizing morality of Seneca, Epictetus, and Marcus Aurelius. Cleanthes' pantheistic hymn to Zeus has a certain moral impressiveness and is tolerable, but only tolerable, poetry. Walter Pater, by a trick of translation, converts its loose verbose rhetorical Greek hexameters into the plausible likeness of an Old Testament psalm:

Thou O Zeus art praised above all gods: many are Thy names and Thine is all power for ever.

The beginning of the world was from Thee: and with law Thou rulest over all things.

Unto Thee may all flesh speak: for we are Thy offspring.

Therefore will I raise a hymn unto Thee: and will ever sing of Thy power.

The whole order of the heavens obeyeth Thy word: as it moveth around the earth:

With little and great lights mixed together: how great art Thou, King above all for ever!

Nor is anything done upon earth apart from Thee; nor in the firmament, nor in the seas:

Save that which the wicked do: by their own folly.

But Thine is the skill to set even the crooked straight: what is without fashion is fashioned and the alien akin before Thee.

Thus hast Thou fitted together all things in one: the good with the evil:

That Thy word should be one in all things: abiding for ever.

Let folly be dispersed from our souls: that we may repay Thee the honour, wherewith Thou hast honoured us:

Singing praise of Thy works for ever: as becometh the sons of men.[38]

Seneca, Epictetus, and Marcus Aurelius have been bedside books and books of edification for many generations of readers. But they are in no proper sense Stoics. Seneca is an eclectic who quotes Epicurus as often as any Stoic. He likes to display his ingenuity in defense of Stoic paradoxes and enjoys the affectation of Stoic austerity at the court of Nero or in a millionaire's villa. But many of his finest sentiments are direct reminiscences of Plato, and like Plato and unlike Professor Murray's Stoic sage, he indulges his fancy in pictures of immortality and what awaits the spirit released from the prison house of the flesh. The ethical religion of Epictetus and Marcus Aurelius is, in the main, the religion of Socrates, collected from Plato's *Apology*, *Crito*, *Gorgias*, and *Phaedo*, with touches from Xenophon's *Memorabilia*. To this, Marcus Aurelius adds his wistful and imaginative alternation between the Tennysonian two voices, the voice of Plato whispering hope and the voice of negation proclaiming that all is atoms and void.

These elementary truths, as I deem them, are persistently overlooked in the majority of popular and even philological expositions of Stoicism. Professor Murray's brilliant lecture, sometimes reprinted as a radical tract, idealizes Stoicism throughout as a system of moral idealism, poetical pantheism, and unflinching rationalism. He practically ignores its pedantries, its inconsistencies, and its plagiarisms, pays no attention to the chronology of four hundred years, and mentions Plato and Platonism but once, and then disparagingly and with an error of about a hundred years in the chronology, which makes the use of Plato's name meaningless in the context. Mr. Henry D. Sedgwick's interesting volume on Marcus Aurelius and Edwyn Bevan's *Stoics and Sceptics* likewise overlook the part of Platonism in Stoicism and treat Seneca, Epictetus, and Marcus Aurelius as the typical Stoics. Professor Wenley's readable little monograph on Stoicism and its influence, and more scholarly works such as Arnold's *Roman Stoicism*, with its useful collection of passages from Roman literature, the excellent treatise of Hicks, *Stoic and Epicurean*, and even the admirable book of Barth, *Die Stoa*, are only a little better in this respect. They do not bring out what I deem to be the essential facts of the relationship. That may be partly unacquaintance with the facts, but in the popular expositors it is perhaps mainly a desire to make the most of their subject, and an instinctive perception that the juxtaposition of Platonism, as one says of colors and works of art, kills Stoicism. Their attitude is that of a deliberate or temporarily affected partisanship. The popular appeal of Stoicism was, and is, largely due to the very fact of its intellectual, and in a sense moral, inferiority. Humanity sometimes likes to be fed from a low crib. Men go to the Stoics somewhat as a shrewd businessman or a university professor might go on Sunday to let his mind be relaxed or roused and edified by the exhortations of an uneducated country preacher, his in-

tellectual inferior. Men grow weary of the very perfection
of Plato, the polished surface of the unfailing literary art,
the mastery of an inevitable dialectic, the sense of intellectual adequacy or superiority, the perfect reasonableness,
the entire absence of pseudo science and a technical and
system-building terminology for the mind to play with, the
ironical evasion of unprofitable discussion of ultimates in
symbolism and myth. And so they find a certain pleasure in
the Stoic pedantry and commonplace.

But there is a higher, intellectual, point of view from
which Stoicism is really, as I have said, an episode, a form
of ethical culture for matter-of-fact and semicultural minds,
something that does not really count when compared with
Plato and Aristotle on the one side or even with Plotinus
and the Neo-Platonists on the other. The pedantic terminology satirized in Cicero's *Pro Murena*, in Horace, and in
Macaulay's *Essay on Bacon*, the curious mixture of pantheism borrowed from the pre-Socratics with allegories of
and concessions to popular religion, the hairsplitting termi-
nological elaboration of the Platonic dialectics and the Aristotelian logic and rhetoric, the loose combination of inac-
curate and undigested erudition and folklore, these things
belong to the specialist and have no absolute or humanistic
value. The only thing of permanent interest is the Stoic
ethics, the Stoic attitude towards life, and that is not un-
fairly characterized in Cicero's remark that all the Stoic
paradoxes are Socratic, or in Gilfillan's epigrammatic saying that "the Stoic was only the stony similitude of a Platonist."[39]

That nothing is absolutely ours and in our power except
the moral will; that so-called external goods and the vicis-
situdes of pleasure and pain are neither good nor evil in the
higher sense, and cannot deflect the resolute soul; that
peace, contentment, and happiness are to be found only in
the complete self-possession that liberates the sage from all

concern for unconcerning things; that the sensuous tyrant can never be happy; that the true king, whether crowned or uncrowned, the true ruler, whether he wins or loses the election, is he who rules himself and knows how to rule others —these and similar truisms, paradoxes, or ideals are dramatically appropriate and convincing in the mouth of a Socrates rebuking his unjust judges, resisting the importunities of Crito that he bribe the jailer and break prison, or controverting the ethical nihilism and cynical man-of-the-world philosophy of a Callicles or the Machiavellianism of a Thrasymachus. They have a certain pathetic as well as historic interest when repeated from Plato's *Gorgias* in Boethius' *Consolation of Philosophy*, from which the Middle Ages took them. But the droning iteration of them in a terminology that recalls the style of a twentieth-century doctor's dissertation in sociology is more apt to be felt as pedantry or cant. It can impose only on tired minds, or minds incapable of receiving this moral inspiration in any finer form. Others will prefer to take it directly from the *Apology*, the *Crito*, and the *Gorgias* of Plato, or from such a passage of the *Republic* as the following, which anticipates nearly everything of genuine spiritual significance in the absolute ethical idealism of the Stoics:

"In what way then and on what principle, Glaucon, shall we say that it profits a man to be unjust or licentious or do any shameful thing that will make him a worse man but bring him more wealth or other forms of power?"

"In no way," he said.

"And how that it pays him to escape detection in wrongdoing, and not pay the penalty? Is it not true that he who escapes detection becomes a worse man, while in the one who is discovered and chastened the brutish part is lulled and tamed and the gentle part liberated, and his soul as a whole returning to its nature at the best, attains to a much more precious condition in acquiring soberness and righteousness with wisdom than the body does when it gains strength and beauty conjoined with health, as the soul is more precious than the body?"

"Most assuredly," he said.

"Then the wise man will bend all his endeavors to this end throughout his life. He will, to begin with, prize the studies that will give this quality to his soul and disprize the others."

"Clearly," he said.

"And then," I said, "he not only will not abandon the habit and nurture of his body to the brutish and irrational pleasure, and live with his face set in that direction, but he will not even make health his aim, nor regard as the chief thing the ways of becoming strong and healthy and beautiful, unless these things are likely to bring with them soberness of spirit, but he will always be found attuning the harmonies in his body for the sake of the concord in his soul."

"By all means," he replied, "if he is to be a true musician."

"And will he not deal likewise with the ordering and harmonizing of his possessions? He will not let himself be dazzled by the felicitations of the multitude, and pile up the mass of his wealth without measure, involving himself in measureless evil."

"No, I think not," he said.

"He will rather," I said, "keep his eyes fixed on the constitution of his soul and, taking care lest he disturb anything there by excess or deficiency in his possessions, will direct his course and add to or detract from his wealth on this principle so far as may be."

"Precisely so," he said.

"And in the matter of honors and office, too, this will be his guiding principle. He will gladly take part in and enjoy those that he thinks will make him a better man, but in public and private life he will shun honors that may endanger and overthrow the established constitution of his soul."

"Then if that is his chief concern," he said, "he will not willingly take part in politics."

"Yes, by the dog," said I, "in his own city he certainly will, yet perhaps not in the city of his birth, except in some providential conjuncture."

"I understand," he said; "you mean the city whose establishment we have described, the city whose home is in the ideal; for I think it can be found nowhere on earth."

"Well," said I, "perhaps there is a pattern of it laid up in heaven for him who chooses to contemplate it, and so beholding to constitute himself its citizen. But it makes no difference whether it is now or ever will be. The politics of this city only and of none other will be his concern" (*Republic* 591 A-592 B).

It is perhaps a matter of taste whether we prefer this or the genuine older, unplatonized Stoic style. Becomings are actions the performance of which admits of plausible justification. The effectuation of the becoming is that which is appropriate and akin to natural endowment. Perfect becomings are rectitudes, such as intelligence and justice. They are possible only to the Stoic sage, who is an ideal that has never been realized. Imperfect becomings are intermediates, such as marrying, being an ambassador, or engaging in argument. All intermediates are indifferents. But we must distinguish such indifferents from absolute indifferents, such as paring your nails, cutting your hair, or brushing the dust from your coat. Indifferents may be divided (like stocks) into preferred and nonpreferred, or preferables and unpreferables. Money is an indifferent; but in certain situations it may be a preferable or preferred. The toothache is an indifferent; but it is unpreferable.

The Stoics took over from Aristotle the ambition for encyclopedic exhaustiveness, an illusion from which Plato was preserved both by his intelligence and by the resources of his literary art. They divided philosophy or the knowledge of things human and divine under three heads: logic, which included dialectic and rhetoric; physics, including religion; and ethics, including politics. This classification is sometimes referred to Aristotle. It is distinctly, though not technically, implied in Plato.[40] The detail of ancient science belongs in a book of reference. It is neither readable nor rememberable by anybody but a few specialists. It is only the larger aspects of the Stoic physics and their relation to Platonism that concern us. Ostensibly, the Stoic physics attached itself to the pre-Socratic philosopher Heraclitus, who said that all things move or flow, who spoke vaguely of some logos or law that governed it, and who uttered many aphorisms or epigrams on the paradoxical identity of contraries in God. But in the elaboration of that so-called Heraclitan system the Stoics took much from Aristotle and perhaps were even more influenced by Plato's *Timaeus*. The *Timaeus* is, with the *Republic* and the philosophy of love in the *Symposium*, the most influential, historically, of Plato's works. We shall meet it again in connection with Neo-Platonism, the Christian Fathers, and the Platonism of the Middle Ages and the Renaissance. It is Plato's summary of fourth-century science, a prose poem on the nature of things, and a teleological view of the universe. Zeno, the founder of Stoicism, is reported to have studied it, and the long line of commentaries and interpretations of it began with the commentary of Crantor, a contemporary of Zeno. The chief ideas that Stoicism seems to have taken over from the *Timaeus* were the teleological view of nature, to which we shall return later, and a confirmation in Plato's doctrine of a world soul, of the pantheism which they found or read into Heraclitus.

Their system, omitting details which are of no interest to us, may be summed in a convenient sentence: Our world is derived from a mass of living fire (whatever that may mean) containing within itself the seminal reasons (whatever that may mean) of all things. Out of this have come all things,

and into it they will be reabsorbed in a final conflagration
with which the cycle will begin anew and everything will
repeat itself. This fire they called Zeus or God, and its
transformations take place in a series determined by inevitable and unchanging law. This is what is called pantheism, and it calls forth distressing outpourings of rhetoric
from the admirers and expositors of Stoicism. These expositions are really about on the level of Poe's *Eureka*, which
will give the modern reader a fair notion of their quality.
One sentence of Poe will suffice: ". . . that God—the material *and* spiritual God—*now* exists solely in the diffused
Matter and Spirit of the Universe; and that the regather-
ing of this diffused Matter and Spirit will be but the re-
constitution of the *purely* Spiritual and individual God."[41]
Poe probably got this from some exposition of Stoicism.
Professor Murray finds in the system Bergson's *élan vital*
and his *évolution créatrice*. As the sentimental bard of evolution puts it,"Some call it evolution and others call it God."
In Professor Murray's account it is *Phusis* or Nature, with
a capital letter. "It is," he says, "like a soul, or a life-force,
running through all matter."[42] Vergil said it more prettily
in the sixth book of the *Aeneid*. In fact, the Stoic word for
that which holds matter together was *hexis*. "This view,"
Professor Murray tells us, and the conception of God that
results from it,"is so sublime and so stirring that at times
it almost deadens one's power of criticism."[43] That perhaps
explains why many interpreters of Stoicism, including Professor Murray himself and Mr. Sedgwick who follows him
in this, give the system credit for two incompatible and ir-
reconcilable teachings and tendencies. They first praise it
for the rigid rationalism and scientific materialism that re-
duces all things to one chain of causation and does not, like
Plato, entertain the multitude with the illusion of immortality. Then they turn about and commend the prudent
and kindly concessions to popular superstition in which

Stoicism went far beyond Platonism, and claim as one of the chief lights of Stoicism Seneca, who paints the delights of the New Jerusalem with a rhetoric beside which that of Plato pales. Such inconsistencies are of the very essence of rhetoric; and the pantheism which in this case calls them forth is not a term of science or philosophy, but of rhetoric. And since pantheism is a topic that will meet us frequently in these chapters it will be convenient to digress here for a moment, and dispose of it by anticipation.

The doctrine that God is all in all and all is God, is a confusion of thought that still survives in literature, theology, and philosophy. It is the theme of some good poems, as Emerson's *Brahma* and Swinburne's *Hertha*. It is the source of innumerable epigrams and paradoxes on the identity of contraries, including sometimes the identity of good and evil, and their reconciliation in God, from Heraclitus to Hegel, Victor Hugo, and Walt Whitman. As a philosophy or theology, it is quite meaningless. It does not alter the universe a particle to call it God, and it does not make God any more real or bring Him nearer as helper or consoler to identify Him with the world. Yet it must be admitted, as a matter of personal psychology, that an astonishing number of thinkers, theologians, and poets have found satisfaction in this equivocal rhetoric. They seem to feel that there is something inherently irrational and debasing in anything that may be styled dualism, in any admission of a possible distinction between soul and body, or God and the world. And so they pour themselves out in dithyrambic praise of any philosopher who seems to transcend these distinctions and thereby attain to unity, monism, the epigrammatic identity of contraries, and the abolition of all isolating and undemocratic distinctions. This rhetoric of pantheism is applied indiscriminately to the Stoics, to the Platonizing Stoic Posidonius, who is conjectured to have elaborated a magnificent system of monism (of which traces are to be

found in the literature of the two centuries that center in
Cicero and Seneca), to Neo-Platonism, to John Scot Erigena, to Giordano Bruno, to Nicolaus of Cusa, and to Spinoza. Spinoza is a test case. It was wrong to persecute him
for atheism, and since he was threatened with persecution
he was justified in his evasions. But his persecutors were
quite right in their suspicions concerning his real opinions,
and now that nobody is in danger of persecution, the critics
who persist in calling Spinoza a "God-intoxicated man" are
either silly or insincere. The unction of his theological language is either the self-delusion of his own rhetoric or a
conscious camouflage of his real opinion. But to return to
antiquity.

There is practically no pantheism in Plato. Plato's God
is taken over from the popular national religion, and the
conception is purified and elevated by his rejection of immoral anthropomorphism and his well-known canons of all
future theologies. But Plato does not attempt to work the
idea of God into a complete metaphysical system, or adjust
it to one, and the endeavors of later Platonists to do this for
him and to foist such a system upon him are among the
chief causes of the misinterpretation of his writings. For
Plato, God is a supreme category of the moral ideal and a
word of edification, and that is all there is to it. He does not
identify God with the Idea of Good, the idea of unity, the
idea of pure being, the mythical Demiourgos of the *Timaeus*,
or any other abstraction, principle, or symbol in his philosophy.

But though pantheism is absent from Plato, it occupies a
great place in the history of Platonism, and it remains to
explain how this came about. There are two main causes;
the world soul of the *Timaeus* is obviously suggestive of a
poetical pantheism. It acted in this way upon the imagination of the Middle Ages and so became the source of many
philosophical and poetical heresies combated and finally

suppressed by the orthodox doctrine. Something of the same influence can also be traced in some of the poetic philosophies of the Renaissance, notably in Giordano Bruno. More widespread and lasting is the influence of the Theory of Ideas. Plato himself did not deduce all other Ideas systematically from one highest and all-comprehending Idea, as the Idea of Being, of Unity, or of Good. But throughout the history of philosophy and scholarship it has repeatedly been asserted that he did. And from such interpretations a plausible argument leads straight to what may be called a logical or dialectical pantheism. If real being belongs only to the Ideas, and if the amount of being is proportional to the generality and abstractness of the Idea, then the being of the most abstract, the most general, the most comprehensive Idea includes all the others, and they exist only in and through it. This pantheistic interpretation of Platonism was transmitted from the Neo-Platonists, sometimes through Arabic and Jewish mystics, to the Middle Ages, where it sometimes blended with the poetic pantheism derived from the *Timaeus*. Thence, if we care so to speculate, we may trace it to Nicolaus of Cusa and Spinoza, where it stirs a—to me—incomprehensible enthusiasm in many modern critics.

Our current histories overestimate not only the value of Stoicism but also its influence. Of course, a philosophy that retained its vogue for four hundred years left its traces on both thought and expression. But an occasional touch of Stoic terminology is no proof of adherence to Stoicism even during the period of its predominance, and still less later. We do not class as a Kantian today any writer who speaks of categories, antinomies, transcendentalism, and the distinction between reason and understanding. One is not a disciple of Spencer by virtue of an allusion to the instability of the homogeneous, and not everyone who speaks of the unconscious or the libido is a Freudian. The Stoics coined an enormous pseudoscientific terminology; and then, as now, such terms were eagerly adopted by those who wished to be in the fashion, and insidiously insinuated themselves into the vocabulary even of their opponents. This, I think, is the main reason why even Zeller greatly exaggerates the part of Stoicism in the Platonist Philo Judaeus, as the Chicago dissertation of Dr. Billings shows,[44] and why he even finds a large measure of Stoic doctrine in Plotinus himself. The same tendency manifests itself in some histories of modern philosophy. A notable example is the learned work of that acute scholar W. Dilthey on European culture and philosophy since the Renaissance and Reformation.[45] Platonism, though the chief, was not the only revival of ancient philosophy in the Renaissance. Every system had its historian and its professed advocate. Gassendi devoted his life to the philosophy of Epicurus and Lucretius, and the philosophy of the Stoics was expounded and advocated in the learned treatises of Justus Lipsius, Gerardus Vossius, Scioppius, and others.[46]

Starting from the influence of these treatises on Montaigne, Dilthey tries to show the dependence on Stoicism of nearly everything of pantheistic or monistic tendencies in modern philosophy, of all modern natural religion and liberal theology, and of much modern ethics. What he actually shows is the enormous influence on modern thought of the reading of Cicero and Seneca by all educated men for three centuries, which is a very different thing. But to return to antiquity and to the history of the later postclassical centuries of Greek culture and philosophy, which for these lectures are only a transition to Neo-Platonism. My conception of that history is that it is chiefly marked by the gradual infusion of other systems with Platonism and by the progressive increase in the influence of Platonism, due mainly to the fact that Plato was readable and was therefore read. And my argument is that this simple interpretation is obscured by the apparent predominance of Stoicism, by the

attribution of too much significance to the use of Stoic terminology resulting from this fashion, by the historical interest of the lives of the noble Roman Stoics whose defiance
of imperial tyranny and whose deaths are described by Tacitus, and by modern overvaluation of the Stoic elements in
such Platonizing Stoic moralists as Epictetus, Seneca, and
Marcus Aurelius.

The full evidence of this would be the rewriting of the
entire history from this point of view. The earlier post-
Aristotelian literature is mostly lost, and has to be recon-
structed by supposed imitations in later writers. But in the
fragments there is sufficient testimony, as well as proof,
that the earlier Stoics made ample use of Plato in the construction of their system and their terminology, and the influence of Plato is easily traced in the one great prose writer
of this period who has been preserved, the historian Polybius, on whom Livy so largely drew. Polybius' philosophy
of politics, and his theory of the law that governs the cycles
of forms of government, are plainly derived from the account of the evolution of constitutions in the eighth book of
Plato's *Republic*, though too many historians of the science
of politics overlook the fact. When we get down to Panaetius
and Posidonius, the Stoics whom Cicero knew and to whom
he owed so much, we are explicitly told that they were constant readers of Plato and that in a number of the most important matters they adopted Plato's views where they
differed from the orthodoxy of the Stoic sect.

Cicero himself is the earliest extant and best example of
the transmission of Platonic thought by great Platonists. I
even think that, if time permitted, I could make it plausible
that some suggestions of Platonism in Shakespeare are derived from Cicero's *Tusculans*. Cicero everywhere proclaims
his allegiance to Plato as the supreme philosopher. He even
says, to the horror of some literal-minded modern physi-
cists, that he would rather err with Plato than be right with

mechanistic Epicureans.[47] He translated some dialogues of Plato, including apparently the difficult *Timaeus*.[48] He has numerous latent reminiscences of Platonic passages besides the explicit references that scholars have collected, and we need not waste time on the hypothesis that because, like everybody else, he sometimes quotes at second hand, he knew Plato only in the quotations of Panaetius, Posidonius, and their likes. The Stoic ethics that some of his treatises transmit to the Middle Ages and the modern world, is everywhere, like the ethics of Seneca, infused with Platonism, and indeed with explicit quotations from the *Gorgias*, the *Phaedo*, and the *Republic*. There is still room for a monograph on Cicero as a transmitter of Platonism.[49]

Still more copious sources of secondary Platonism are Plutarch and Philo Judaeus, who knew Plato almost by heart and whose Platonism has been studied in two University of Chicago dissertations.[50] But who will undertake the perhaps impossible study of their later influence, and the enumeration of all the Platonic references in secular European literature and in the writings of the Christian Fathers that are due to the one or the other? Another cause of the diffusion of Platonic influence I can only mention. For eight hundred years ancient culture and education were based on the study of either philosophy or rhetoric, or both. The philosophers, of course, knew Plato. But it is to be remembered that all students of rhetoric also knew him through the reading of the two dialogues that discuss rhetoric, the *Gorgias* and the *Phaedrus*, or at least from listening to lectures on them.

To complete the transition to Neo-Platonism there would be needed another chapter on three or four topics which I can only enumerate. First, the whole Pythagorean or Neo-Pythagorean tradition—the notion about which books are still written, that there was an occult mystical philosophy which Pythagoras received from the Orient and which Plato transmitted to the Neo-Pythagoreans and Neo-Platonists. I shall dismiss this immense but to me distasteful topic in the next lecture by merely enumerating the Platonic passages and the features of Plato's literary art that have given rise to this superstition. Next, would be to consider two groups of Platonists, besides the Platonizing Stoics we have already touched upon: first, Platonizing moral essayists such as Dio Chrysostomus and Maximus of Tyre, excerpts from either of whom would supply matter for a readable essay; second, the more technical and conjectural study of the fragments of those predecessors of Plotinus who influenced his special interpretation of Plato and the construction of his system. Lastly, in a broader summary, we might identify the Platonism of these centuries with that religion of philosophy by which, in the decay of the ancient religions, the finer minds of the Greco-Roman empire kept their souls alive, the religion of which Cicero wrote: "O Philosophy, guide of life, pursuit of virtue, redeemer from sin, what would we, what would the life of man be without thee? . . . To thee we fly for refuge, to thee that hast ever held out thy arms to us we yield ourselves entire. One day well spent in obedience to thy precepts is to be preferred to an eternity of sin" (*Tusc. disp.* V 2.5). That religion was, doubtless, a composite of many elements drawn from Matthew Arnold's four prophets of the religion of the imaginative reason, the Greek poets Aeschylus, Sophocles, Pindar, and Simonides, as well as from the noblest and most heartening teachings of all the philosophic schools. But its Messiah was the Platonic Socrates; its fourfold gospel was the *Apology, Crito, Gorgias*, and *Phaedo*; its Holy Ghost was the Platonic idealism, and its spiritual fervor was Plato's moral eloquence.

CHAPTER II

PLATONISM IN ANTIQUITY—NEO-PLATONISM

NEO-PLATONISM is the form of Greek philosophy which in
the decline of Stoicism and Epicureanism dominated the
last three centuries of Greco-Roman literature. A historical
study of Neo-Platonism, then, would be the enumeration
or the story of a long series of names and books—the predecessors of Plotinus running back from Numenius, in the
second century, to Plutarch, the Neo-Pythagoreans, Philo
Judaeus, the lost Posidonius, whom German ingenuity re-
constructs, and finally to the immediate pupils of Plato,
Xenocrates and Speusippus, and then, again, forward from
Plotinus himself, the first and greatest of the Neo-Platonists, his disciple Porphyry, his successors Iamblichus, the
emperor Julian, Proclus, and so on down through the schools
of Athens and Alexandria and the last Greek commentators
on Aristotle, to Dionysius the Areopagite, and others who
handed on fantastic and superstitious elaborations of the
doctrine to the Arabs and the Middle Ages. The consequence was that ancient philosophy and culture were thus
transmitted to the Middle Ages in interpretations, commentaries, and textbooks that even when not explicitly
Neo-Platonic were colored by the Neo-Platonic spirit and
terminology. The great Platonists of the Renaissance, Gemistus Pletho, Ficino, and Pico della Mirandola, unlike the
Neo-Platonists of today, knew intimately the texts of Plato,
but they read them through Neo-Platonic spectacles. Thus
something of the Neo-Platonic interpretation was transmitted to the modern world, and so today even in the writings of those who, like Coleridge, protest against the confounding of Plotinist with Platonist, Neo-Platonic ideas are
persistently and mistakenly attributed to Plato himself,
and it is almost impossible for criticism to eradicate them.

[36]

A detailed history of Neo-Platonism would fill many volumes. Obviously, I cannot expound to you here the systems of those whom Thomas Taylor, the British Platonist, styles "the great Plotinus, the most learned Porphyry, the divine Iamblichus, the most acute Syrianus, Proclus, the consummation of philosophic excellence, the magnificent Hierocles, the most elegant Sallust, and the most inquisitive Damascius." The interpretation of Plotinus alone would be a specialty for a lifetime. His latent quotations of Plato, Aristotle, and the Stoics are so numerous that a complete understanding of his system presupposes an intimate knowledge of these preceding philosophies, which, so far as I have observed, none of the writers who are interpreting Plotinus to the public in our day possess. Certainly not Dean Inge or Bergson or Maeterlinck or Guthrie, and probably not MacKenna, for all the beauty of his translation, or Whittaker, for all the good sense and practical sufficiency of his excellent book on Neo-Platonism.[1] Fortunately, a completely critical interpretation of the details is not necessary to a fair understanding of the Neo-Platonic system of philosophy. The shorter way that I am suggesting to the adequate comprehension of Neo-Platonism requires first a few generalizations about what I call Neo-Platonism as a state of mind, and second an observation of those features in Plato himself of which it is the exaggeration.

The first thing to note in the psychology of the Neo-Platonic type of mind is the delight in what we mistakenly call dialectics. In Plato dialectics simply means discussion, argument; and the skill with which Plato in his dialogues makes the written word perform the function of the spoken word, is, in this respect, one of the chief though least often recognized values of the study of Plato. Plato's dialectic may often seem to the modern reader to exhibit those weaknesses which Faguet so deliciously parodies in his book

[1] Superior figures refer to notes which will be found on p. 241.

Pour qu'on lise Platon. I need not return to that point. But, at its best, Plato's realistic reproduction of argumentative conversation is a real verification of, and check upon, the processes of thought. We are required to pause at every disputable, obscure, or ambiguous proposition until an intelligent and representative interlocutor understands and accepts it with or without qualification. That, of course, is not as good a check and verification as the modern scientific tests in the laboratory; but in many fields of thought it is still the best check and verification that we have, and the Platonic dialogues are still its best illustration and expression in literature, and the best encouragement and discipline of this habit of mind.

But the thing which the historians of philosophy call dialectic is the precise opposite of this and develops an altogether different habit of mind. The Platonic dialectic is the challenging and checking of equivocation or ambiguity at every step and stage of the process of thought. In this sense Montaigne is the true Platonist when he says "*distinguo* is the most universal member of my logic,"[2] and Locke, the conventional antithesis of Platonism, is, so far as it can be done without dialogue, one of the chief practitioners and teachers of the Platonic method. On the other hand, the imitations in Schelling's *Bruno* and in Hegel of certain parts of Plato's *Parmenides* and *Sophist* which Plato probably meant as illustrations of bad metaphysics, are, in their effect upon the mind, the opposite of true dialectics or rational discussion. The Hegelian dialectic, conversancy with which John Stuart Mill, with less than his usual temperate courtesy, says tends to deprave the intellect, is the indeterminate and uncontrolled concatenation of equivocal and ambiguous words in long chains of unverified and unverifiable ratiocinations. And to this general type the dialectic of Plotinus and the Neo-Platonists belongs.

Plato, in the *Phaedo* (68 C; 69 A ff.), denouncing with

Ruskinian or Carlylean eloquence utilitarians and the calculus of pleasures and pains, had said that true virtue knows nothing of these prudential calculations but is a purging or purification of the soul from all sensuous desires and selfish interests. Plotinus turns this fluid rhetoric of ethics and religion into dialectics thus: "We must enquire whether the purification is identical with the virtue or the virtue is an accompaniment and a sequence of the purification. Does the virtue consist in being purified or in having been purified? Is the purification all that is needed if the object purified was good before it became impure? We must remember, however, that the good is not the purification, but what remains after the purification. But that cannot have been good *per se* and essentially. For, by hypothesis, it is capable of both good and evil, while the good *per se* repudiates all community with evil. It is not enough, either, to say that it resembles the good. For it must abide always with the good. Its goodness, then, consists in its association with that which is akin to it. Purification is required to enable it so to associate. And it will so associate by virtue of conversion. This opens the inquiry whether it is converted after the purification or whether we must say that when purified it is *ipso facto* converted" (*Enn.* I 2.4). And so on *ad infinitum*.

There are literally hundreds of pages of this sort of thing in Plotinus and his successors. This is in fact a very easy specimen dealing with a simple ethical idea. It is child's play compared to what we get when this sort of dialectic is applied to problems of logic, epistemology, or eschatology. Neo-Platonism, then, in its historic, philological aspect is a kind of scholasticism in the form of a pseudodialectical exegesis of Plato. It can be understood in its technical detail only by students who are willing to plow through several volumes of this sort of verbiage after having first learned by heart the *Metaphysics* and *De anima* of Aristotle and those more difficult Platonic dialogues which Matthew Arnold scorns as bar-

ren logomachies. The Neo-Platonic mind combines with its
dialectical impulse certain needs and aptitudes vaguely designated by such words as scholasticism, mysticism, enthusiasm, asceticism, pantheism, symbolism, and the imaginative personification of abstractions. The dialectic yields
pleasure from the mere exercise of ingenuity in the process,
and from the cumulative intensity of the emotion of conviction which this semblance of reasoning generates. This
subjective feeling is so strong that it requires little confirmation from without. Hence the imperturbable self-assur-
ance of the Neo-Platonic type of mind—the almost comic
innocent serenity with which these "babe-like Jupiters," in
Emerson's phrase, Plotinus, Proclus, Olympiodorus, Syne-
sius, and the rest, sit on their clouds and from age to age
prattle to each other and to no contemporary.

But these dialectical exercitations are not all. Abstraction is strangely akin to the poetic imagination, metaphor,
symbolism, and the mythopoeic faculty. Plato, as if in di-
vinatory anticipation of the Neo-Platonists and the Hege-
lians, calls the pseudo dialectics of the One and the Many
an eternal disease of language in the human mind.[3] But the
disease of language, like the disease of the oyster, yields
pearls. Max Müller called mythology a disease of language.
But the peoples who have no mythology have no metaphors,
no true poetry, no imaginative eloquence.

> For no thought of man made gods to love or honour
> Ere the song within the silent soul began.
> Nor could earth in dream or deed take heaven upon her
> Till the word was clothed with speech by lips of man.

Lafcadio Hearn could not get his Japanese class in English
literature to understand Tennyson's *Tithonus*. And they
could not conceive the meaning of the line:

> She is more beautiful than day.
> (*The Beggar Maid* 8)

You cannot have the glorious exuberance of Shakespearean metaphor except at the price of Shakespeare's bad puns. The logic chopping and the cloudy sophistries of the sophists were precipitated by the reasoning of Plato and Aristotle into the crystals of logic. The scholasticism of the Middle Ages created the terminology of modern philosophy and disciplined the European mind for science. It may be, as Jowett says, that the habit of mind that makes necessary distinctions will go on to make unnecessary ones. But the habit is none the less indispensable for the creation of either philosophy or science. And so, naturally enough, this fallacy, this game of realizing abstractions, is indissolubly associated with the poetries, the mythologies, the religions, of Europe.

There is an order of minds in which imagination and feeling are more stimulated by the abstract and the vague than by the concrete and particular. The large abstraction is a barren blank check to barren literal minds. But poets and Platonizing philosophers fill it out for sums that no earthly bank can pay; and their art or artifice keeps this unreal currency in circulation. The orders of intelligible and intelligent gods, intra- and extracosmic divinities of Iamblichus and Julian, the "thrones, dominations, princedoms, virtues, powers" of Dionysius the Areopagite, are of the same family as Shelley's Desires and Adorations, Winged Persuasions, and Veiled Destinies (*Adonais* XIII 1-2), or Tennyson's The Great Intelligences fair/That range above our mortal state (*In Mem.* LXXXV 21-22). And the play of abstractions not only gives pleasurable exercise to the logical instinct, and stimulates the personifying imagination in poetry, but the abstractions become to the Neo-Platonic mind symbols of otherwise ineffable and inexpressible meanings. The Neo-Platonist is, like Dante, Milton, Swedenborg, Blake, Shelley, and Plato himself in some moods, a symbolist. As Milton expresses it:

> and what surmounts the reach
> Of human sense, I shall delineate so,
> By likening spiritual to corporal forms,
> As may express them best; though what if earth
> Be but the shadow of heaven, and things therein
> Each to other like, more than on earth is thought?
>
> *Paradise Lost* V 571-576

"The world of imagination is the world of eternity," says Blake. ". . . There exist in that Eternal World the Permanent Realities of Every Thing that we see reflected in this Vegetable Glass of Nature."[4]

> Life, like a dome of many-coloured glass
> Stains the white radiance of eternity,

says Shelley.[5]

"But of the heaven which is above the heavens," says Plato,"what earthly poet ever did or ever will sing worthily? . . . There abides very being, the colorless, formless, intangible essence visible only to mind—beauty not in the likeness of a face or hands or in any form of speech or knowledge or animal or particular thing in time or place, but beauty absolute, separate, simple, everlasting—the source and cause of the perishing beauty of all other things."[6]

Accepted in this way, Neo-Platonism is perhaps the most beautiful of philosophic systems. In the eloquent language of Mr. Alfred Benn: "Nothing can be imagined more imposing than this wondrous procession of forms defiling from the unknown to the unknown—from the self-developing consciousness of Reason as it breaks and flames and multiplies into a whole universe of being and life and thought, ever returning, by the very law of their production, to the source whence they have sprung—onward and outward on the wings of the cosmic Soul, through this visible world, where they reappear as images of intellectual beauty in the eternal revolutions of the starry spheres above, in the everlasting reproductions of organic species below . . . till the utmost limits of their propagation and dispersion have been reached, till the last faint rays of existence die out in the dark and void region that extends to infinity beyond."[7] Or better yet, let us take it in the more exact and scientific language of a poet, Matthew Arnold, who has summed up both the system and the moral ideal of Plotinus in a single strophe:

> If, in the silent mind of *One* all-pure
>   At first imagined lay
> The sacred world; and by *procession* sure
> From those still deeps, in form and colour drest,
> Seasons alternating, and night and day,
> The long mused thought to north, south, east, and west,
> Took then its all-seen way.
> O waking on a world which thus-wise springs!
>
> . . . .
> . . . . O waking on life's stream!
> By lonely pureness to the all-pure fount
> (Only by this thou canst) the colour'd dream
>   Of life remount!
>   *In utrumque paratus,* 1 ff.

Arnold's last words suggest a third aspect of this play of abstractions which is constitutive of Neo-Platonism. The association, namely, of abstractions with ideas of purity, immateriality, spirituality, transcendence, escape from the body, repose in the bosom of unity, mysticism. I will postpone that topic or these topics for the conclusion of the chapter. And since Neo-Platonism is, after all, essentially a special interpretation of Plato, I will first present the chief elements in Plato's writings that seem to justify this interpretation, and then summarize briefly and less poetically than Benn and Matthew Arnold the resulting system.

All that the ordinary mind esteems concrete real things, then, the Neo-Platonic mind treats as symbols and suggestions of abstractions which may be half personified in a faint, pale, metaphysical mythology and built up into ingenious systems or strung out in hierarchies stretching from the lowest demon to the supreme and ineffable unknown and unknowable God. But the nobler Neo-Platonism is aware that in this it is only playing with symbols. At the most it dallies and coquettes with superstition and the concrete supernatural. In its later degenerate forms Neo-Platonism tends to become mere system mongering and vain multiplication of terminology, or descends to table rapping and levitation. Now, there emanates from Plato, or is attached to his name, a huge literature of liberal theology, natural theology, theosophy, pantheism, mysticism, higher and lower, Neo-Pythagoreanism, occultism, and superstition. The easiest way for me would be to ignore everything except what I regard as the only true Platonic tradition—liberal theology and natural theology. The true and typical Platonists in this domain are such men as Cicero, Plutarch, Schleiermacher, Matthew Arnold, and Martineau, with perhaps in second line the writers who may be represented by the ideas of Pope's *Essay on Man* and Leibnitz' *Theodicy*, to whom we may add, if we please, the Cambridge Platonists, Dean Inge, and Dr. Fosdick.

But this would be too arbitrary, for the various schools of Platonizing mystics and occultists, though they misrepresent Plato, fill a large place in the history of Platonism. Something must be said of them, and the best way to avoid the impossible, the wearisome, the repetitious detail, without falling into a meaningless vagueness and abstraction, will be to describe each type first and chiefly in terms of the passages of Plato on which it rests its claim to be called Platonic. That will at least be something definite and concrete, however inadequate it may seem to the ideal of an exhaustive historical erudition. It is at any rate the procedure I shall use in the present chapter on Neo-Platonism, and in the next succeeding two.

There is, first and chief, the second part of the *Parmenides*, a concatenation of abstractions about the one and the many, being and nonbeing, the whole and the part, the same and the other, the like and the unlike, which Plato intended partly as an illustration of the vanity of absolute metaphysics, partly as an elementary lesson in logic, partly, perhaps, as his anticipatory version of Herbert Spencer's Unknowable.[8] The Neo-Platonists took it as an exemplar of true dialectics, leading up to the intuition or spiritual apprehension of the ineffable One. All the dialectic of Neo-Platonism is in the *Parmenides*. Plato put it there to get rid of it, instead of spilling it all over his philosophy like Hegel and Aristotle. Then there is the awe-inspiring poetic prose of the *Timaeus* with its symbolic story of creation, its Demiourgos, its world-soul, its suggestion of the Neo-Platonic trinity of soul, intellect, and the one, the good, or God, its conception of the world as an infinite living thing, and of the stars as the abode of the souls, and its ironical but seriously accepted acceptance of the gods of the mythology as inferior ministers of the supreme God.[9] There are the eloquent passages of the *Phaedo* (69 A ff.) about the purification of the philosophic soul from the clogs of appetite and sense and its flight to communion with God. There is the prenatal vision of the Ideas outside the world, beyond our bourne of space and time, in the *Phaedrus* (247 C-D); its symbolization of the soul under the figure of a winged charioteer with one unruly and one orderly steed (*ibid.* 246 A ff.); its loss of the power of the wing and its descent into the world of sense, its fall. There is the doctrine in the *Meno* (82 B ff.) and the *Phaedo* (72 E ff.) that all our knowledge here is reminiscence and imperfect recapture of the heavenly vision. There is the Pythagorean idea of the transmigration of souls in the *Phaedo* (81 E-82 B), the *Phaedrus* (248-249), and the myth that concludes the *Republic* (617 E ff.).[10] There is, in the *Republic* (508 A ff.), the comparison of the

Idea of Good to the sun which both illumines and creates, and the picture of ordinary human life as a firelit, shadow-haunted cave from which philosophy releases the soul to find its way up to the true sunlight and the contemplation of reality (514 A ff.). There are all the myths of creation, immortality, and the judgment to come. There is the moral eloquence of the *Gorgias*, and the little sermons scattered through the *Laws*. There is, in the *Republic* (475 C ff.), the portrait of the philosopher who is spectator of all time and existence, and who, it is said in the *Theaetetus* (172 C; 173 C ff.), hardly knows the way to the City Hall. All this poetry and symbolism which Plato as a literary artist and man of the world holds in due subordination to the logical reason and relieves opportunely with serious argument and practical, common-sense criticism of life, the Neo-Platonists made the theme of obsessed meditation or of hairsplitting refinements of dialectics. To these are to be added all the passages in which Plato as a literary man plays with the symbols of the Eleusinian mysteries and the language of Pythagorean or of Orphic tradition, but which later super-stition to this day takes as a specimen of mystic and secret doctrines handed down from prehistoric revelation. Such are the *daimonion* of Socrates,[11] the divine voice of inner admonition that never urges but sometimes checks actions, not for the sake of so-called material goods but in the spir-itual interests of the soul; the doctrine of daemons,[12] of whom he whom the multitude call the great god Love is one, mediator and interpreter between the gods and men (*Symp.* 202 DE); the doctrine of the inspiration whereby the poet and the statesman achieve things inexplicable by their conscious mind (*Ion* 533 E ff.), and Socrates' own pre-tense of inspiration in the *Cratylus* and the *Phaedrus* (243 AB); the doctrine of the divine madness of prophecy, poetry, and love, in the *Phaedrus* (244-245); the figuring of the stages of knowledge as the grades of an initiation, and its consummation as the beatific vision; the prophetic dream of Socrates at the beginning of the *Crito* (44 AB) and the voices that ring in his ears like those heard by the Corybants at its end (54 D); the description in the *Phaedo* (81 D) of the earth-freighted souls of the sensuous, haunting their old abodes and materializing as apparitions at tombs; the ironic description in the *Timaeus* of the liver as a mirror of prophecy (71 D ff.); the play with number symbolism, which Emerson calls "throwing a little mathematical dust in the reader's eyes"[13]; the apparent acceptance of the oracles and the rebuking of youthful skepticism; the apparent willingness to interpret any desired meaning into ancient and poetic texts by the allegorical method; the attempt to elicit profound truths from the derivation of words; the allusions to Orpheus, Musaeus, Pythagoras, Epimenides; the frequent references to the transcendent wisdom of ancient poets, sages, and prophets; the lore in the *Philebus* (16 C ff.) that is handed down with Promethean fire from the wiser ancients, and that turns out to be essentially one of the main precepts of Baconian logic;[14] the references in the *Charmides* (156 B ff.) to a disciple of the Thracian Zamolxis, who gave Socrates a charm for the headache but swore him to impart it to no one whom he had not first examined on the state of his soul; the description in the *Alcibiades* (121 ff.) of the education of the Persian princes in magic by the Magi; Diotima in the *Symposium*, the prophetess who taught Socrates the lore of heavenly love (201 D ff.); the elevation and solemn unction of style, half playful, half serious, with which Plato speaks of these things, and so forth.

A critical and flexible literary interpretation discovers no trace of concrete superstition in any of these passages. Literary ornament, irony, harmless concessions to popular religion when it is not immoral, and the willingness to use traditional symbols for the faith that there is something more than mechanism in the universe, explain them all. But

they have been and still are endlessly quoted in the literature of superstition and mysticism by the mob of incredible
twaddle-churners, fanatical and hypocritical ascetics, maud-
lin mystics, and table-tipping thaumaturgists who have
made Platonism a byword with rational men.

These impressions have been confirmed in both camps by
the exaggeration of these Platonic traits in some of the
spurious letters, as, for example, the affectation of a secret
inner doctrine which must not be revealed to the vulgar,[15]
and the assumption that knowledge can be transmitted
from mind to mind by mere physical contact or even by
absent epistolary treatment; the pure jargon of certain
references to an ineffable and vaguely trinitary deity; the
caricature of the passage of the *Phaedrus* (275 D ff.)[16] that
exalts the spoken above the written word in the statement
that Plato's real philosophy never was and never could be
written down. It is the misunderstanding of such passages
that has served to confirm the belief, still prevalent in some
quarters, that Plato is only the next link after Pythagoras
in the chain that transmits primitive revelations from Zoroaster, Orpheus, and Musaeus, to Plotinus and his successors. They are, also, a chief cause of the distrust of Plato in
the minds of many men of science who, having no leisure
for fine discriminations, feel that traditional Platonism has
too often been the ally of the obscurantist forces that ham-
per science and block the pathway of progress.

Zeller's summary analysis of Plotinus' system fills more
than 160 pages of German text and fine-print notes.[17] My
promised abstract must be briefer still.

Everything exists by virtue of the inherent tendency of
the plenitude of ungrudging Being in the higher to radiate,
illuminate, emanate, overflow, and impart itself to the
lower. In this process or procession the higher remains un-
changed while the lower turns back towards and reflects
that which brings it forth, somewhat as, psychologically

speaking, the mind turns back to and reflects upon itself. The highest is the ineffable One (of Plato's *Parmenides*) identical with the Idea of Good in the *Republic*, though in its unknowable unity it cannot properly be said to be either good or intelligent. The second principle, emanating from this, is the Nous, or intellect, answering to the Demiourgos, or creator, in Plato's *Timaeus*. The ideas that are the proto-types of all created things and constitute the intelligible world are in this Nous. They are the thoughts of God, or, to put it in Aristotelian terminology, the intellect is identical with its ideas, and God is self-thinking thought. In the poetical, cosmogonical myth of Plato's *Timaeus*, the Demi-ourgos creates the soul of the world; that is, in Plotinus' translation, soul is the emanation of intellect and the third and last member of the triad or trinity. Human souls, though endowed with freedom, are parts or detachments of the soul. Extended first matter is the final and faintest irradia-tion of Being, and as such, through its weakness, the ulti-mate principle of evil, which is merely negation, and noth-ing positive. All good, true, and beautiful things are ex-plicable as the restoration of the soul to its native purity, or the dominance and irradiation of the material by the ideal. All evil and unbeautiful things are the clogging and imbruting of the soul, or the obscuration of the idea, by matter. The order here set forth as in time really belongs to timeless eternity, and expresses the true nature and abiding relations of existence.

Such an abstract, of course, does injustice to the system. Though it can, for the most part, be deduced from the too literal interpretation of Plato's imagery, or the too fanciful interpretation of his dialectic, some new elements have en-tered in. Plato, it is true, had already opposed and defini-tively refuted dogmatic materialism. But after the domina-tion of ancient thought for four hundred years by the materialistic systems of Stoicism and Epicureanism, the

statement of the spiritualistic argument is much amplified
in Plotinus. His chapters on the soul, perhaps the earliest
of his book, and the starting point of his system, are much
more explicit than Plato in the demonstration of the impossibility of explaining or explaining away the soul in terms
of matter, so much so that he is sometimes wrongly credited
with being the first to proclaim this truth. His discussion of
the soul also contains many interesting psychological observations and analyses. He brings out the idea of self-
consciousness more clearly than any of his predecessors,
and sometimes approximates to the ideas and the methods
of Cartesian and Berkeleian psychological idealism. Though
his theory of beauty (*Enn.* I 6) is derived from the *Phaedrus*
and the *Symposium*, it is more nearly a philosophy of aesthetics than anything in Plato. He speaks quite eloquently
and poetically of the beauty of the world (*Enn.* II 9. 4).
Though his ethics and theodicy are, in the main, Platonic,
they are enriched by Stoic and perhaps Christian ideas,
and the spiritual experience of the first two Christian centuries. Lastly, though Neo-Platonism and the Neo-Platonic
emphasis on the mystical side of Plato in alliance with
orientalism fostered the development of superstition in the
later empire, Plotinus is nearly as free from the concrete
supernatural as Plato.

We have no time for the system builders that followed
Plotinus. The psychology of their methods and their tricks
of procedure are all that concern us. Hairsplitting dialectic
multiplies distinctions and abstractions. Each of these is
embodied, personified, hypostatized, and identified with
some Platonic image or category, or some figure of the Greek,
the Oriental, or the Egyptian mythology. The supreme God,
Being, the Good, the Unknowable, is, following a hint of
Plato's *Timaeus*, exalted above all contact with the gross
work of creation. This is a well-known principle of the psychology or the rhetoric of religion. The worshipers of an

inferior and more human divinity in the hyperboles of devotion transfer to him all the epithets and the immunities of the supreme god, and it then becomes necessary to invent another, subordinate, deity to do his dirty work and maintain contact with this mundane sphere. Thus the sublunar world is left to inferior delegates, easily identifiable with the daemons and angels of popular superstition or exotic cults. The way is thus prepared for theurgy, thaumaturgy, levitation, materialization, thought transference, in short for Mr. Sludge the medium, and Mrs. Piper.

> Non ragioniam di lor, ma guarda e passa—

observing only that some of the Neo-Platonic writers who employ this language are very slightly, if at all, affected by the taint; the emperor Julian, for example. On this point, our histories of philosophy are quite untrustworthy. A special investigation is required for each writer, beginning with Plato himself.

A test case is supplied by a notable page of the Theodicy in the tenth book of Plato's *Laws*. What Plato in effect says there is that the heavens declare the glory of God, that the order of the universe presupposes a divine mind, and that it would be better that the people should believe in Apollo and his chariot than that they should accept mechanistic atheism. His position might be summed up in Bacon's saying, that he would rather believe all the fables of the Talmud than that this universal frame is without an author.[18] But a majority of modern interpreters, taking Plato's rhetoric literally, have read into the passage Plato's personal belief in the chariot of the sun god, star worship, and even the Stoic paradox that the years, the seasons, and the months are gods. I give a paraphrase or free translation of the passage that honestly and critically represents its meaning: "Every man," Plato says, "sees the body of the sun, but no one its soul. For soul is not apprehensible by sense but only by thought. If soul is the cause of the motion of the sun, we have three alternatives: either the soul inhabits its body and moves it as our souls us, or it dwells in some external body that communicates its motion, or, independently of all body, it guides the sun by some transcendent power. But whether such a soul, mounted on its chariot, drives the sun, or in whatsoever way it accomplishes this, man must conceive of it as god. And as of the sun, so we must say of all the stars, the moon, the years, the months, and the seasons, that since it has been proved that soul or souls possessed of all excellence are the causes of these things, we must affirm these souls to be gods, whether as living things dwelling in bodies they order all the heavens, or in whatsoever way and manner they operate. No man who admits these principles can refuse to say with Thales that 'all things are full of Gods' " (*Laws* 898 D-899 B).

Now, it is natural that uncompromising materialists should refuse to discriminate, and should see in this passage nothing but the superstition, as they deem it, that there is something more than mechanism in the universe. But it is incomprehensible that critics who themselves admit any religion in any shape, or any form of belief in soul, should fail to perceive that the affirmation of that general faith is Plato's only concern here, and that the alternatives which he proposes do not describe or define his own positive belief but only express his willingness to let the unsophisticated retain the faith in any form, rather than abandon themselves to the propaganda of crude dogmatic materialism claiming to speak in the name of science. How can anyone who recalls the skeptical passages about the "magnified non-natural man" and the divinities of the mythology from the *Phaedrus* and the *Timaeus*, and who takes note of the repeated phrase here, "soul, in whatsoever way or manner exercising its powers," suppose that Plato is here referring to his personal belief in the chariot of Apollo, or star worship, or the literal divinity of the months and seasons of the year? Yet this is precisely what sometimes seems to be done by scholars of the rank of Cumont, Murray, C. C. J. Webb, and many others.[19]

A historian of Platonism cannot overlook the fact that what is perhaps the most readable and widely read English book on Greek religion today is, in its perspective and its emphasis, a complete misconception of the cultured Greco-Roman intelligence in the eight post-Platonic centuries, and of that religion of Greek philosophy of which I spoke too briefly in my previous lecture. Professor Murray's chapter on what he calls "The Failure of Nerve"[20] systematically misuses the rhetoric of Greek religious and philosophic literature to impute to the better writers the superstitions of the multitude. The procedure which I am deprecating is peculiarly irrational in an age that publishes horoscopes in its daily papers, prints scores of volumes of psychical research, and numbers among its favorite books and authors Professor James's *Will to Believe*, and Maeterlinck, who accepted as genuine miracles the performances of the horse "Kluger Hans." Professor Murray himself, if the London newspapers can be trusted, alternates parlor demonstrations of his gift of mind reading with lectures to rational societies, disparaging the superstition of Plato in comparison with the rigid rationalism of the Stoics, though even they, he says, deviated from the true scientific attitude in admitting the possibility of a friend behind phenomena. He and we, surely, cannot have it both ways.

One aspect of later Neo-Platonism cannot be passed over. The entire theology of the unknown God and the metaphysics of the Unknowable goes back through these Neo-Platonists to Plato's *Parmenides*. The teleological philosophy of the unknowable exalts the divinity of pure being by stripping it of limiting affirmations until nothing but negations remain. It then turns around and explains that the negations are all to be taken in a Pickwickian sense, as implying higher transcendental affirmations. This is the procedure described in Berkeley's *divine visual language* as the "method of growing in expression and dwindling in notion."[21] It can be traced from Plato through Philo Judaeus, Plutarch, the Christian Fathers, and the Neo-Platonists to Hermes Trismegistus, Dionysius the Areopagite, and Scotus Erigena, down to Sir Thomas Browne's quaint statement that "nothing can be said hyperbolically of God, . . . Trismegistus's circle, whose center is everywhere and circumference nowhere, was no hyperbole."[22] From Sir Thomas Browne we might follow it to Pope's universal prayer and Mansel's philosophy of the Unconditioned, the inspiration of Sir William Hamilton and Herbert Spencer. The Pickwickian sense always accompanies it, as the *deus ex machina* for the resolution of all difficulties.

When Parmenides speaks of the one as resting in the same place, says the Neo-Platonic commentator Simplicius, he does not mean the rest that is the opposite of motion, but the abiding that is exalted above both rest and motion. This is the Neo-Platonic μονή, or abiding in its place, of the higher principle, at the same time that it emanates or goes forth in creation. It is derived from one sentence about the Demiourgos in Plato's *Timaeus*,[23] and is endlessly repeated and elaborated in Neo-Platonic and Christian exegesis. It is found in the lines at the end of the twenty-ninth canto of Dante's *Paradiso*: "And the amplitude of the eternal, since it hath made itself so many mirrors where it is broken, one in itself remaining as before,"[24] which recalls the lines quoted above from Matthew Arnold (cf. *supra* p. 42), and also a well-known Platonic passage in Shelley's *Adonais* (LII 1):   The One remains, the many change and pass.

One of the latest echoes of the conceit is Milton's: "for he also went/invisible, yet stayed" (*Par. Lost* VII 589-590).

The Pickwickian sense, though especially characteristic of Neo-Platonism, is the mainspring or, if you will, the safety valve of all abstract and absolute metaphysics. It functions regularly on every page of Hegel with the aid of the double meaning of "aufheben," and is a favorite device of Descartes. "Substance cannot be used unifically," he says, "of finite and infinite being. God is cause of himself, but never effect." Even Aristotle, defending slavery, argues that the slave is of the master, but the master is not of the slave (*Pol.* 1254 a 11-13). This Pickwickian sense is what Roosevelt called "the use of weasel words." It is still a favorite evasion of philosophers. Kantians tell us that Kant's *a priori* is not really *a priori*, and that his design does not imply intention. Huxley says: "Let me remind the reader that I use anarchy in its philosophical sense." Innumerable writers have explained that freedom is obedience to the higher necessity, and Miss Jane Addams once announced that patriotism is to be taken in the cosmopolitan sense. Christ is said by some prohibitionists to have turned the water into unfermented wine. The Stoics said sensation is an impression on the tablets of the mind but not an impression in the sense of convexity and concavity, and a modern neurological psychologist goes them one better with the remark that the synapse is a functional junction but that it is not necessary to decide whether it is an anatomical junction. Which is as if a railroad president should say: "We have a functional switch at Bird Center Station. But I don't know whether there are any rails there." The culmination is achieved in Cora Lenore Williams' *Creative Involution*. "You have passed into the fourth dimension of spatial realization," says Cora. "Time is past, you shout aloud, and laugh to find yourself in the inside of externality."[25]

Closely analogous to this negative theology is the metaphysics of the Unknowable, which culminates in the last great Neo-Platonist, Damascius, who tangles himself and his readers in a coil of contradiction and antinomy compared with which Spencer's Unknowable and Kant's antinomies are lucidity itself. Damascius admits that if it is unknowable we cannot properly speak of it at all, yet he insists that we have at least a yearning or travail towards it.[26] The word ὠδὶς, "travail or birth pangs," comes from the passage on the Idea of Good in Plato's *Republic*, and, like μονὴ and μένειν above, shows once more that these philosophies, from one point of view, are merely the conversion of Platonic metaphors into metaphysics.

Whatever the cause, the long postclassical centuries of the Roman Empire seem to us a protracted decadence and decline. Whatever interest we may feel in Seneca, Tacitus, Juvenal, and Plutarch, Epictetus, Lucian, and Marcus Aurelius, terminates, like our school-day acquaintance, with the dates and names of the emperors up to the accession of Commodus. Thereafter we dimly descry what Renan calls "that hell of a half-century," a progressive degeneracy and disintegration into chaos and medieval night. Yet it was after the year 200 that Plotinus excogitated this new interpretation of Platonism, which became the fashionable philosophy of the intelligentsia, making Stoicism and Epicureanism obsolete; which was elaborated for three centuries in a succession of ingenious and ever more complicated metaphysical systems that make child's play of Hegel and Schelling; which colored the thought and the language of all educated men, including the Christian Fathers; which passed by various underground channels to the philosophy and theology of the Middle Ages; which emerged with the revival of Platonism at the Renaissance, became the source of German mysticism and British liberal and symbolic theologies, accompanied Platonism as its shadow through the following centuries, and is today imbibed by readers innocent of Plato and Plotinus from Emerson, Maeterlinck, Bergson, and Dean Inge.

We have now finally to consider Neo-Platonism as a last phase of ancient idealism and the literature of escape or flight from reality. Today the heroes of Mr. Sherwood Anderson seek escape in running away from the factory, the accounting room, and the wife, in the emancipation of instinct and the breakdown of inhibitions that check what Whitman calls "native moments" and their expression in the ordinary decent citizen. Mrs. Virginia Woolf, in her booklet *Monday or Tuesday*, finds her escape from the tiresome restrictions of common sense and consecutive thought by way of the Joyce *parole intérieure* chaotic soliloquy, and by an occasional lapse into the indecency of which she avows that she grows fonder the older she grows. But the human spirit is infinitely various. The Neo-Platonists looked for escape in the opposite direction—of pure thought, as they termed it. They were not troubled by the double meaning of pure: independent of the perceptions of sense, and free from sensuality. They found that ambiguity already in the last discourses of Socrates in Plato's *Phaedo*, and they sincerely believed that there is a real connection between devotion to pure, abstract thought and the moral *katharsis*, that is, emancipation from appetite and desire. There was no Freud to tell them that if Plotinus was ashamed of having a body it was only because his subconscious was obsessed by the body's libidos, if that is the proper Freudian plural and proper false quantity as warranted by the bard of *Spoon River* in the exquisite line:

> You call it lust, we call it libido,

followed also, I see, by the recent prize-winning ode to Freud:

> you know
> There is no exit for my libido.

We fortunately do not have to determine here whether the purity of pure thought is necessarily an illusion or may

sometimes be a fact of experience. It was true enough for
poetry and philosophy and a literature of idealistic escape
for Hellenic thinkers in a brutal Roman world deliquescing
into barbarism. Though Matthew Arnold is, as I said, out
of fashion, I must again take as my text here his definitive
description of this aspect of Neo-Platonism:

> . . . O waking on life's stream!
> By lonely pureness to the all-pure fount
> (Only by this thou canst) the colour'd dream
>   Of life remount!
>
> *In utrumque paratus* 11-14
> (cf. *supra* p. 43)

But pure thought outside Plato, its inventor, is dangerously akin in some of Plato's imitators to pure jargon. The
faculty of language, developed we may suppose for the practical purposes of communication, becomes in the hyper-
trophy of abstract words an end in itself. The machine functions in the void with no grist to grind but with a soothing,
hypnotizing power in the sound of its clapper and the droning of its wheels on the axles. Remoteness from sense imparts a feeling of detachment and purity and of remoteness
from the strife and turmoil of the world. As Pope put it:
"And quitting sense call imitating God."[27] Unintelligibility
is mistaken for profundity. Neo-Platonism is much more
than this; but it is also the supreme historical example of
this psychological trait of the paradoxical creature, man.
It is, as already pointed out, what Plato profoundly calls an
eternal and ageless disease of the very faculty of speech and
discourse of reason within us.

Our scientific century is by no means immune. The thing
is still with us the basis of prosperous and dividend-paying
religions, the stock in trade of the most widely advertised
philosophers, the key to the success of best-selling books of
pseudo science, and of some popular expositions of real science. It accounts, for example, for all popular interpreta-

tions of Professor Einstein's theories, and for the theories themselves apart from their strictly technical and physical meanings, which are intelligible only to a few experts. I once saw an audience of fifteen hundred people apparently listening to Professor Einstein himself for a stricken hour; not ten of them understood a single paragraph or sentence, yet they were edified. A brilliant English critic, J. Middleton Murry, writing on the eternal theme of the disintegration of the old morality in the minds of the younger generation, says, "To some the Einstein theory may show the way of reconciliation." That is pure jargon, it is absolutely meaningless; yet a majority of his readers are probably thrilled. Reconciliation is an idealistic word, and the Einstein theory is as good a name as another for the unknowable that shapes our destinies, for whatever gods there be. The audiences at the Lowell Institute must have been similarly affected when Professor Whitehead told them, "For Berkeley's *mind* I substitute a process of prehensive unification[28] . . . this realized togetherness is the achievement of an emergent value defined." I have addressed Lowell Institute audiences myself, and unless they have greatly changed it is quite impossible that they should have understood the mystico-mathematico-philosophical parts of either Professor Whitehead's or Mr. Bertrand Russell's lectures. Yet they were fascinated, thrilled, edified, hypnotized. So Mr. Sherwood Anderson tells us how Mrs. Gertrude Stein's book, called *Tender Buttons*, excited him. "Here," he says, "was something purely experimental and dealing with words separated from sense."

Before we smile at the devotion of three centuries to the concatenation of abstract terms, the interlocking divine hierarchies, the pure galimatias, as it may seem to us, of the later and lower forms of Neo-Platonism, we should remember that there is today a considerable body of readers from Maeterlinck and Dean Inge down who are excited, inspired, soothed, by sentences such as these, which I take not from Mrs. Eddy or Aimee McPherson or Emerson or Rousseau or Mr. Post of Battle Creek and Postum Cereal, but from Mr. Stephen MacKenna's translation of Plotinus:

"Let every soul recall, then, . . . the truth that soul is the author of all living things, that it has breathed the life into them all, whatever is nourished by earth and sea, all the creatures of the air, the divine stars in the sky; it is the maker of the sun; itself formed and ordered this vast heaven and conducts all that rhythmic motion. . . . That great soul must stand pictured before another soul, one not mean, a soul that has become worthy to look, emancipate from the lure, from all that binds its fellows in bewitchment, holding itself in quietude. Let not merely the enveloping body be at peace, body's turmoil stilled, but all that lies around, earth at peace, and sea at peace, and air and the very heavens. Into that heaven, all at rest, let the great soul be conceived to roll inward at every point, penetrating, permeating, from all sides pouring in its light. . . .[29] Thus, the Soul unlit remains without that vision; lit, it possesses what it sought. And this is the true end set before the Soul, to take that light, to see the Supreme by the Supreme and not by the light of any other principle. . . . But how is this to be accomplished? Cut away everything."[30]

Perhaps they are not altogether mistaken. Even for readers who can attach no definite meaning to the words, the repetition of such formulas may, like the Buddhist prayers in the *Light of Asia*, seem to withdraw the soul from the harsh contacts of reality, purge the thoughts of earthly dross, numb the nerves of pain, create what Dante and Schopenhauer and Rousseau and Wordsworth and Tennyson in his mystic moods would call the ineffable sense of being; elevate, fortify, and calm, and reconcile the soul to the renunciation of that individual existence to which it so fiercely clings, and teach it to welcome self-annihilation and absorption into the Infinite One, "when the dew-drop slips

into the shining sea and the lone takes flight to the lone."
Neo-Platonism once did that for Goethe, when he wrote in
paraphrase of Plotinus:

> Wär' nicht das Auge sonnenhaft,
> Die Sonne könnt' es nie erblicken;
> Läg' nicht in uns des Gottes eigne Kraft,
> Wie könnt' uns Göttliches entzücken?[31]

> Were there no sunlight in our eyes,
> To yon bright sun they would be blind;
> To thoughts of God how could we rise
> Were there no God within the mind?

It brought consolation to the unhappy British poet, Lionel
Johnson, when he wrote in darkest London:

> Do what thou wilt, thou shalt not so
> Dark Angel! triumph over me.
> Lonely, unto the Lone I go;
> Divine, to the Divinity.[32]

It seems to have done this for the Greek scholars and philosophers of those three hundred years of final decadence.
And who can say that it was wholly an illusion? The feeling
is eternal. The expression is a matter of taste. And those
who do not care for these flights of rhapsody in Stephen
MacKenna's Plotinus, or Edwin Arnold's *Light of Asia*, or
Mrs. Eddy, may still respond to the French poet Joachim
du Bellay's Platonic version of the theme.[33]

CHAPTER III

PLATO AND CHRISTIANITY

INTO THIS WORLD of Greco-Roman thought within which
we have been trying to define the place of Platonism, en-
tered the moral idealism of Jesus, the establishment of the
Christian Church, the development of Christian dogma
from the Sermon on the Mount to the Nicene Creed, and
the growth of Christianity in rivalry with other Oriental
cults that in the decline of the old religion competed for the
favor of the populace, and its final triumph and proclamation as the religion of the state by Constantine. The battle
of the reaction against this decision was fought under the
banner of Neo-Platonism, and (such are the ironies of history) under the leadership of a better and greater man than
Constantine, his nephew Julian, the so-called Apostate.
Julian and his sympathizers were unable to recognize the
superiority of Christianity over the religion to which they
attributed "the glory that was Greece and the grandeur
that was Rome." Celsus, friend of Lucian and author of the
first clever, critical, Voltairean attack on Christianity, cannot comprehend the Christians' devout enthusiasm for a
god whose theophany is the son of a Jewish carpenter, and
as an educated Greek he could see nothing but foolishness
in the argument of the Christian Father, Lactantius (*Div.
inst.* VII 14), that Plato was mistaken in saying that the
world had existed for countless generations, when in fact,
since it was created in six days, it obviously can and will
endure six thousand years and no more.

As the populace must have symbols, the Hellenists felt,
as Renan and Swinburne have felt in our own day, that the
symbolism of the Greek mythology was the more beautiful.
And they sincerely believed that the interpretations read
into it by Neo-Platonism were a higher form of moral and

[62]

religious idealism than anything that the theology of the contemporary Christian bishops could offer. They fought a losing battle. It is a pathetic and interesting story, for which, however, there is no space in so brief an outline as this must necessarily be.

The present chapter, entitled *Plato and Christianity*, is of course not a history of Christianity during these five centuries. It is at most an outline of the relation of Platonism to Christianity. This will involve, first, a brief statement of Plato's own religious philosophy; secondly, a consideration of both the real and the fanciful analogies between Platonism and Christianity; and lastly, a survey of the Platonism of the Christian Fathers and a few of their modern successors, mainly in the form of an enumeration of the thoughts and sayings of Plato that are most frequently quoted by Christian writers.

There is no lack of exhaustive works that discuss and compare in a highly abstract style the supposed metaphysics of Plato's philosophy of religion and the metaphysics of Christian theology.[1] But I have already in the first chapter stated my opinion that metaphysics and religion are connected in Plato only so far as the refutation and repudiation of materialism is the presupposition of anything that can honestly be called religion. If there is something more than mechanism, if there is a possibility of a purpose in the universe, if there is something more than a "harmony" of the elements or a nervous system in the mind or soul of man, that something more, however little we may know of it, opens up infinite possibilities for religious aspiration and hope. Without it there is nothing.

Whether this be true or not, it was Plato's opinion. It is on this that he lays the main stress in the treatise on Natural Theology in the tenth book of his *Laws*, and this is the chief purpose of his psychological analysis in the *Theaetetus*

---

[1] Superior figures refer to notes which will be found on pp. 242-243.

and elsewhere in the dialogues. But apart from this fundamental basis, Plato's treatment of religion is independent
of his metaphysics and cannot be deduced from it. It is to
be found in the *Euthyphro* on piety, in what I have called
the fourfold gospel of the religion of Socrates, in the *Republic*, the *Laws*, and a few sentences of the *Timaeus*. The minor
dialogue, the *Euthyphro*, is ostensibly an attempt to define
piety. It is also a satire on popular religion and on Euthyphro, who is partly an embodiment and partly a type of the
vain and fanatical innovator. "Piety," says Euthyphro na-
ively,"is doing what I do, trying to punish my father for
impiety regardless of the fact that he is my father" (*Euth.*
4 BC). Piety is what pleases the gods. But Socrates wishes
to know which gods, the tribal gods of Greece or Troy, of
London or Berlin, and does Euthyphro really believe that
there is dissension and difference of opinion among the gods?
and war, such as is depicted on the peplus of Athena? As
Ruskin's beautiful rendering of the passage puts it: "And
think you that there is verily war with each other among
the gods? and dreadful enmities and battles, such as the
poets have told, and such as our painters set forth in graven
scripture, to adorn all our sacred rites and holy places; yes,
and in the great Panathenaea themselves, the Peplus, full of
such wild picturing, is carried up into the Acropolis—shall we
say that these things are true, Oh Euthuphron, right-minded
friend?"[2]Again, is right loved by the gods because it is right,
or is it right because the gods love it?—a question debated
in the Middle Ages and by some theologians still.[3] And
lastly, if piety is justice towards the gods, what justice can
there be between man and god, and what service can man's
insignificance render to a being who needs nothing? Is religion a commercial transaction, an exchange between man
and god, of so much worldly prosperity in return for so much
honor, incense, and sacrifice? The dialogue is full of suggestions, but no conclusion is reached.[4]

The *Republic* was the storehouse from which the Christian Fathers drew nearly all their arguments against the old religion, including Plato's admission, so embarrassing to later Hellenists and apologists for Homer, that the mythology could not be justified even as allegory.[5] Plato's censorship of Homer was based on the three famous canons for what a Kantian would style the critique of all possible future theologies: (1) God is the author of good only; (2) there is, with him, no variableness, neither shadow of turning; (3) he does not deceive. The repetitions and paraphrases of these canons in European theology would fill a volume. The *Republic* does not attack dogmatic atheism, a problem which is reserved for the *Laws*, but, in anticipation of the *Laws*, it condemns as practical atheism the later Epicurean doctrine that the gods are careless of mankind (365 D-E), and it denounces as more dangerous than atheism the claim of priestcraft that the judgments of the gods can be bought off by incense and sacrifice and prayer.[6] This was one of the points on which the emperor Julian the Apostate maintained the superiority of Platonic theology over Christian. The heathen priests, he said, refused absolution to the murderer Constantine. The Christians granted it.

The main thesis of the *Republic* is that virtue is its own reward and needs no external sanction in this world or the other.[7] Lactantius censures Plato for this. "The one supreme good," he says, "is not virtue, but immortality."[8] He is of Tennyson's opinion:

Truth for truth, and good for good! The Good, the True, the
                        Pure, the Just—
Take the charm 'For ever' from them, and they crumble into dust.
                (*Locksley Hall Sixty Years After*)

But Plato, having, as he thinks, established the independence of the moral law, withdraws the immense concession of the hypothesis that the good man is usually misunder-

stood, reviled, persecuted, crowned with thorns, and crucified. Even in this world it is normally true that, in the long
run, the righteous man is *not* forsaken and his children do
not beg their bread. And at the bar of eternal justice where
the stripped and shivering soul appears naked and scarred
before the judge, virtue is secure of her crown. Let us, then,
give her—give her the wages of going on and not to die.

The tale told at the end of the *Republic* by Er the son of
Armenius is the chief of the sublime myths in which Plato
embodies what he believes to be a rational and salutary
hope. With the myth that concludes the *Gorgias*, the myth
of the *Phaedo*, and the myth of the *Phaedrus*, it must be
read entire in the text or in Professor J. A. Stewart's *The
Myths of Plato*. The myths are introduced by a show of
arguments which differ from one another more than the
myths themselves. The Christian Fathers while approving
Plato's conclusions usually ridicule his arguments and affirm that Christian faith is the one solid basis of a belief in
immortality.[9] Plato was as well aware as are the Ingersoll
lecturers of today that he could prove nothing except what
he elsewhere does prove, the breakdown of the negative
case of dogmatic materialism. Eight or nine hundred years
after Plato, the Byzantine poet Agathias Asianus resumed
the results of ancient speculation in some such terms as
these:

> I questioned once Nicostratus the Sage,
> The Plato and Aristotle of our age,
> One cunning with sheer logic to divide
> A hair 'twixt northeast and 'twixt northwest side:
> "What think you of the soul? Come, make reply.
> Is it immortal or condemned to die,
> Matter or spirit, only known to sense,
> A mixture or a pure intelligence?"
> The sage consulted many a learned scroll,
> The stagirite's three books upon the soul,

resemblance of St. Paul's contrast between the earthly crown of the athlete and the Christian crown (1 *Cor.* 9. 24-25) to an eloquent passage in the last book of the *Republic* about the rewards of the just man in this life (613 C). On the border line and perhaps to be styled accidental rather than fanciful is the parallel sometimes drawn between the crucifixion, and the torture and final impalement of the perfectly righteous man described in the second book of the *Republic* (361 E-362 A). Rousseau's Savoyard Vicar in his famous profession of faith says: "When Plato describes his ideal just man covered with all the opprobrium of crime and worthy of all the prizes of virtue, he depicts trait for trait Jesus Christ. The likeness is impossible to miss, and all the Fathers of the Church have felt it."[17] An eloquent passage of Tertullian applies the language and imagery of Plato here not to Christ himself and the crucifixion, but to the typical Christian, and to the body of Christian believers as persecuted and tortured by the rulers and populace of the Pagan Empire.

We need not take seriously the hypothesis frequently met in Jewish, early Christian, and medieval literature, that Plato was the Attic Moses and learned the philosophy of Moses from Jeremiah in Egypt.[18] In the polemics of the third century each side had learned to use the weapons of the other. Both Christians and pagans, for example, practiced allegory uncritically to defend the rationality of their own mythologies, and sometimes rejected, almost in the critical spirit of a modern scholar, the allegories of their opponents. Similarly, while Christians contended that all the finest things in Plato were borrowed from the Hebrew Scriptures, their philosophic and Neo-Platonic adversaries reversed the contention and argued that the coincidences in thought and moral sentiment only proved that the Christians were plagiarizing Plato.

A few specimens of these uncritical and fanciful analogies

and parallels must represent them all. Justin Martyr, commenting on the text, "The sword shall devour you," says it is not a literal sword, but the wrath of God, that punishes those who chose the wrong. Hence he innocently adds, it is the same as Plato's "The blame is with the chooser, blameless is God" (*Rep.* 617 E).[19] Tertullian (*De anima* 16) tells us that Plato's tripartite division of the soul into reason, anger, and appetite is anticipated in the person of Christ. Christ teaches the way of salvation by reason; he denounces the scribes and Pharisees in anger; he eats the Last Supper in the company of his disciples with appetite. Plato, describing the myth of the Golden Age, when men were shepherded by gods and understood the language of the animals, says ironically, "We cannot know whether they were really happier than we. If they merely abandoned themselves to self-indulgence and the enjoyment of leisure, they were less happy. If they studied to learn all that the animals had to teach them, they were happier" (*Politicus* 271 A ff.). Eusebius (*Praep. ev.* 12.14) quotes this to prove that the serpent could talk with Eve. Minucius Felix identifies with Christian practice Plato's famous sentence, "The father and the maker of this universe is hard to discover and impossible to proclaim to all men" (*Tim.* 28 C). "We too," he says, "know God as father and creator and we don't speak of Him except when questioned" (*Oct.* 19.14),[20] and many of the Fathers take Plato's word "impossible" in the sense of "dangerous" as inviting persecution. The treatment of the body as a mere hindrance to the soul in the *Phaedo* (82 C; 114 C) and all suggestions of asceticism in Plato, already exploited by the Neo-Platonist, were interpreted in the sense of similar aspects of Christianity, and a story repeated in many medieval sermons had it that Plato deliberately selected a malarial site for his Academy in order to suppress the rebellion of the flesh in himself and his students,[21] and the word Academy itself was sometimes derived from *achos* = ache and *demos* = people.

The influence of the Platonic *Republic* in shaping the Christian idea of a City of God tempts me to a digression for which there is little space.[22] "The wise man," says Socrates, in a passage quoted in an earlier chapter,[23] "will not take part in politics except at some imperative providential call. He belongs to another city, the city of the ideal whose pattern is laid up in heaven, of which whoso will may constitute himself a citizen" (*Rep.* 592 AB). When the Church grew strong, St. Augustine and others rightly affirmed that their City of God was the actual Church of God both on earth and in heaven. The Platonic passage is merely a general expression of the idealist's withdrawal from the world (ἀναχώρησις, from which "anchorite" is derived, is the Platonic and Neo-Platonic word) and as such is one of the few Platonic thoughts directly quoted by Kant. Modern philosophies of history have also found in the Platonic state interesting prefigurements or prophecies of the organization of medieval society under the Catholic Church, with the three classes of clerics, warriors, and workers, and the education in the *trivium* and *quadrivium* derived from the Platonic course of study prescribed for the guardians.

But I must dismiss this portion of the fanciful analogies of our subject with a word on the theological doctrine of the Trinity and the λόγος question.[24] The comparison was at once suggested by Plotinus' trinity of the one, the intellect, and the soul, and the innumerable triads invented by the later Neo-Platonists. To symbolists and allegorists, the very first sentence of the *Timaeus*—which begins, "one, two, three" —was proof positive that Plato knew the Trinity, and a bit of jargon in one of the spurious letters, often quoted by the Fathers, comes still nearer to it.[25] And with this clue it was as easy to discover triads of principles in Plato's philosophy as it is by Hegelian, Coleridgian, or allegorical methods to find a triad or a trinity in any philosophy or system of ideas. That is all we need say of a matter that fills volumes of dusty disquisition.

The λόγος question also demands either a treatise or a paragraph. For us a paragraph must suffice. I cannot undertake to follow the specifically Christian dogma of the λόγος from Philo Judaeus, Justin Martyr, the Epistle to the Hebrews, and the Gospel of John through the Greek Fathers to its final authoritative definition by the great Councils of the fourth century. Nor am I competent to adjudicate the controversy over the relative contributions to its human formulation of Greek philosophy on the one hand and purely Hebraic and Old Testament influence on the other. To a matter-of-fact philological mind the question is quite simple. The word λόγος is a perpetual stumblingblock and difficulty in every Greek classroom. The tyro never knows how to translate it. It means word and thought in one, and discourse, argument, discussion, reason, principle, and definition, and many other things. A philologist in Plato is not a lover of words but a lover of discussion. The word is prominent in Stoicism, in Plato, and in Heraclitus, and the Christian Fathers friendly to Greek culture attributed to them some measure of inspiration by the λόγος. In Plato, the λόγος or course of the argument is constantly personified,[26] and in one passage it even veils its face and hurries past a difficult point in the discussion (*Rep.* 503 A). In the *Timaeus* the λόγος or reasoning principle by which the Demiourgos creates the world is in one sentence substituted for the Demiourgos himself as creator. And since the word is divine and in a sense a secondary god, Jowett is unable to resist the temptation of paraphrasing one such sentence by the words, "The thought of God (he might have said the word of God) made God."[27]

Philo Judaeus combined with this Platonic way of speaking the Old Testament—personified rhetoric that uses the Wisdom of God as a periphrasis for God, or God in his wisdom. Humanly and philologically speaking, the λόγος doctrine seems to derive from the blending of these two tradi-

tions in Philo, and culminates in the identification of the
λόγος with the person of Jesus the coeternal son of identical
and not merely similar substance with the father. To pure
pagans and Hellenists this was and remained mere foolishness. How could the Supreme Unknowable God or His Reason incarnate Itself in a carpenter's son of Judaea? This was
one of the main points in the book of the Platonist Celsus
against Christianity.[28] Platonizing Christians friendly to
Greek philosophy placed allegorizing Hegelian or Coleridgian interpretation upon it and found anticipations of it in
the Stoics, Heraclitus, and Plato himself, who, they said,
were partially inspired by the λόγος. It is delightful, says
Coleridge (*Table Talk*), it is delightful to think that the be-
loved disciple was born a Plato. The more austere and dogmatic theologies gloried in the abasement of proud human
reason before the mystery of faith and definitely proclaimed:
Credo quia absurdum—I believe it because it defies mere reason.[29] Our general comparisons thus concluded, we are now
ready to enter upon the brief historical survey for which
they have prepared us and which they have in some measure anticipated.

Many earnest Christian scholars have devoted long lives
to the study of the Fathers and prize them in proportion to
the labor expended upon editions, commentaries, and texts.
Many historians of postclassical literature opine that this
Christian literature was more vital, more forward-looking,
more significant, than anything that imitation, rhetoric,
and philosophy could produce in those waning centuries of
the old civilization. They prefer Justin Martyr, Athenagoras,
Minucius Felix, Tatian, Tertullian, Arnobius, Lactantius,
Irenaeus, Clement of Alexandria, Origen, Basil, the Gre-
gories, St. Jerome and St. Augustine, to Plutarch, Dio Chrysostomus, Tacitus, Epictetus, Lucian, Marcus Aurelius,
Maximus of Tyre, Plotinus, Porphyry, Julian, Libanius,
and Proclus. On the other hand, there are critics who find

the whole tone and temper of the Christian Fathers distasteful and feel that the co nporary pagan writers were
scholars and gentlemen tics in comparison with these
irascible and denunc   edants, and some eminent modern writers have given singly drastic expression to this
distaste. George Eliot i *Adam Bede* (p. 64) explains this as
the natural result of a classical education at Oxford. She
says of a British clergyman: "His mental palate, indeed, was
rather pagan, and found a savoriness in a quotation from
Sophocles or Theocritus that was quite absent from any
text in Isaiah or Amos. But if you feed our young setter on
raw flesh how can you wonder on its retaining a relish for
uncooked partridge in after life?"

If your heart is really with Sophocles, Plato, Cicero, and
the emperor Julian, you will write the History of Christianity in the spirit of Havet's excellent though now forgotten book,[30] and try to show that all that is best in Christian ethics is anticipated by, and derived from, the ethical
philosophy of the Greeks. If you genuinely prefer the spirit
and temper of St. Augustine, St. Francis, Thomas Aquinas,
Luther, and Calvin, the feelings and doctrines that distinguish Christianity from Hellenism will seem infinitely more
significant to you than any coincidences in ethical principles. But we have not, here, to dispute on this question of
taste.

An exhaustive critical study of the quotations from Plato
in the Christian Fathers would fill an erudite monograph
and would, perhaps, be unreadable. Many of the quotations
were taken at second hand, as quotations from Plato in
French literature are borrowed from Bodin or Montaigne,
and in English literature from Cudworth. Only a few of the
Greek Fathers, especially those contemporary with the Neo-
Platonic revival, were widely read in Plato's own writings,
and none had any critical understanding of his thought as a
whole and its relation to his age. To some, Plato was the

author and source of heresies, the inspirer of dangerous forms of liberalism that sophisticated away the essentials of the gospel of Christ crucified, or he served to illustrate how far inferior to Christianity was this ideal of Hellenic wisdom. Others represented Plato as the schoolmaster unto Christ and sought by symbolism, allegory, and strained interpretation to identify a liberal and intelligent Christianity with Platonic philosophy. Others, still, may have more or less consciously used these arts of interpretation to conceal the fact that they were at heart Platonists or Neo-Platonists, as much as Christians.

After what has already been quoted, it will be enough to group and classify a few by types. There are only a few typical attitudes and points of view. All the relevant arguments were formulated in the first two or three Christian centuries, and all the apt quotations excerpted. The chief things which the Christian Fathers approve in Plato are, as we have seen, his censure of the mythology in the *Republic*, which they quote verbatim by the page; his ideal morality, as for example the principle that the good man will not harm his enemy, and that it is better to suffer than to do wrong; his rejection of materialism and affirmation of the primacy of soul, including the immortality of the soul and the mythical pictures of future rewards and punishments; his proclamation of one God, father and maker of all things, whom it is hard to discover and impossible to declare to everybody; a large part of the cosmogony of creation in the *Timaeus*, including especially the goodness of the creator as its cause and his beneficent design as manifested in the universe (29 E), as well as most of the ideas and many of the phrases of the theodicy or principles of natural religion in the tenth book of the *Laws*. To these might be added many of the things that we have classified as fanciful analogies—the *logos*; the trinity; the doctrine of daemons, which could be used to justify both the Christian angels and the opinion that the gods of the mythology were evil daemons; and the comparison of Plato's just man crucified with Christ.

Among the chief things for which they censured Plato were his concessions to the popular religion, as for example at the beginning of the *Republic* his representation of Socrates as attending the worship of Diana,[31] and at the end of the *Phaedo* his asking Crito to sacrifice a cock to Aesculapius; his belief in the preëxistence and transmigration of souls, as opposed to the Christian doctrine of their creation at birth; his assumption of a preëxisting Chaos which the creator reduced to order, instead of a creation out of nothing. Platonism, then, divides the Christian Fathers into two broad groups. On the one side are the philhellenes and cultured latitudinarians and liberals who constantly quote and approve Plato even while they reluctantly admit his divergencies from the true faith. On the other side are the strict dogmatists and the Latin obscurantists, jealous of Greek learning, who denounce Plato as the seductive source of heresies, or take him as the type and symbol of the pride of the intellect and the futility of all human philosophy. The early apologists, Aristides, Justin Martyr, Athenagoras, Minucius Felix, belong in the first or liberal class both by virtue of their Hellenizing culture and sincere admiration for Plato, and because it was good taste, at first, to present the new religion as merely the consummation and completion of the highest religious and philosophic thought of the old culture. St. Paul's "Whom therefore ye ignorantly worship, him declare I unto you" seemed only the natural development of the great sentence in Plato's *Timaeus*, "The Father and Maker of this universe is hard to find out and impossible to reveal unto mankind" (28 C).

The early Latin apology of Minucius Felix is a little Ciceronian dialogue containing a defense of natural religion, some latent quotations from Plato, and hardly an allusion to anything specifically Christian in dogma. Christ, I believe, is not mentioned once. The Greek apologies of Justin Martyr and Athenagoras are more explicit in frequent, ver- batim quotations from Plato, and much more explicit in de- fense of the Christians against the charge of superstition and immoral practices. But apart from their contributions to the λόγος doctrine, they contain little positive dogma, and little that would either offend the taste or excite the in- tellectual curiosity of the philosophic emperors to whom they were addressed. The great Christian catechetical school of Alexandria whose leaders were Pantaenus, Clement of Alexandria, and Origen, was almost as much a school of Platonism as was that of the contemporary Neo-Platonists. Clement and Origen refer to Plato on almost every page, and excerpt long passages verbatim from the *Republic*, the *Laws*, the *Phaedo*, and other dialogues. The two schools at- tended each other's lectures and debated controverted points in a comparatively friendly spirit, up to the time when the conversion of Constantine and the apostasy of Julian took the controversy from the schoolroom out into the bloody field of imperial politics.

Yet, as we have observed, this liberal Platonizing Chris- tianity which always tended to deviate into heresy even in the best intentioned of the liberal Greek Fathers, was re- garded with suspicion by the more dogmatic spirits and es- pecially by the more rigid Latin mind. The Hellenists tended to make the Church a sort of Choir Invisible or international congress of religions of all the great and good thinkers of the past. Latin Christianity sought to organize it as a defi- nite closed communion of the faithful on earth; and for this it was necessary to define its dogma more precisely. Thus it came about that the doctrine of the Church was, in large measure, defined and formulated in opposition to heresies. The heresy is always something too vague and obscure to be conveniently taught in a catechism; or its implications are incompatible with the supreme authority of the Church or indeed with any authority, discipline, and order; or it tends to antinomianism and makes the moral government of mankind more difficult by exalting emotionalism, private judgment, enthusiasm, or the inner light. Platonism thus by its double challenge and stimulus to the free inquiry of the intellect and the romancing divagations of the mytho-poeic imagination was the most prolific source of heresies. More specifically, the undogmatic, colorless, Platonizing, natural religion of the early apologists may, as we have said, have been good tactics in the first presentation of Christianity to educated pagans. But it involved no recognition of the divinity and special mission of Christ or the authority of the Church. Hence writers like Tatian and Tertullian, while admitting that there are some good things in Plato, frequently denounce or deplore the support he gives to heresies. "Let them look to it," exclaims the fiery Tertullian (*De praescriptione* 7), "who have produced a Stoic and Platonic and dialectic Christianity. We need no curiosity who have Jesus Christ, no inquiry who have the gospel."

Thus Plato, as the chief name in ancient philosophy, is often taken as the text and symbol for the denunciation of the pride of intellect and distrust of secular learning which can be traced through the Christian Fathers and the Middle Ages to the fundamentalist of our own day. One example is as good as another. The best known is the anticipation of Shakespeare's Jack Cade in a letter of Gregory the Great: "I blush to mention, my brother, that you are guilty of the grave and unspeakable crime of teaching grammar."[32] Medieval sermons are full of such exclamations as "What need have we of Pythagoras, Socrates, Plato, and Aristotle?"[33] "All the assertions of the philosophers about the eternity of the world and *hyle* and the ideas, and that soul of the world that they call *noys* are utterly destroyed and confounded by the first chapter of Genesis."[34] "What folly to teach in the school of Christ this vain and secular philosophy!"[35]

"How much more estimable the philosophy that does not discourse idly of the stars and the nature of things in the style of Plato, but treats humbly and usefully of the correction of morals and the practice of the virtues."[36] The culmination is achieved by one Gauthier, prior of Saint-Victor, in his discourse against modern heresies.[37] He there defines logic as the art of the devil. Before we laugh at the Middle Ages, we might profitably recall the passage in which Romain Rolland (not, however, in the interests of Christianity) denounces the syllogism as a sophistical weapon of so-called antiquity, or the fact of which a colleague here reminds me, that that eminent American critic, Mr. Mencken (again, not as an advocate of Christianity) attributes to Socrates the invention of the syllogism that strangled thought.

The later history of Platonism and Christianity will be glanced at from time to time in the survey of our lectures. The Byzantine middle age is distinguished from the contemporary Latin Christianity by the simple fact that the Byzantines knew Greek. As a famous sentence of Gibbon puts it, "In their lowest servitude and depression, the subjects of the Byzantine throne were still possessed of a golden key that could unlock the treasures of antiquity; of a musical and prolific language, that gives a soul to the objects of sense, and a body to the abstractions of philosophy."[38] It is true that they did not always use that key to unlock or to unsphere the spirit of Plato. But scholars habituated to the reading of the Greek Fathers, and exercised in the subtleties of theological debate, could read Plato after a fashion, if they chose. There were, in the course of the Byzantine centuries, occasional revivals of classical literature and of Platonism, marked by such names as Photius, Georgios Monachos, Psellus, and finally, Gemistus Pletho, whom we shall meet as the inaugurator of the revival of Platonism in the Italian Renaissance. All this would supply ample material for a lecture, a dissertation, or a book. But despite repeated rehabilitations of the Byzantine empire, the number of people interested in the cultural history of Byzantium today is very limited. So I will dismiss this topic with one quotation illustrative of the fact that the literary quarrel in the Renaissance between Platonists and Aristotelians was an inheritance from this Byzantine literature.

"For the miserable Aristotle, even while Plato lived, openly and shamelessly opposed him and took up war against the Academy. He did not honor the instruction which he had sought and enjoyed in a spirit of emulation and ambition. Nor did he reverence the fame or fear the logic of that great man, but insolently and unblushingly the moonstruck disciple revolted against his teacher, though his own teachings were not better, but far worse. For while Plato taught that the tripartite soul is immortal and divine, Aristotle said that it is mortal and subject to decay. And while Plato said that the providence of God extends to all things, Aristotle . . . affirmed that the divinity comes down only to the moon, and that all things below are subject to fate and chance. And he imposes a constraining necessity on all men, whereby murderers and burglars and prostitutes engage in every kind of lawlessness contrary to their better judgments. And many other impious, outrageous, and monstrous doctrines the wretched man promulgated for the overthrowing of the teachings of his teacher."[39]

The Latin middle age will be the theme of the next chapter. Here I need only remind you of the paradox that, in spite of the obvious fact brought out in the passage of Georgios Monachos just quoted, the Catholic Church has usually found it easier to accommodate systematic theology to the logic of Aristotle than to the religious eloquence of Plato. The reasons for this attitude would take us too far. Perhaps Platonism is too stimulating to the mythopoeic and religious imagination; too provocative of mystical and pantheistic aberrations in some minds, or of broad-church

liberalism in others; too hard to regulate. From the point of
view of dogmatic and institutional Christianity, if one kind
of Platonism erred by defect, there was another kind that
went astray by excess. Theosophy, asceticism, enthusiasm,
and mysticism are the reactions of a certain type of mind to
Plato's myths and his religious eloquence. The Church has
always distrusted these things except when regulated by
her own shrewd and beneficent policy. She too affirms a
Platonic supernatural order or world of ideas. But if every
heated imagination is free to people that world with the
hypostasies of its own fancy, the result is chaos, not a teach-
able catechism.

The Platonic flight from the world and repudiation of
the flesh may be allowed as a counsel of perfection for the
few when regulated and systematized in the convent and
the nunnery, but if accepted as the absolute philosophy it
would annihilate the world which the Church wishes to
control and guide, not destroy. Mysticism adds to these
two dangers the notion of an inner illumination and personal
identification with the absolute being which tends to render
all ecclesiastical intermediation superfluous. There have, of
course, been many devout Catholics who prefer Plato, and
I think that today an increasing number of educated Catholics are beginning to perceive that in spite of the ingenuity
of Thomas Aquinas' harmony of Aristotelianism and systematic theology, Plato is, in the situation that now confronts the Church, a more helpful ally of essential religion
than Aristotle.

The various oppositions and points of view that we have
thus far noticed persist through European theological literature to our own day. "Abélard," remarks St. Bernard drily
(*Epist.* 19, 4), "sweats dreadfully in the attempt to make
Plato a Christian." This did not deter the great Platonists
of the Italian Renaissance from similar attempts, even as
the experience of their predecessors did not deter some of

them from quarreling about Plato and Aristotle and others
from producing a harmony of the two. Marsilio Ficino's
parallelism of Platonism and Christianity in the introduction to the translation of the *Crito* is as plausible as that of
Bauer, the modern German scholar, and misses few of the
essential points. In Socrates' refusal to escape from prison
and his submission to death he finds a confirmation of
evangelical doctrine and a justification of the martyrs. Pico
della Mirandola, his disciple, contributed much to the diffusion of this Platonizing, liberal, and allegorizing Christianity throughout Europe, and especially in England. But
the theologians of the Catholic reaction were suspicious of
this Platonizing Christianity of the Florentines, and after
the capture of Rome in 1527 forbade Muretus to lecture on
Plato's *Republic* there.

The Platonism of Ficino and Pico passed, with other gifts
of the Renaissance, to the countries beyond the Alps, and to
England. To the atheism and Machiavellianism of Hobbes
the famous school of seventeenth-century Cambridge Platonists opposed the spiritualism and the ethical religion
of Plato, and unfortunately, sometimes, the superstitions
of degenerate Platonists. "They have brought the Church
back to her old loving nurse, the Platonic philosophy," it
was said of them. But at the same time English evangelical
dogmatists denounced and English skeptics alluded with
thinly veiled irony to the Platonic philosophy as it is now
"accommodated to" Christianity. Throughout the seventeenth and eighteenth centuries the generalized natural
Platonic religion of Socrates and of Cicero found much
acceptance in liberal and broad-church circles. The fundamentalist Young in his *Night Thoughts* repels all such latitudinarian assimilations of Socrates to Christ with the fierce
counterblast: Talk they of morals? O thou bleeding Love!
Thou maker of new morals to mankind!
The grand morality is love of Thee.

As wise as Socrates, if such they were,
(Nor will they 'bate of that sublime renown)
As wise as Socrates, might justly stand
The definition of a modern fool.

Night Fourth 781 ff.

These polemics and the bitterness of the Christian Fathers
have no meaning for us today when the real issue is the survival of religion in any sense. The fundamental difference
between Christianity and Platonism, between Socrates and
Christ, is not likely now to be overlooked by either Christian or agnostic. Platonism is intellectual and aristocratic
in its appeal, as a drastic sentence of Emerson has already
told us. Christianity is emotional and popular. Nietzsche
said that Christianity is Platonism for the people; and some
of the Christian Fathers said it before him, though in a very
different spirit. Plato describes conversion as a turning about.
of the eye of the mind from transitory and material to abiding and ideal objects. For popular Christianity it is a change of
heart. It was the Sermon on the Mount and the beauty and
the unity of Jesus' life that in the course of the second and
third centuries gradually drew over to Christianity a majority of the more earnest moral natures and so, since morality is of the nature of things, assured its ultimate triumph.

"It is impossible that the multitude should be philosophers,
should truly love wisdom," says Plato.[40] "Come unto me, all
ye that are weary and heavy laden," is the call of Jesus(*Matt.*
11.28). "In Cicero and Plato," said St. Augustine,"I meet
with many things acutely said. But I do not find 'Venite ad
me.' "[41] Greek philosophy, said Lactantius,[42] taught only
one woman, a few slaves, and one barbarian. The Gospel
teaches all. Socrates, says Justin Martyr,[43] persuaded no
man to die for his faith. Christ persuaded not only philosophers, but ordinary men as well, to give their lives for him.

CHAPTER IV

PLATONISM IN THE MIDDLE AGES

OUR MODERN CIVILIZATION, if we date it from Columbus and
Ficino's Latin translation of the whole of Plato, has lasted
about four hundred and fifty years. Greco-Roman civilization, from Aeschylus to Justinian, has a span of about a
thousand years, and if we go back to Homer, of fifteen hundred. The so-called Middle Ages, from Boethius to Columbus, cover about a thousand years. It would, obviously, be
impossible to expound the cultural history of ten centuries
in a chapter, even if I knew it. The value of an attempt to
sketch the relation of Platonism to that culture will depend
on whether the writer talks jargon or something intelligible,
as far as it goes, and whether he knows or divines enough to
present his selection of facts and illustrations fairly.

We need not enter into the endless debate between the
admirers and the detractors of the so-called Dark Ages. I
could fill half my space at once with eloquent denunciations
of the Middle Ages by enthusiastic devotees of the Renaissance. "In all the nine hundred years before Dante," writes
one of them, "is nothing but ghosts and shadows moving in
the mist. . . . They have fine names, some of them wore
crowns, and some were great saints, and great men of all
kinds, St. Louis, and Alfred, Benedict, Charlemagne, Theod-
oric, Stilicho—but there is not one whom I feel that I
know or care about." And, on the other hand, I could quote
equally eloquent rehabilitations of the centuries that produced Dante, St. Thomas, and the cathedrals, by Mr. Ralph
Cram, and Dr. J. J. Walsh, author of *The Thirteenth, the
Greatest of Centuries*, not to speak of Professor Rand's edi-
torial pronouncement in the very first number of *Speculum*,
the American journal of medieval studies.[1] The men of

[1] Superior figures refer to notes which will be found on pp. 244-245.

that time might rear glorious cathedrals and create new forms in literature from the fruitful chaos of their ignorance, but whatever else they could do, they could not read widely or critically. We may measure the difference in this respect between them and us by the fact that they tell us with bated breath that Vincent of Beauvais, the compiler of the medieval *Encyclopaedia Britannica*, actually consulted twelve hundred books. Antiquity, looming large through the fogs of ignorance, might stir their imagination; they could not understand it. We may be interested in knowing how Platonism, known to them only in a translation of the first half of the *Timaeus* and in the allusions and quotations of Cicero, and, later, Aristotle, Boethius, Apuleius, St. Augustine and other Christian Fathers, stimulated their thought, but they cannot help us to interpret Plato himself.

Some of the medieval philosophers may have been acute and profound thinkers; not to speak of the influence of Aristotle and Cicero, the presence of a translation of Plato's *Meno* and *Phaedo*, of Diogenes Laertius' *Story of Philosophy*, of Sextus Empiricus' Encyclopaedia of Skepticism, of Bishop Nemesius' suggestive treatise on the *Nature of Man* in the library of some isolated monastery might account for almost any seemingly accidental anticipation of modern thought in some individual medieval thinker. But in general the condition of the medieval mind in relation to the history and philosophy of the past was that of hopeless befuddlement. The men of this age were as much muddled by too little literature and criticism as modern professors of the pseudo sciences and the victims of the new education are by indigestion of the too much which they have too hastily bolted. Professor Kittredge, in an essay on Chaucer,[2] draws up an entertaining list of medieval howlers about ancient art, literature, history, and philosophy, which would match any of the anecdotes that gloating professors tell one another of the performances of their students on examinations. A Latin manuscript, published a few years ago, supplies equally good examples. The author tells us that Alcibiades was a seductive damsel wooed by Alexander and Aristotle, a new view, which, if it had only been communicated to Mrs. Atherton, might have supplied material for a brilliant episode in her novel, *The Jealous Gods*. Epicurean is derived from the Greek *epi*, under, and *guros*, a pig, and means a man who leads the life of a porker. Socrates was poisoned by the king Got, in the presence of Plato, because he refused to destroy two virtuous men, Filatus and Omer. Vessius, that is, Mount Vesuvius, is a furiosity who reigns in hell. The references to Aristotle's *Book of the Behinds* baffled the French editor. It meant the *Posterior Analytics*.

But there is little point in trying to make the Middle Age ridiculous. I could quote almost equally good examples from books published in the last twenty years. Anything may happen when a careless and confident sciolist mixes his notes and his memories. And it is easy to exaggerate the deficiencies of the Middle Ages. Roger Bacon, who was an advanced thinker and a faultfinder in his day, complained that the translations of Aristotle were so bad that it would have been better if he had not been translated at all. That was a good deal of a bluff. A few years ago, a special graduate student, educated at a Catholic college, brought me a copy of the new Italian edition which now makes generally available Thomas Aquinas' commentary on Aristotle's *Metaphysics*.[3] We studied it together with the Aristotelian text, and I found that the translation, though, of course, sometimes incorrect, was by no means impossible; that Thomas himself had gathered from Aristotle a very fair notion, as far as it went, of the issue between Aristotle and Plato about the ideas; and if I had the choice of putting into the hands of a student of Aristotle the commentary of Thomas or the book of some recent interpreter of Aristotle, I would choose the medieval schoolman as more educative in sensible methods and less likely to mislead and confuse the student.

To turn from these preliminaries to the substantive history of ideas, the three chief lines of Platonic tradition in the Middle Ages were (1) the all-pervading, often indirect, influence of the widely diffused later mystical and superstitious Neo-Platonism; (2) the controversy about the nature of general ideas or universals; (3) the impression on the medieval imagination of the story of creation as told in Chalcidius' Latin translation of the first half of the *Timaeus*. We have already considered Neo-Platonism in antiquity, but need to remind ourselves that its dominance through the centuries of the decline and fall gave to nearly all the classical heritage of the Middle Ages a Neo-Platonic tinge. The Middle Ages received Plato not only through the philosophic and theosophic treatises of degenerate adherents of that school, as for example the pseudo Dionysius the Areopagite, but from St. Augustine, Macrobius, Boethius, the later Christian Fathers, the Neo-Platonic commentaries on Aristotle, and the mystic pantheism of their Arabian interpreters. This is one of the chief sources of mysticism and mystical heresies in the Middle Ages—of what the Italian historian Rotta calls the *platonico-mistico-patristico* tradition as distinguished from the *peripatetico-rationalistico-scolastico* stream of thought.

Mysticism is a tendency of the human mind and a variety of religious experience which needs no literary source. But, as a matter of fact, the higher mysticism of the Middle Ages was, as we have said, associated with the indirect tradition of Platonism through Neo-Platonism. I have looked through the book of Gardner on *Dante and the Mystics*,[4] have read Josef Bernhart's *Die philosophische Mystik des Mittelalters*,[5] the Italian Tocco's *Heresy in the Middle Ages*,[6] turned over the pages of two or three of Evelyn Underhill's popular books on the history of mysticism, and glanced at many essays on the pantheists David of Dinant, Amalric, Bernard of Clairvaux, Gundissalinus, and St. Bonaventura, and on the relation of the German mystics to this whole tradition. But I was not interested enough to remember much of it, and I do not know enough to write the critical chapter on Medieval Mysticism for which there would be no room here if it were written. I should, in any case, begin like Socrates in Plato by asking for a definition. "Mysticism," says John Stuart Mill, "is the abuse of abstract language." Plato does not do that. "Mysticism," says Clough, "is letting the feelings run on without thinking of the reality." That is not Plato's way. "Mysticism," says Professor Stewart, "is the dream consciousness." Plato is no dreamer. His very definition of the philosopher is, the man in whom reason is awake, not dreaming. "Mysticism," says Mr. Bertrand Russell, not very consistently with his elsewhere professed contempt for it, "is in essence little more than a certain intensity and depth of feeling in regard to what is believed about the universe." Clifford expressed that more briefly by his phrase "cosmic emotion," and Plato's *Timaeus*, as we shall see later, is the chief source of cosmic emotion in European literature. "Mysticism," says Mr. Chesterton, ". . . is only a transcendental form of common sense." It "appeals to realities . . . which have no place in the argument except as postulates." That is the mysticism of Tennyson's *The Ancient Sage* (v. 60):

For nothing worthy proving can be proven.

That is only half-Platonic. Plato does use myths in supplementary expression of rational hopes. But he never sets intuition above reason, in the fashion of modern mystics. The reader of the Platonic myths may say with Sir Thomas Browne, "I am now content to understand a mystery, without a rigid definition, in an easy and Platonic description."[7] "By mysticism," says a recent historian of the subject, "I shall always understand ecstasy." Ah yes! But whose ecstasy? The ecstasy of the dancing dervish, of the sentimentalist

Rousseau, of the sensualists Verlaine and Oscar Wilde, or the ecstasy of the spirits finely touched to fine issues? Of Plotinus, Pico della Mirandola, Giordano Bruno, Wordsworth at Tintern Abbey, Jonathan Edwards and Emerson returning to their studies from a walk in the New England woods? All depends on that. As Burns says (*The Holy Fair* 27),

There's some are fu' o' love divine,
There's some are fu' o' brandy.

"Mysticism," says Emerson, "consists in the mistake of an accidental and individual symbol for an universal one."[8] Emerson himself did not think Plato a mystic in this objectionable sense, and Alcott and other American Neo-Platonists sometimes made Emerson very weary. He writes in a letter to Miss Hoar: "With what security and common-sense this Plato treads the pinnacles and cliffs of Parnassus, as if he walked in a street, and came down into the street again as if he lived there! My dazzling friends, the New-Platonists, have none of this air of facts and society about them."[9]

Plato, then, was himself temperamentally and intellectually not a mystic. The pattern even of his myths is as clean-cut and sharply defined and unambiguous as a piece of Greek geometry.[10] The only hint of mysticism is in the passages enumerated in an earlier chapter[11] that suggest pantheism or the unknown and ineffable God, and the two passages, one in the *Symposium* (210 B ff.), and one in the *Republic* (517 BC), which describe the consummation of knowledge, the apprehension of the Idea of Beauty and the Idea of Good, as a sort of ecstasy and beatific vision. From these passages to medieval mysticism the path is very indirect, and by way, as we have said, of Neo-Platonizing and Arabic commentators on the self-thinking thought of Aristotle's God and the active intellect that is either common to all humanity or flashed upon humanity from the mind of

God. Plotinus told his pupil Porphyry[12] that he had four times during his discipleship attained to union with the One and caught sight of the transcendental God that has neither form nor visual aspect. He perhaps meant something like the experience of which Tennyson speaks in *In Memoriam* XCV:

> And all at once it seem'd at last
> His living soul was flash'd on mine
> And mine in this was wound, and whirl'd
> About empyreal heights of thought,
> And came on that which is, and caught
> The deep pulsations of the world.

We cannot delay to illustrate further these various aspects of mysticism in the literature of the Middle Ages. But in place of that, I will say a few words about a philosopher who, though perhaps not personally and emotionally a mystic, is one of the chief transmitters of mystical, pantheistical, and heretical ideas to the later Middle Ages and the Renaissance—John Scot Erigena, the chief representative of philosophy and the only writer who knew Greek in the band of scholars that Charlemagne gathered about him.

Erigena[13] occupies much more space in the histories of philosophy and in the notes collected for this book than I can give him here. He is an important transmitter of a few Neo-Platonic and pantheistic ideas to the Middle Ages and the Renaissance from Nicolaus of Cusa to Spinoza. But his interest to the modern reader is a matter of personal taste. If you like the semblance of an exhaustive, metaphysical system and a seemingly severe dialectic leading to a blend of pantheistic mystic and yet rationalistic conclusions, you will be deeply impressed by the *De divisione naturae*, which is sufficiently analyzed in the histories of philosophy and in special monographs.[14] If you regard metaphysical system as an illusion, pantheism as rhetoric, dialectic—except the Platonic, Socratic dramatic type—as verbiage, and prefer the direct to the allegorical, mystical, or pantheistic expression of liberalism in theology, you will feel that whatever his historical significance, Erigena is, taken by himself, a much overrated writer. He undoubtedly says some interesting things; for example: God does not know himself, for that would be to define himself, and definition is limitation. God does not know evil, for evil would really exist if God knew it. The whole act of creation is in the words, "God saw that it was good." This derives, directly or indirectly, from the famous sentence in Plato's *Timaeus* (29 E): "Let us declare for what cause the Maker of this universe composed it. He was good. And no spirit of grudging dwells in any being that is good." Man is a thought eternally created in the mind of God. This may be loosely connected with the interpretation of Plato that makes all Platonic ideas thoughts of God. All that God creates is immortal. Elsewhere, speaking of the Christian theologians, Erigena contradicts this. The idea, probably, came to him from the passage in which the Platonic Demiourgos turns over the creation of the mortal soul to the inferior deities (*Tim.* 69 C-D) because, if he made it, it would be immortal. Paradise is not a place but a state. The future punishment of the wicked is spiritual. The distance between the saved and the lost is not a distance of space. These commonplaces of modern liberal theology are all in Plato's *Laws*. Whether and how they were thence transmitted to Erigena, I do not know. The sleep of Adam is the turning away of the soul from the contemplation of the creator; that is, it is an allegory of the Neo-Platonic development that starts at each stage with the turning away of the lower from the higher. Evil is not eternal. It will cease to exist "when God hath made the pile complete" (Tennyson, *In Mem.* LIV). All things return to unity with one another and with God. This Neo-Platonic principle Erigena expresses by the word *adunatio*, which occurs also in Bernardus Silvestris. For all things yearn towards their cause. God is nothing. Not the nothing which is privation of existence, but the nothing that surpasses all knowledge.[15] This is merely one more example of the Pickwickian sense and the negative theology that runs through the entire history of the Neo-Platonic forms of Platonism.

It is the business of the historian of philosophy to trace these and similar utterances to their sources in St. Augustine, from whom most of Erigena's Neo-Platonic thoughts are derived, or to the pseudo Dionysius the Areopagite, whom he translated and in whom he found confirmation or, some think, the source of his philosophy, to Chalcidius' translation of the first part of the *Timaeus*, which was all he knew of Plato, and to the various other Greek Fathers whom he quotes or to whom he alludes. In one form of the Platonic tradition, then, he is a significant link. But in the true, Platonic tradition of literary charm, dramatic interest, wide-ranging, concrete reflection on all the problems of the moral, the social, the political, the aesthetic, the spiritual life of humanity, he plays no part.

The relation of Plato's theory of ideas to the interminable debates of medieval scholastics may be dismissed briefly. As told in the ordinary histories of philosophy, the controversy about universals, the question of nominalism, realism, and conceptualism, is a very simple matter.[16] The Platonists taught that the universal, the idea of tree, for example, is a real thing which existed from all eternity in itself or in the mind of God. It was *before* the thing. The Aristotelians maintained that the idea was in the tree as its form and was thence extracted by the human mind. The universal was *in* the thing. Lastly, there were some Aristotelians and hard-boiled rationalists who argued that the idea or universal was not even in the thing at all, but was collected by the mind from the comparison of many things, or, to go still further, was nothing but a sound, nothing but the common name tree, that designated all trees. The debate, it is usually

added, was started by an incidental remark of the Neo-
Platonist Porphyry in his introduction to the translation of
a minor treatise of the Aristotelian logic. "I will not stop to
discuss the question," says Porphyry, "whether the ideas
exist in themselves or only in the objects or are only our
thoughts."[17] Boethius translated this into Latin, but in his
commentary refrained from intervening between such mighty
opposites as Plato and Aristotle. As the rhyming Latin verses
of Godefroi de Saint-Victor put it:

> Puzzled by their fierce debate Boethius sits beside them,
> Hearing what each has to say on the problem that divides them.
> But to which side his mind inclines he cannot tell you rightly,
> And won't presume to arbitrate the contest definitely.[18]

The medieval philosophers, having abundant leisure, did
stop to discuss it and kept up the discussion for six hundred
years.[19] To ignore minor predecessors, the trouble began, it
is sometimes said, with one Roscelin in the eleventh century, who taught nominalism and was accused of heresy,
because, if the abstract or universal has no real existence
and the material object is the only real thing, it is impossible
to account for the unity of the trinity or the transubstan-
tiation of the bread and wine.[20] Some nominalists got around
this by the distinction between truths of faith and truths of
science, which, seriously or ironically meant, continued to
play a great part throughout the Middle Ages but was rejected by Thomas Aquinas and condemned by the Church.
Others, I believe, devised ingenious arguments to prove that
conceptualism and realism were as dangerous to dogma as
was nominalism.

From century to century the controversy flared up and
died down. Roscelin was opposed by St. Anselm, who, however, had little or no acquaintance with Plato, and whose
Platonism is grossly exaggerated by most students of medieval philosophy. William of Champeaux first developed ex-

plicitly and with some reference to Plato the arguments for realism.[21] The famous Abélard, more famous as the lover of Héloïse, pupil of both Roscelin and William of Champeaux, victoriously attacked the realism of the latter, but, whether from prudence or from conviction, did not go all the way with Roscelin in nominalism. Hence he is sometimes classed as a conceptualist and sometimes as a nominalist. To have a right to an opinion one must have studied all his works and be a trained psychologist. The question passed on to the great systematizing scholastics of the thirteenth century, and to the rationalizing English scholastic of the decline, the supposed nominalist William of Occam, and Duns Scotus, who, though a king of rationalists, expressed his rationalism in what seems to be the language of the most extreme Platonic realism. That, supposing I have got it approximately right, makes a smooth, simple story, and there is no living scholar who knows enough to get it entirely right. To begin with, the problem today is as hotly debated among psychologists as it was in the Middle Ages, and there is no more prospect of agreement. There are behaviorists and materialists who think that the nature of abstract and general ideas is a very simple matter, and that the power of the human mind to use them is a perfectly natural development from the evolution of sensitive protoplasm, and is completely explained by reflex action and the nervous arc. So Aristotle, when hard put to it, thinks he explains the formation of abstract ideas by saying, "The human mind is so constituted as to be able to do this," and the American author of a widely read textbook of psychology says that a general idea is merely a particular idea plus a feeling of generality. But in spite of their assurance other psychologists and reputable philosophers continue to pour forth volumes of subtle and conflicting disquisitions on the same old problem. In the second place, there is no agreement concerning what Plato and Aristotle thought about it. I, for

example, regard it as certain that Plato knew perfectly well
what he was doing and that his maintenance of the paradox
that the idea exists eternally outside of space and time, and
that our knowledge of it is reminiscence and recapture of
the rapture of a prenatal vision of this supernatural world,
was often only a poetic way of rejecting the ancient equivalent of our modern behaviorist's too simple material explanation. It was Plato's way of affirming that human beings
do possess both ideals and ideas, and have to think in abstract and general terms, which are, somehow, something
more than movements of the larynx. It was also a convenient and, I believe, conscious relegation of all the still in-
solvable puzzles of metaphysics to one all-comprehending
mystery. If the comparison were not too frivolous, we could
liken Plato's attitude to that of the Duke of Wellington
telling his story of the rat in the bottle of champagne. "It
must have been a very small rat," ventured a dazed sub-
altern, timidly. "It was a damn big rat," the duke fiercely
replied.

But other modern interpreters insist that Plato could not
have believed anything so foolish, and that the Platonic
ideas were only thoughts in our mind.[22] Others still hold,
with many of the ancients, and most medieval writers, that
the ideas were the thoughts of God[23] which served him as
models and patterns in the creation of the world. They exercised their ingenuity in adapting this doctrine to the Aristotelian theories of matter and form. In Plato, and usually
in Aristotle, idea and form are synonyms. The Middle Ages
distinguished the ideas as the preëxisting patterns in the
mind of God from the forms, the more or less perfect copies
in things. We need not attempt to follow them in their further refinements on the theory of forms, as, for example, the
question whether in Socrates there dwells a special form of
Socrateity as distinguished from the general form of humanity. This is what the American reporter used to satirize

as the Concord School of Philosophy's doctrine of the "bean-fulness of the bean." But Duns Scotus many centuries before outbid the Concord School of Philosophy. He explained that when a man died it was because the form of organic corporosity departed from him and the form of corpserosity entered in in its stead. Other modern interpreters opine that Plato was merely a simple, primitive, childish thinker, who did not understand our elementary modern psychology of the formation of abstract ideas and the way in which the reactions of the nervous system build them up. Their exegesis has not got beyond Voltaire's airy remark, "The great defect of all Platonic philosophy is the mistaking of abstract ideas for real things."[24]

Similarly of Aristotle, I believe that while working at logic and biology and in a mood of reaction against his teacher he tried to discard Plato's ideas altogether and explain universals simply as generalizations of the mind, whatever that may mean, in terms of psychological analysis or brain anatomy. But when Aristotle came to discuss metaphysics and the ultimate nature of things, he found the matter not so simple. Just what is the form that constitutes the essence of the thing? How does it get into the thing, and how does it pass from the thing to the mind, and what, precisely, is it when it is in the mind? When Aristotle asked himself these questions, he found himself slipping back into a theory of absolute forms finally identified with the thoughts of God who thinks himself. That was little better than the most mystic doctrines attributed to Plato. Aristotle himself never got clear on these points, and his commentators have made the confusion worse confounded. That is my interpretation. But there are many others, and, again, there is no prospect of agreement.

Suppose, now, that a scholar had mastered these problems, that he understood the nature of universals, and had fixed the definitive interpretation of Plato's and Aristotle's

teaching about them. He would still be only at the thresh-
old of his task. Superficial surveys have classified the medieval philosophers as realists, nominalists, and conceptual-
ists. But there are innumerable intervening shades and
confusions of opinion. John of Salisbury, the acutest historian of the movement, reckons no less than ten distinct
positions on the main dialectical problem, and this enumeration is not exhaustive. Dr. C. R. S. Harris, the author of
an excellent two-volume work on Duns Scotus, describes
the confusion thus: "This baffling and stupendous mixture
of would-be Platonism, metaphysical realism, and logical
conceptualism . . . we find . . . still unsifted and unclarified
in the writings of Albertus Magnus and Thomas Aquinas.
. . . The result is a confusion of a nature so complicated that
it is almost impossible to arrive at any clear conception of
their real meaning."[25] Thus, to determine correctly the precise opinion of any medieval thinker, it would be necessary
to study his writings attentively.

None of them could understand Plato or Aristotle critically and historically. Here and there an acute thinker may,
by sheer force of thought, have attained to perfect clarity
and consistency about the nature of universals, or at least
may have said things that leave that impression on a modern psychologist who agrees with him. The majority were,
probably, hopelessly muddled. The first step towards writing a really critical history of the subject would be to study
and not merely to skim the entire medieval literature about
it. That would be the task of many studious years. It has
never been done. As H. O. Taylor says, "the extant Latin
classics could be tucked away in a corner" of medieval Latin
literature.[26] "Traces of conceptualism," says Poole, "there
certainly were long before Abailard's time. We may find
them in the ninth century in the glosses of Heric of Auxerre."[27]
Doubtless we may find traces of conceptualism, nominalism, and realism in glosses and manuscripts all over the

shop from the ninth century to the fifteenth; but who is going to look for them there?

Our flourishing new American school of medievalists are interested in other aspects of the medieval world, and lack the indispensable preparation for this particular task. The new Catholic Scholasticism, based on the revived study of Thomas Aquinas, has produced many useful and smooth textbooks but has not yet gone to the bottom of this question. Professor De Wulf, the brilliant lecturer on medieval philosophy at Harvard and Louvain, is far too clever to waste his energies in trying to get to the bottom himself or to drag his students there. He probably feels about this problem as President Stanley Hall did about Berkeleian idealism. "We should not try to teach that doctrine to our students of philosophy," President Hall argued. "It will only confuse them. We should tell them flatly that our senses directly perceive the external world as it is, and let the matter rest there." So Professor De Wulf is probably content to give his students Aristotle's explanation: "The human mind is so constituted as to be able to do this." And so John of Salisbury in the mid-Middle Ages protests against the excessive attention paid to the problem of universals in the schools, and says that Abélard simplified it, as popular lecturers simplify Einstein today, to make it intelligible to his students.

There is, then, I presume, no living scholar who has the knowledge to write a detailed and critical history of medieval philosophy. Perhaps it is not worth doing. Who cares for the precise notions about the psychology or ontology of universals entertained by Roscelin, William of Champeaux, Abélard, Albert the Great, St. Thomas Aquinas, William of Occam, Duns Scotus, and their countless disciples and followers? But the division of labor and the ceaseless quest for new subjects in our universities will some time set some specialists upon this task, if only in the spirit in which my old teacher Prantl wrote his *Geschichte der Logik*. "I wrote it," he says in his preface, "so that nobody would ever have to read those books again."

There are five or six Platonic dialogues any one of which would serve as the text for a cross section of the history of European literature. Not to speak now of the *Apology* and *Crito* or the *Protagoras* and *Gorgias*, there is the *Republic*, prototype of all ideal states from More's *Utopia* and Campanella's *City of the Sun* to *Looking Backward* and Mr. H. G. Wells. It, also, anticipates all modern discussions of the place and function of women, and its expurgation of Homer is the starting point of all debates on the censorship of literature and art and supplies the main content of the Christian Fathers' protests against the pagan mythology. Its banishment of Homer is the challenge that called forth the entire literature of the defense of poetry. It is the chief source of all political philosophy from Aristotle to Polybius and Cicero, from Cicero to Bodin, and from Bodin to John Stuart Mill. There is the *Phaedo*, initiator of all speculations about the immortality of the soul, the *Phaedo* in which Mr. Burnet and Mr. Taylor have discovered, recently, that Plato is Socrates, a paradox endlessly discussed because it is obviously not true but it is so easy to talk about. There is the *Symposium*, which those who proclaim it to be the last word on the heights of heavenly and the depths of earthly love are not willing to leave the last word, but endlessly paraphrase, imitate, and comment, from Marsilio Ficino, whose commentary four centuries ago spread the gospel of Platonic love throughout Europe, and Leo Hebraeus, to Miss Jane Addams, who preaches from it in her *Spirit of Youth and the City Streets*. There is the *Theaetetus*, the earliest and still the most suggestive of psychological inquiries, long neglected by all but professional philosophers, and today the center of the controversy between relativism and absolutism, pragmatism and antipragmatism. There is, above all, the *Timaeus*, a prose hymn of the universe, the story of creative evolution as the inadequate science of his time presented it to Plato's imagination, his rewriting of the nature philosophies of the pre-Socratics with the retention of all their poetry and stimulating largeness of view, but with the substitution of the affirmation of mind and purpose for their negations—the *Timaeus*, identical in poetic spirit with its counterpart, the *De rerum natura* of Lucretius, but sounding through the ages the other of the Tennysonian *Two Voices* to which men alternatively incline their ears.

Nothing perhaps so impressively reveals the extent and persistency of Plato's hold on the thought and imagination of mankind, as the history of this book. The story of Atlantis, on which it and the *Critias* are based, the island seat of an ancient civilization sunk in the Atlantic—Atlantis alone has provoked a whole library of literature to which ponderous volumes are still being added.[28] Mr. Preemby in Wells's *Christina Alberta's Father*, you will remember, was always muddling around with esoteric ideas, thinking about Atlantis and reincarnation. The *Timaeus* has been the theme of endless commentaries,[29] from Crantor to Posidonius, Cicero's translation, and Plutarch, and from Plutarch to the seven-hundred-page commentary of the late Neo-Platonist Proclus, and from Proclus to the seven-hundred-page commentary of A. E. Taylor, not to speak of the hundreds of essays and monographs of which the latest, but not the last, is my *Recent Interpretations of the Timaeus*.[30] The references, direct and indirect, of Aristotle to it, would fill a chapter, and though he had no sympathy with and no understanding for the poetical and mythical form, its ideas on cosmogony, chemistry, if we may so call it, and physiology profoundly influenced his own thought.

The Christian Fathers, as we have seen, found there the Trinity in the first sentence, the Cross of Christ in the crossing of the ecliptic and the equator like the Greek letter Chi,

the unity of God, the creation of the World, the key to
Genesis, the fountain of heresies, the Unknown God that
Christianity revealed, and, according as they interpreted
it, Plato's ironic repudiation or his cowardly acceptance of
the gods of the mythology. Gnosticism and other superstitions discovered in it their Demiourgos and their eons and
the hierarchies of subordinate deities employed in the lesser
works of creation. The first half of the Middle Ages, which
knew the first half of the *Timaeus* in the Latin translation
and commentary of Chalcidius,[31] and knew, as yet, only the
minor logical works of Aristotle,[32] regarded Plato as the
philosopher and theologian *par excellence*, and Aristotle as
merely a logician. As Fulbert of Chartres, the medieval ver-
sifier, puts it:

> This thinker says there are many gods,
>   and that one says there are none,
> But Plato, greater than them all,
>   affirms there is only one.[33]

The shortest cut to the study of the philosophy of the
early Middle Ages is to commit the *Timaeus* to memory.
Otherwise you can never be sure that any sentence that
strikes your attention is not a latent quotation from the
Timaeus, or a development of one of its suggestions. If a
medieval writer states that the expression is necessarily determined by the thought, or affirms his belief in the law of
causality, that everything must have a cause, he states
these commonplaces in one of the sentences with which
Plato began his story of creation. The medieval writers
paraphrased and glossed and quoted the *Timaeus* endlessly.
They read into it all that the Christian Fathers found there,
and much more, and after the Christian Fathers they used
it to interpret and allegorize the Mosaic account of creation
in the so-called hexaemeral literature describing the six
days' work of the creator or Demiourgos, a literature most
fully discussed in the Chicago dissertation of Frank E.

Robbins.[34] The Platonic philosophy of the four elements
was the basis of their physics and chemistry and they observed its resemblance to the atomic theories of Democritus
in anticipation of the Cambridge Platonist Cudworth and
those twentieth-century German scholars who fancy that
they were the first to perceive it. Some of them identified
Plato's soul of the world with the Holy Ghost, and others
more poetically, pantheistically, and heretically interpreted
it as nature personified, or nature as the created minister of
God. The nous or intellect of the soul of the world these
theologians sometimes identified with the Logos or second
person of the Trinity; and the pantheists and poets and
mystics personified the nous as the Noys, to whom they
attributed many surprising adventures and conversations
in a mystico-poetical world of realized abstractions.

The best illustration of this is the *De mundi universitate*
of Bernardus Silvestris,[35] a great educator who anticipated
in his teaching the classical culture of the Renaissance. But
our concern is with his story of creation. Like Boethius'
Consolation of Philosophy or the *Satyricon* of Martianus
Capella, it is written partly in verse and partly in prose. It
falls into two books, the Megacosmus, or the world as a
whole, and the Microcosmus, or man. Bernard invokes as
his Muse the nous of the *Timaeus* under the medieval name
Noys, precisely as Milton calls upon the Holy Spirit to tell
him how in the beginning God laid out the order of the
world. Natura laments the confusion of primal Chaos and
begs Noys to reduce it to order. Noys does so in conjunction
and conversation with Physis and her two daughters, The-
orica and Practica, with Silva or Hyle, matter, with Usia,
substance, with Endelechia, as Bernard spells the Aristotelian entelechy, with Urania, Unity, and Diversity, and a
supreme divinity Tugaton, who occupies the height nearest
to God, and in whom, after some hesitation, I recognized
the Platonic *to agathon*,[36] or Idea of Good. When she has

completed her main task, Noys turns over the remainder of the work to these ministers in a speech that partly recalls the speech of Plato's Demiourgos to the inferior divinities, but whose main theme is an anticipation of Hamlet's "What a piece of work is a man!" (II 3.315), or the great chorus of Sophocles' *Antigone* (332 ff.).[37]

I cannot elaborate further. But enough has been said to show that for the first half of the Middle Ages Plato was philosophy and the *Timaeus* was Plato. For this reason the fundamentalists who distrusted all secular learning, who took to heart St. Paul's warning against the vain oppositions of science, who preached Christ crucified and Him only, viewed it with suspicion. As Werner of Basel, in his poem "Paraclitus," summed it up, "Whoever believes that the world has a soul, and reads the *Timaeus*, does not love God."[38]

The Renaissance, while acquainted with the interpretations of the Fathers and the Middle Age, emphasized rather the poetical and pantheistic suggestions of the *Timaeus*. The world soul meant for them that nature is one with God and that all nature is allied and interconnected and sympathetic in all its parts. From one point of view, as I have said, the *Timaeus* is at the opposite pole from the pre-Socratics and Lucretius' poem *On the Nature of Things*; for it inculcates throughout the idea of design which they tried to banish from nature and science. But the poetical philosophy of the Renaissance felt the resemblance rather than the difference between Plato and the pre-Socratics and Lucretius' Epicurean poem. They were all alike in their large, vivid, animated, vital conception of nature and the universe as a living whole. This, at any rate, is the spirit of the typical Renaissance poet-philosopher Giordano Bruno and his Italian predecessors and of Nicolaus of Cusa, from whom something of the feeling was transmitted to Spinoza and modern German philosophies of pantheism and monism.

After the Renaissance came the Latinized centuries of
the narrow, disciplined, pseudoclassic, Latin culture of the
Scaligers, the Boileaus, and the Popes, imperfectly appre-
ciative of the supreme literature of Greece. What we call
the eighteenth-century spirit was quite incapable of understanding what my friend Dr. H. O. Taylor calls "the divine
fooling of the *Timaeus*."[39] The histories of philosophy current in the seventeenth and eighteenth centuries presented
a hard, matter-of-fact, unintelligent, unsympathetic view
of Plato and Platonism, and Voltaire's jibes and the un-
friendly caricature of the *Timaeus* in La Harpe's widely
read *Cours de littérature ancienne et moderne* are fairly representative of the notions of this aspect of Platonism entertained by the educated general reader. There were some
exceptions. Barthélemy's once much-read but now forgotten summary of Greek culture entitled *The Voyage of Young
Anacharsis* makes Plato take his stand on "Sunium's marbled steep" to recite the *Timaeus*,[40] a scene which became
the suggestion of a poem by Lamartine.[41] The scholars of
the German revival of Greek in the second half of the eighteenth century included the *Timaeus* in their enthusiasm
for all things Greek. Goethe greatly admired it, and spoke
with reverence of the sacred awe with which Plato ap-
proaches the study of nature.

Emerson, a lifelong Platonist, shared and perhaps inherited Goethe's feeling, which, however, he could also have
derived from his reading in the Neo-Platonists. He says of
the *Timaeus*: "The scholar must look long for the right
hour for Plato's *Timaeus*. At last the elect morning arrives,
the early dawn,—a few lights conspicuous in the heaven, as
of a world just created and still becoming,—and in its wide
leisures we dare open that book."[42] But the nineteenth century as a whole, while recovering the sense for Greek literature in general, still retained much of the eighteenth-century
attitude towards the *Timaeus*. Its typical point of view is

that expressed in the condescension of Jowett's Introduction to the immaturity of Greek thought and his failure to discriminate in this respect between Plato and the pre-Socratics. It is still more apparent in the dry, matter-of-fact summary of Grote. His enumeration of the scientific errors, or what he takes for the absurdities, of the *Timaeus* has been the arsenal from which men of science whose science did not include the critical interpretation of literature have drawn the weapons for commencement addresses on the passing of Plato, whom they innocently took as the type of the antiscientific spirit. As some of the Christian Fathers took seriously Plato's recital of the thirty-nine articles of the Greek mythology, so these uncritical spokesmen of modern science are outraged by the irreverent parody of the reversed evolution in which Plato solemnly explains how the foresight of the Demiourgos endowed man with the rudimentary structure of nails and hairs because he foresaw that in the gradual downward evolution, out of the species man, of women and other animals, there would be need of claws and fur (*Tim.* 76 B ff.). But every decline of Platonism brings a revival. And the transcendental physical and mathematical philosophers of the twentieth century, as represented by Professor Whitehead and Professor Russell, are now coming around to the view which I must be permitted to say that I expressed long before the close of the last century,[43] that the *Timaeus* rightly understood and interpreted is more in harmony with the spirit of modern science than Aristotle or almost any other philosophy of the past. That is too technical a topic for elaboration here. I have developed it in a paper on *Platonism and the History of Science*[44] already referred to.

For the rest, throughout history and even in the periods when the *Timaeus* was most grossly misunderstood, there were kindred spirits who felt its poetry and imaginative breadth. I have mentioned *The Voyage of the Young Ana-*

charsis, and Lamartine and Goethe and Emerson. 'Way back in the decline of Roman literature, a forgotten minor poet of the fourth century, Tiberianus, was inspired by it to this result:

> Almighty God, the ancient heavens to thee
> Look up abiding in changeless unity
> Amid thy myriad aspects; nor can man
> By weight or measure thy timeless essence scan.
> Thou art the first and last, the many and one,
> The sole survivor of the world undone.
> Boundless, the gliding ages thou dost bound,
> Watching the destinies in the eternal round
> Renew the cycle of birth, and take away
> The life they lend to creatures of a day.
> What birth took from the stars, the fates restore
> To feed the flux of mortal bodies once more.
> Thee who art all in one, and one in all,
> By what name best may please thee, do I call.
> And if so much, Father, I may presume,
> Pray thee my spirit's darkness to illume.
> Grant me to know the great primordial cause
> Of this great world, and by what wondrous laws
> Thou didst sustain the heavens from pole to pole,
> And of what substance thou didst weave the soul;
> What numbers link the Other to the Same
> In that which quickens this swift-moving frame.

> *The Oxford Book of Latin Verse,*
> Oxford 1921, pp. 374-375

Plato had said that God created the world soul of essence, the Same, and the Other, mixed and distributed in proportions of harmonious numbers, and by forcing the recalcitrant Other into reluctant union with the Same. It has, I think, not been observed that this and other ideas of the poem are reminiscences of the *Timaeus*. In some parts which I have omitted there is further pantheistical and Stoic coloring. My translation is designed to bring out the

references to the *Timaeus* and make them clearer. But it is
not unfaithful to the meaning.

There is no time to illustrate further the enthusiasm for
the *Timaeus* of Giordano Bruno and other poetic and pantheistic philosophers of the Renaissance. But a little poem
of Lorenzo de' Medici's may exemplify its more general influence on Renaissance literature. It matters not that Lorenzo's direct inspiration is, perhaps, rather Boethius' *Consolation of Philosophy* than the original text of Plato. My
paraphrase abbreviates and condenses the poem in places,
but brings out fairly, I think, the curious mixture of Platonism and Christianity, of the *Timaeus* and the Bible, that
Lorenzo derived from the Platonic Academy and Ficino's
treatises on the Christian religion and on the Platonic
theology.

> Great God that by thy constant law
> Dost hold the universe in awe,
> Watching from thy eternal place
> Time's seasons pass before thy face,
> Moveless thyself, thou art the cause
> That all things move without a pause.
> No force without bade thee create
> This world of matter insatiate
> That ever seeking new forms flows
> And no rest in its questing knows.
> It was thy goodness and thy love
> That on its heavenly pattern above
> Modeled this beauteous world in kind
> Like to the image in thy mind.
> Great architect, at thy command
> The chaos of water, air, fire, and land,
> Reduced to order, took their place
> In forms of symmetry and grace.
> Thy providence informed the whole
> With one infused and central soul

That spreading to the outmost ring
Made of this world a living thing
Vital throughout; no life can be
Vile, father, that is akin to thee.

Grant that my soul, father, too may mount
Upward and upward to the sacred fount
From which all truth, from which all good things flow.
And as thy sun illumes my eyes below,
So in that higher world give me to know
That supreme good which is its sun, its light,
And makes the world of spirits ever bright,
And there, from all earth's clouds and burdens free,
To find my everlasting rest in thee.

Rime spirituali, II, capitoli, I.
Opere, ed. A. Simioni, Bari 1914, vol.
II pp. 119 ff.

From Boethius and Lorenzo our airplane flight across the
centuries swoops to Swinburne in mid-nineteenth century.
Plato's Demiourgos, it will be remembered, created the immortal part of the soul himself of the same materials as the
soul of the universe. But he delegated to the inferior deities
the formation of the mortal and passionate part of the soul,
"and they," Plato says (*Tim.* 69 C-D), "taking over the
immortal principle of the soul, turned and shaped about it
a mortal body to be its vehicle and container, and therein
they constructed another type of soul, the mortal spirit,
bearing within itself dread and inevitable passions, first,
pleasure, the chief bait of evil, then pains that make men
flee from the good, and thereto confidence and fear, a brace
of foolish counselors, and anger that will not be assuaged,
and hope that is easily led astray; and these they blended
with irrational sensations, and love that attempts all things,
and so driven by necessity composed the mortal soul." The
profound poetic suggestiveness of this did not escape Swinburne, the pupil and friend of Jowett, and in a chorus of

Atalanta in Calydon he expanded Plato's hint with modern excessiveness, to this effect:

> Before the beginning of years
> There came to the making of man
> Time, with the gift of tears;
> Grief, with a glass that ran;
> Pleasure, with pain for leaven;
> Summer, with flowers that fell;
> Remembrance fallen from heaven,
> And madness risen from hell;
> Strength without hands to smite;
> Love that endures for a breath;
> Night, the shadow of light,
> And life, the shadow of death.
>
> And the high gods took in hand
> Fire, and the falling of tears,
> And a measure of sliding sand
> From under the feet of the years;
> And froth and rift of the sea;
> And dust of the labouring earth;
> And bodies of things to be
> In the houses of death and of birth;
> And wrought with weeping and laughter,
> And fashioned with loathing and love,
> With life before and after
> And death beneath and above,
> For a day and a night and a morrow,
> That his strength might endure for a span
> With travail and heavy sorrow,
> The holy spirit of man.

Need we wonder that the *Timaeus* intoxicated the poetic, mystic, and imaginative minds of the early Middle Ages who had little other high philosophy and poetry to feed their imaginations?

Even from these few illustrations it is apparent that a history of Platonism might use the *Timaeus* and Boethius'

Consolation of Philosophy to effect the transition from the Middle Ages. For they were no less, though less excessively, studied in the Renaissance. Philosophical historians sometimes think it necessary to remind us of the truism that historical epochs and periods are only mnemonic conveniences. History is a continuity, and every age is an age of gradual transition. If I should survive to write an unreadable six-volume history of Platonism, I might be tempted to try to fill the apparent gap between the Middle Age and the Renaissance with exhaustive studies of the later scholastics, Occam and Duns Scotus and their followers, Petrarch, Bessarion, Gennadius, Nicolaus of Cusa, Ramus, Rudolph Agricola, Ludovicus Vives, and the rest. But enough is enough; and if any of my readers survive this chapter they will probably be grateful if in the next I plunge directly into its main theme, the revival of Platonism in the Italian Renaissance, and some of its effects on European literature.

However, before I conclude the present one I should like to subjoin a few additional remarks to the short account of Platonism in Byzantium given at the end of the last chapter. Despite the fact that the Byzantines were tolerably conversant with the literature of classical antiquity and could read Plato's masterpieces in the original, they were unable to appreciate the wit, the subtleties, the poetry, the free life of the spirit of Plato. They read the works of Christian Fathers who wrote a degenerate kind of Platonic Greek, and sharpened their wits on a theology that bore remote resemblance to Neo-Platonic interpretations of Platonic metaphysics. There was a library and a tradition at Constantinople, and from time to time there were minor revivals of learning. The first of these reawakenings, after a period of obscurity, attaches itself to the name of the patriarch Photius in the ninth century. We still possess his so-called *Bibliotheca* or Library, a huge compilation of summaries of the books he had read, with his criticisms of their substance or their style. He also contributed notes to Greek lexicography and conducted at his home a sort of academy or philological seminary. He is by temperament an Aristotelian, and his ideals of style are as formal and rigid and matter-of-fact as those that inspire the hostile criticism of Plato in Dionysius of Halicarnassus.

From both points of view and also as a Christian theologian he censures Plato sharply, and we may, if we please, date from him and his contemporary, George Hamartolos, who is equally severe upon Aristotle, the beginning of the long quarrel between Platonists and Aristotelians which Byzantium passed on to the Italian Renaissance. Photius' criticisms and his lexicographical notes testify to considerable familiarity with the Platonic writings. He may have interpreted Plato to his students and may have annotated his own text. There are references in our manuscripts to the "book of the patriarch," which can hardly refer to anything else.[45] Coincidences with Photius' readings are thought to prove that our best manuscripts, the Parisinus (A) and the Bodleianus (B), are copies of editions made in the circle of Photius' disciples. To this group of scholars are also probably due, for the most part, the extant scholia on Plato, a collection of variants and marginal notes from these and other manuscripts, which often go back to the older lexicons and commentaries.[46] Together with a few good remarks on language and style, they offer, by way of literary criticism, denunciations of the temptations which the sensuous pictures of Plato present to youthful readers, and attacks on Greek polytheism and Plato's concessions to it.

The impulse given to classical studies by Photius never wholly died out. But the first name that need detain us is that of the would-be Platonist, Michael Psellos, in the eleventh century. Psellos tried to write in the style of Plato, read Christianity and the Trinity into him by allegorical interpretation, disparaged Aristotle, wrote commentaries

on the theory of ideas, the creation of the world soul in the
Timaeus, and on parts of the *Phaedrus*, and propagated
through his many pupils a regular cult of Platonism. One of
his pupils, Gregorios Magistros, is the author of the Ar-
menian translation. His influence was perhaps felt in the
Greek culture of the kingdom of the two Sicilies, where,
about 1156, one Henricus Aristippus, archdeacon of Ca-
tania, translated into Latin the *Phaedo* and the *Meno*.[47]
From this point the Byzantine tradition ran on to Georgios
Gemistus Pletho and the group of scholars who in the fifteenth century transmitted it to Italy. At the age of eighty,
having spent the second half of his life in the Peloponnesus,
Gemistus attended the Council of Ferrara in Florence in
the year 1439 to discuss the procession of the Holy Ghost
with the champions of the Latin Church. For the procession
of the Holy Ghost, except as an exercise in dialectics, he
cared as little as he did for the reunion of the Greek and
Latin churches. His inner feeling was, "A plague on both
your houses." His real religion was that of the emperor
Julian and of educated Greeks in every age; it was ancient
Hellas, the Greek language and literature, and Platonism.
His god was the unknown unity, source of the Neo-Platonic
emanations and hierarchies which as symbols he preferred
to what he deemed the mythologies of the Greek and the
Catholic churches. In his chief work, the *Laws*, he constructs
a complete religion and cult, fantastically embodying a
scheme of Platonic categories of thought in the divinities
of the old Hellenic Pantheon. The mythological scheme invented by Pletho is merely a to us quaint but to him entirely
natural expression, first, of Hellenic patriotism and distaste
for official Christianity; second, of genuine personal faith
in some sort of divine immanence and the conviction that
the people must have a mythology and a cult; third, of the
dialectician's delight in the ingenious exercise of so con-
structing such a mythology as at the same time to sym-

bolize the chief categories of his metaphysical speculation. For the rest, the *Laws* is one of the long series of Utopias or ideal states inspired by Plato's own *Republic* and *Laws*.

Another work of Pletho's, representative of a now obsolete literature, is his comparison of the philosophy of Plato and Aristotle.[48] The Neo-Platonists of antiquity, when they were driven to choose, preferred, in particular issues, Plato's opinion to Aristotle's. But they preferred to harmonize the two masters by a syncretism which was quite as near the truth as is the statement in the eleventh edition of the *Encyclopaedia Britannica* that Plato makes us think first of the supernatural, and Aristotle of the natural. It is quite true, in a sense, that every man is born either a Platonist or an Aristotelian; but hitherto all attempts to define in precisely what sense it is true have failed, because the difference is not really an opposition of thought, but is, in Plato and Aristotle themselves, a difference of genius and literary style, and in their followers, a difference of taste and temperament.

The debate between the Byzantine Platonists and Aristotelians was stirred to a flame of controversy by the contrast between the Latin Aristotle of Western scholasticism and the Platonic revelation of which the Greeks were then the sole depositors. The fifteenth-century polemic on this question, associated with the names of Cardinal Bessarion, Theodorus Gaza, Georgios Trapezuntios, and other forgotten worthies, bulks as large in the early Renaissance as the controversy between the Ancients and the Moderns does in the literary history of seventeenth-century France, and has been the subject of as many erudite monographs and now fills a perfunctory chapter or page in every history of philosophy.

CHAPTER V

PLATONISM AND THE RENAISSANCE

A DETAILED CONSIDERATION of the influence of Platonic philosophy on the several aspects of the Renaissance would call for a volume of essays. Lack of space forces me to condense my material into one short chapter and begin by enumerating topics which are indispensable but which I can ask you to take for granted. There is, first, the Renaissance itself, the eloquent description and praise of the Renaissance by enthusiasts who regard it as an awakening of the human spirit from medieval darkness and Christian asceticism. Then, there is the counterblast of those who for any reason dislike and wish to minimize the Renaissance. Mr. H. G. Wells, who hates the classics, simply leaves the Renaissance out of universal history. For him, like the Roman empire, it does not exist. Medievalists, like Mr. Cram and Dr. Walsh, who regard the thirteenth as the greatest of centuries, cannot admit that there was any need of a Renaissance. And lastly, all critics adopt a tone of disparagement towards it who, like Oscar Wilde, prefer Gothic to Palladian architecture, mysticism to clarity, and feel a distaste for modern Latin poetry, pseudo classicism and the eighteenth-century style. Assuming all this as a background, I must confine myself, first, to a brief account of the external history of the revival of Platonism, and second, to some indications of the three or four ways in which it chiefly, though of course not solely, influenced subsequent European literature.

The spark that kindled the Platonic revival in Italy is usually attributed to the Greek Gemistus Pletho, who attended the council of the Eastern and Western churches in 1439 and lectured on Plato to enthusiastic Italian audiences. The impression of his eloquence and his venerable philosophic beard may be compared to that produced by Rabin-dranath Tagore on the Women's Clubs in America. The result was that some of the Florentines were moved to learn Greek so that they might study Plato in the original, and this led to the foundation of the Platonic Academy. This is the traditional account of the matter.[1] But I do not know how much the Florentines understood of Pletho's Greek lectures, and the considerable interval between Pletho's visit and the dedication of Marsilio Ficino to the Platonic studies that culminated in his translation of Plato into Latin and the formation of the little club that it amused him to call "Platonic Academy," leaves room for some skepticism of the legend.

We may suspect that the time was ripe and that weari-ness of the praise of Plato in Cicero, Boethius, Macrobius, Apuleius, and the more learned of the Christian Fathers, and of scholastic Aristotelianism, would have brought about a revival of Platonism in any case. However, what we are told is that the recollection of Pletho's lectures many years later led Cosimo de' Medici to select the son of his physician, Ficino, to be educated as a Platonist and dedicated to the task of presenting the real Plato to the Western world. The story of Ficino's life and education, his so-called Platonic Academy, and his translation of Plato, is told superficially and with forceful rhetorical flourishes in nearly every book and essay on the Italian Renaissance, from Roscoe's *Life and Pontificate of Leo the Tenth* and his *Life of Lorenzo de' Medici*, to Symonds' *Renaissance in Italy*, Villari's *Life and Times of Niccolò Machiavelli* and *Life and Times of Giro-lamo Savonarola*, Seebohm's *Oxford Reformers*, and the latest French or English histories of the Renaissance.[2] For the student who wants details and the actual facts, most earlier accounts were superseded by the huge, richly docu-mented, somewhat chaotic work of some 900 pages of Della

[1] Superior figures refer to notes which will be found on p. 246.

Torre.[3] It traces, in minutest detail, largely from unpublished documents, the education of Ficino, the progress of Greek studies, the literary history of the culture and the scholarly coteries and academies of Florence and all Italy during his life. The book is, also, an exhaustive study of the history of the word "academy."

Notable for the history of Platonism is the fact that Ficino wrote a book upon Plato before he knew much Greek or had begun the serious study of the Platonic text. He was able to get together from Cicero, Apuleius, Macrobius, and the Christian Fathers a very respectable body of Platonic doctrine. This transmission of Platonism through secondary sources is, as I have already said, a fundamental fact never to be lost sight of in the history of Platonism.

The so-called Platonic Academy, its meetings and dinners, its banquets, its celebrations of Plato's birthday, its burning of incense before Plato's bust, its nights and feasts of the gods in gardens and villas in the beautiful Arno Valley, is a tempting theme for rhetoric, developed in many histories of the Renaissance. A well-known passage from Macaulay's essay on Machiavelli in his Warren Hastings style will represent them all. "With peculiar pleasure, every cultivated mind must repose on the fair, the happy, the glorious Florence, the halls which rang with the mirth of Pulci, the cell where twinkled the midnight lamp of Politian, the statues on which the young eye of Michel Angelo glared with the frenzy of a kindred inspiration, the gardens in which Lorenzo meditated some sparkling song for the May-day dance of the Etrurian virgins."[4] Ficino's institution was hardly an academy. It was rather a group of friends who occasionally met to honor or humor Ficino's enthusiasm. Two or three of them, notably Pico della Mirandola, were genuine scholars who would carry on the tradition. The others were intelligent amateurs who liked to talk about Platonic love and the creation of the world soul and the music of the spheres and metempsychosis and the harmonization of Platonism and Christianity, and other themes such as I illustrated in the last chapter by the poetry of Lorenzo de' Medici and might illustrate by the sonnets of Michelangelo and the fine line:

The might of one fair face sublimes my love.

The complete Latin translation of Plato with introductory essays to each dialogue appeared in 1482, and its publication was one of the greatest events in European literary history. For three centuries it was to all educated Europe what Jowett's *Plato* has been to the England and America of the past forty years. It was the Plato of Montaigne, of Vico, Rousseau, Macaulay, and numerous other European poets and thinkers. It is the fashion with literary essayists who have perhaps never read Ficino to break epigrams on him and to sneer at the excess of his enthusiasm for Plato, his allegoristic fancies, his sometimes mystical rhetoric, and his endeavors to formulate a religion that will be at once Christian and Platonic. Even George Eliot says that his brain was a little pulpy from an excessive diet of Platonism. But it is not safe to condemn a writer's intelligence because of his willful or naïve employment of method which an ideally sane modern critic would reject. I have studied Ficino and I think I could find as many mistaken renderings and as many fantastic interpretations of Plato in some eminent modern Platonists as in his translations and introductions. In other words, his playing with allegory and his passion or prudent necessity for reconciling Plato with Christianity and with Aristotle do not prevent his translation from being substantially correct, and his introductory essays are, on the whole, excellent summaries of those aspects of Platonism of which he prefers to treat.

By far the most important of these for the literature of the Renaissance is the gospel of Platonic love and enthusiasm, with the associated topics of the defense of poetry against Plato's banishment of the poets by Plato's own doctrine of poetic inspiration. But before I take them up, I must allude briefly to three other chief aspects of Renaissance Platonism for which there is little space: religion, political philosophy, and education.

The essential features of the Platonic religion and its influence upon European literature have already been touched in the preceding chapters. The Renaissance merely developed them with fuller firsthand knowledge. Those who did not read Plato himself could always read Ficino's comparison of Christianity and Platonism in his introduction to the translation of the *Crito* or his Latin treatises on the Platonic theology and on the Christian religion. There are fairly good analyses of Ficino and considerable extracts from these works in several histories of Renaissance philosophy. It comes to this: Ficino wished to be orthodox and stand well with the Church. Like Raymond of Sebonde, whom Montaigne translated, his natural theology nominally included the whole dogma of the Church. He has a chapter to prove that the Incarnation was a reasonable thing and to be expected. Like the Christian Fathers, he said that Plato erred in not admitting creation out of nothing and he formally tried to demonstrate the rationality of the whole Christian creed including the Trinity, which he supported by the spurious Platonic epistles. But his essential personal religion was a liberal Platonizing and Ciceronian ethical Christianity, with a few doubtful and perhaps only apparent concessions to superstition in the form of demonology and astrology.

From Ficino and his pupil and friend Pico della Mirandola, who is a much more rational philosopher than he appears in Symonds' *Renaissance* and in the histories of philosophy, similar ideas passed to the England of Colet, Grocyn, More, Linacre, Fisher, Elyot, Spenser, Sidney, Ben

Jonson, and Shakespeare; the France of Budé and Ronsard; the Germany of Rudolph Agricola and Melanchthon. And this Platonism itself, or the Platonism of Cicero's philosophical treatises, became indissolubly bound up with liberal theology in the European mind—to be regarded as a source of enlightenment or heresy, according to the standpoint of the critic. This tradition, passing through the Cambridge Platonists, the Deists, Tucker's once much-read *Light of Nature Pursued*, Schleiermacher, Martineau, Matthew Arnold, is still a living influence today in such types as Dean Inge, and Dr. Fosdick, and most American preachers of undogmatic and ethical religion. However, it has always been accompanied by an underground tradition of esoteric, mystic, occult, Pythagoreanizing Platonism, on which I have refused to waste much space in these chapters, though inasmuch as it arouses historical curiosity it calls for a monograph. Its only interest to me is that it is the main cause for the distrust of Platonism in some scientific minds.[5]

In the Renaissance and the following centuries, Platonism was used to justify magic, belief in daemons, witchcraft, astrology, the philosopher's stone, and many other charlatanisms and superstitions. A naïve passage of Chaucer will typify this kind of Platonism as well as any later citation.

Telle me the name of thilke privee ston.
And Plato answered unto him anon;
Take the ston that Titanos men name.
Which is that? quod he. Magnetia is the same.
Saide Plato. Ye, sire, and is it thus?
This is *ignotum per ignotius*.
What is Magnetia, good sire, I pray?
It is a water that is made, I say,
Of the elementes foure, quod Plato.
Tell me the rote, good sire, quod he tho
Of that water, if that it be your will.
Nay, nay, quod Plato, certain that I n'ill.

The philosophers were sworne everich on,
That they ne shuld discover it unto non,
Ne in no book it write in no manere;
For unto God it is so lefe and dere,
That he wol not that it discovered be.

Canon's Yeoman's Tale, 1452 ff.

Plato's *Ion* employs the magnesian stone or magnet as a symbol of the attractive and inspirational power of poetry.[6] But there seems to be no connection. The whole mystic tradition is summed up once for all in a paragraph of Ficino's book on the Christian Religion which I translate: "The primitive theology of the Gentiles in which Zoroaster, Mercury, Orpheus, Aglaophemus, and Pythagoras are at one is to be found entire in the books of our Plato. In his letters Plato prophesies that these mysteries can be made plain to mankind only after many centuries. And that was what happened. For it was first in the time of Philo and Numenius that the thought of the primitive theologians, embodied in Plato's writings, began to be understood. That is to say, it was directly after the preachings of the apostles and of the disciples of the apostles, and their writings. For the Platonists used the divine light of Christians for the interpretation of the divine Plato. This is the reason why Basil the Great and Augustine affirm that the Platonists plagiarized the mysteries of John the Evangelist. I myself have certainly found that the chief mystic doctrines of Numenius, Philo, Plotinus, Iamblichus, and Proclus were borrowed from John, from Paul, Hierotheus, and from Dionysius the Areopagite. All the magnificent things they said of the divine mind and the angels and other theological topics, were plainly borrowed thence."[7]

Aristotle's *Politics* was known to the great scholastics of the Middle Ages and commented on by them.[8] The medieval writers knew Plato's *Republic* mainly through Aristotle's unfair criticism and the virulent denunciation by the Christian Fathers of Plato's supposed communal marriage.[9] A translation of the first five books of the *Republic*, begun by Chrysoloras and completed by Uberto Decembrio and his son Pier Candido, was presented to Humphrey, duke of Gloucester, in 1443.[10]After the publication of Ficino's translation, any educated man could gather Plato's political ideas by direct reading of the *Republic*, the *Politicus*, the *Gorgias*, and the *Laws*, or from the convenient summaries of Plato's political theories in Ficino's introductions. Thereafter no scholar wrote about political theory without taking them into account, and apart from the slight imitation of the *Republic* in Campanella's *City of the Sun*, More's *Utopia*, and Bacon's *Atlantis*, the whole early European literature of political philosophy is thickly strewn with references to Plato.

Hardly anybody reads Plato's *Laws* now. But Montaigne has literally scores and perhaps hundreds of quotations from it. To collect the references to Plato in Grotius, Pufendorf, and the rest would demand a monograph. The most important of these sources is Bodin's now forgotten *Six livres de la République*, published in France in the year 1577, and soon after used as a textbook at the universities of Elizabethan England. It held somewhat the place, for that generation, that Barker's *Political Thought of Plato and Aristotle* holds in ours. Our histories of the science of politics do not do justice to this tradition or, indeed, to the political philosophy of Plato himself. Medieval writers attribute to Aristotle ideas that are distinctly anticipated in Plato's writings, but are not so easy to find there as in the more systematic and matter-of-fact Aristotelian treatise. A chief reason, indeed, for the failure to appreciate Plato's full influence on European thought is what I am tempted to call "the fallacy of system." In a lecture, and sometimes in a book, we prefer even a false system, artificially and too ingeniously imposed upon the facts, to the subtleties and complications of truth, because it seems to offer us a clue to the labyrinth, a satisfying explanation in which our minds can rest, and an easily rememberable formula. The mistaking of the appearance of system for profundity is one of the most persistent delusions of the human mind.

Of late, Plato has occupied an ever-increasing place in the textbooks of the history of education. A full treatment of his educational theories would furnish material for a separate essay, but, owing to lack of space in this book of lectures, I can only allude to the subject. It is enough here to remind you that the *Republic* is a treatise on education, the best in the world, according to Rousseau, as well as a treatise on politics. Plato, like all eager reformers, based his hopes for humanity largely on his optimistic estimate of the power of education on plastic human material. Plato has two systems of education: one for the generality, and one for the selected band of students from whom the rulers of the state are to emerge by natural and competitive selection. No man is fit to be a ruler, says Plato, who has not, by many years of severe scientific study supplemented by years of practical experience of affairs, won his way to a vision of the Idea of Good and the best means for realizing it in the measure possible to man.[11] "Every minister," says Dr. Emil Ludwig, "in the cabinet of every nation, should be required to serve his apprenticeship as a chauffeur. For does not his success depend on the very qualities which are needed in driving a car? The twentieth century, you see, has outgrown the visions of the dreamer Plato." But the reformers of education in the Renaissance and after, from Vittorino da Feltre to Mulcaster, Elyot, Roger Ascham, Vives, and Milton, drew their inspiration from this dreamer. They all copied Plato's description of the natural gifts required for the ideal student, his insistence on the blending of music and gymnastics for the production of a sound mind in a sound body, and his warning that severe disciplinary studies are the indispensable preparation for the broader criticism of life and social and political institutions. Plato is also the chief source of inspiration of another type of literature, which the Renaissance took over from antiquity and the Middle Ages, the description of the good or ideal king. This sometimes takes the form of a treatise on the education of a prince, and sometimes that of an encomium of a king to whom are attributed, in order to encourage him in well-doing, all the qualities of Plato's philosophic rulers. This literature would repay a special study for those who are curious about such things.[12] Here I can only mention it and pass on to the two themes which I said were chiefly characteristic of Renaissance Platonism, Platonic love and the defense of poetry.

Platonic love, like Neo-Platonism, is a development of certain passages in Plato, a state of mind, and a chapter in the history of European literature. These passages are mainly found in (1) the *Lysis*, (2) the *Phaedrus*, and (3) the *Symposium*. The *Lysis* is a minor Socratic dialogue on friendship, the Greek word for friendship being sometimes also a synonym for love. In the *Phaedrus*, love is associated with the passion of the elder friend or teacher to help the pupil and friend to develop all his highest possibilities, a noble theme which we must not allow to be spoiled for us even by the somewhat nauseous rhetoric of certain modern scholars about the relations of Plato and Sappho to their pupils. Here is Plato's own version of it (*Symp.* 209 B-C): "And if he, the teacher, meets in conjunction with loveliness of form, a beautiful, generous, and gentle soul, he embraces both at once, and immediately undertakes to educate the object of his love, and is inspired with an overflowing persuasion to declare what is virtue and what he ought to be who would attain to its possession and what are the duties which it exacts." This is an eternal truth and one of the noblest forms of Platonic love—perhaps more practical than

the mystic love of God. I doubt if young students always
realize the intensity of an old teacher's desire to help them
just a little to make the best of themselves. Lastly, and
chiefly, in the *Symposium* a series of after-dinner speeches
in praise of love culminates in Socrates' account of how
Diotima taught him the higher philosophy of love as the
passion of creation, the yearning for an immortality otherwise denied to mortal creatures, and in its highest sublimation, the love of the beautiful, rising by successive stages
from beauty embodied in a single form to the transcendent
beauty of the idea, the great ocean of beauty in which at
last the insatiate soul finds rest.

Even an enumeration of the profusion of thoughts in these
three dialogues exceeds our scope. But the most important
ideas are easily remembered because they have been crys-
tallized in a few notable passages of English poetry, or have
become commonplaces in the history of philosophy and
science. The question debated in the *Lysis* whether friendship or love is the attraction of likes or opposites may be
summed in a stanza of Tennyson's *In Memoriam* (LXXIX):

> And so my wealth resembles thine,
> But he was rich where I was poor,
> And he supplied my want the more
> As his unlikeness fitted mine.

The power of love to purify a man and lift him to his
best is expressed sufficiently for recognition of the idea,
however far below Plato, in Coventry Patmore's *Angel in
the House* and in Tennyson's well-known lines:

> for indeed I knew
> Of no more subtle master under heaven
> Than is the maiden passion for a maid,
> Not only to keep down the base in man,
> But teach high thought, and amiable words
> And courtliness, and the desire of fame,
> And love of truth, and all that makes a man.
>
> *Guinevere* 473 ff.

Love as the symbol of all yearning for great achievements is expressed, not unworthily of Plato himself, in the glorious lines of Spenser:

> The noble heart that harbours virtuous thought
> And is with child of glorious great intent,
> Can never rest, until it forth have brought
> The eternal brood of glory excellent.

Faerie Queene I. V. 1 ff.

The distinction between the heavenly and the earthly love is a commonplace of European poetry and painting, and may be represented here by Lowell's poem *Endymion* and by poems of Baudelaire and Swinburne. The idea that love is a racial or biological *Ersatz* for a denied individual immortality, passed from Plato into Aristotle's biological writings, and thence into the science, the philosophy, and the literature of Europe. The dainty Emerson speaks of organs of procreation which lay hold on immortality, and the conclusion of the *Microcosmus* of Bernardus Silvestris anticipates Emerson's phrase with an Aristophanic frankness which I dare not quote even in these frank days. The gospel of Platonic love was adapted, as by a preëstablished harmony, to the temper and spirit of the age which rediscovered it.

The great Italians of the Renaissance who in one short century recaptured the lost beauty of the ancient world, brought art to its perfection, and laid the foundations of modern philosophy and science were all half-intoxicated by the spiritual ozone of that vivid age. The human spirit, they felt, had drunk of Lethe and slept for a thousand years. Song forsook their tongues who saw the strange God's kingdom come, and Memory, the mother of the Muses, had fled away from earth with her daughters. But at last the great artist had returned to wed once more the raptured eye of the young spirit, as in Tennyson's ode, with large dowries to be led in triumph like a bride of old with music and sweet

showers of festal flowers. Their seething brains held no air-
tight compartments to cabin and confine each sense and
every sentiment in its separate crib. Whatever they did,
they did with their whole souls. They threw the enthusiasm
of the lunatic, the lover, and the poet into their science,
their art, their philosophy, their religion, and their love
alike. In them the need of correlating the sense of beauty
with the sense of conduct and the love of knowledge was im-
perious. They required a philosophy which could justify
their deep inward conviction that all the activities, all the
enthusiasms, all the aspirations of the soul are but many-
tongued flickerings of the one central flame. And this
philosophy they found in the revived Platonism of the Flor-
entine academy. A passage which I have translated from Ficino's preface to his translation of the *Symposium* will illustrate the spirit of the age better than pages of further and
fruitless disquisition:

"Plato, the chief of philosophers, being of the age of
eighty-one years, breathed his last as he lay at banquet
with his friends on the seventh day of November, which
was also the day of his birth. This banquet, which served to
commemorate both the birthday of Plato and the anniver-
sary of his death, was renewed every year by all the old
Platonists down to the time of Plotinus and Porphyry. But
after Porphyry this solemn festival was neglected for one
thousand two hundred years. At last in our days the ever-
glorious Lorenzo de' Medici, wishing to renew this Platonic
banquet, appointed Franciscus Bandinus his master of the
feast. Bandinus selected the seventh of November for the
celebration and on that day entertained with royal magnificence at the villa of Careggi nine Platonic guests: Antonius
Aelius, bishop of Fiesole, Ficinus the doctor, Landino the
poet, Bernardus Nutius the orator, Thomas Bentius, Johannes Cavalcanti, a dear friend of mine whom for the virtue of his soul and the excellency of his mind they called

the hero of the feast, the two Marsuppini, Cristoforo and Carolo, sons of the poet Carolus, and lastly myself, whom Bandinus chose to make the ninth."

I cannot delay to repeat Ficino's account of the speeches delivered at this banquet, which really took place, though he himself composed the speeches afterwards. We may form a general notion of them from the story in Maurice Hewlett's *Earthwork Out of Tuscany* of the poetic discourse on beauty and love at Fiesole that induced the girl to bequeath her beauty to posterity by sitting for Botticelli's Naked Venus. Ficino's report of these speeches in the introduction to his translation of the *Symposium* fills more than fifty huge columns of eloquence, fancy, interpretation, mysticism, allegory, symbolism. It would demand an erudite treatise to expound all the niceties of this doctrine and its relations to Ficino's sources, his own philosophy, and to the literature of the Renaissance to which it gave rise. All the speeches are possible, but sometimes fanciful, developments of those in in Plato's *Symposium*. There were many such banquets and discourses in the Italy of the Renaissance, expressions of the aspiration to "rise on the same stairs to science and to joy." Perhaps the best illustration of this is the fine rhapsody at the close of Baldassare Castiglione's *Cortegiano*.

After a fine description of the Platonic scale of beauty, whereby the soul of the lover, detaching itself from the exclusive devotion to one beautiful body and enlarging its perception to the inclusion of all beautiful sights and sounds, rises to the contemplation of the idea of beauty in music, institutions, and actions, and so by gradual ascent to the vision of the absolute intellectual beauty, Castiglione concludes, in mystic strain: "From this point the soul kindled by the sacred flame of the true divine love takes flight to unite itself with the angelic nature and not only wholly quits the region of sense but no longer has need of the discourse of reason, for being transformed into the angelic nature it understands all intelligible things, and with no veil to cloud its vision looks forth upon the broad sea of beauty divine and receives into itself and enjoys the supreme felicity of the things which eye hath not seen and ear hath not heard. If then the shadowy and unreal beauties that, with cloud-filmed mortal eyes, we daily see in mortal bodies are so fair and lovely in our sight that they enkindle the most ardent fire in our hearts and so delectable that we often repute no felicity comparable to that conveyed by a single glance vouchsafed from the eyes of the lady of our love, with what happy wonder, what blind amaze, will their souls be filled who attain the vision of beauty transcendent.

"This is the beauty which is one with the supreme goodness and which, by its light, calls and attracts to itself all things. Not only does it give intellect to the intellectual and reason to the rational, but to the sensual it imparts, also, the very sense and fine appetite of life, and even in plants and stones it infuses something of its own virtue in their motions and in that natural instinct whereby every created thing tends to preserve itself and fulfill the law of its being. This love is stronger and more blessed than others in proportion to the excellency of its awakening cause. And even as material fire refineth gold, so this most sacred flame enkindled in the soul destroys and burns away all the husks and dross of mortality, and vivifies and makes beautiful the celestial germ that was before mortified by the sense and buried in the sepulcher of the body. This is the flaming pyre on which, as poets feign, Hercules was burned on Mount Oeta and thereby rendered immortal and divine. This is the burning bush of Moses, the divine tongue of flame, the fiery chariot of Elijah. This it is that redoubles the grace and the felicity in the souls of those that are accounted worthy of the celestial vision, when spurning beneath their feet this terrene baseness they take flight for the midheaven."

A rhapsody of words, it may be said, and it is disgust with tasteless exaggeration and repetition of this sort that has at times provoked those intense reactions of so-called common sense against Plato which are also a part of the history of Platonism. Pope's diatribe may stand for them all:

> Go, soar with Plato to the empyreal sphere,
> To the first Good, first Perfect, and first Fair;
> Or tread the mazy round his followers trod,
> And quitting sense call imitating God.[13]
>
> *Essay on Man* II 23 ff.

But life is not so simple as that. Platonic transcendent idealizing rhapsodies and personifications of abstractions, as beautiful women, may disorganize undisciplined minds; but there is the strange fact that only the races and the ages that are capable of these transcendental rhapsodies can achieve the highest things, carve the Parthenon, paint the Botticelli Venus, write the *Iliad* and the *Divina commedia*. The mythology of Homer and all that has come from it is, in a sense, irrational. Would we rather reduce the whole Indo-European world to the common sense of the eighteenth century and the matter-of-factness of Confucius and Lao-tzu? Or do we still find some meaning in the twofold Platonic and Dantesque inspirations of Rossetti?

> This is that Lady Beauty, in whose praise
> Thy voice and hand shake still,—long known to
>   thee
> By flying hair and fluttering hem,—the beat
> Following her daily of thy heart and feet,
> How passionately and irretrievably,
> In what fond flight, how many ways and days!
>
> *The House of Life* Sonnet 77: Soul's Beauty

Now, the young Englishmen who visited Italy in the sixteenth century found there not merely those enchantments of Circe of which Roger Ascham complains, not merely those

wild tales of southern passion and crime that furnished forth
the plots of Elizabethan tragedy, but they also found lin-
gering in the academies and polite circles which a century
later entertained Milton this sage and serious doctrine of
Platonic love; they brought it back to England, and from
Spenser to Shelley it became one of the chief themes of
English poetry, a main inspiration of "these brave trans-
lunary things that our first poets had." From this is derived
Marlowe's "if all the pens that ever poets held" (*Tambur-
laine the Great*, First Part, Act 5 sc. 2); from this the hymn
of Spenser and the allegory of Una, beauty and wisdom in
one. The first English history of philosophy, by Stanley,
presents as one of its most important documents a translation of Pico della Mirandola's commentary on Benivieni's
canzone of love, heavenly and divine,[14] all derived directly
from Ficino.

This doctrine of Platonic love included in its higher and
lower manifestations the *henosis* of Plotinus, the religious
raptures of St. Francis, Dante's love for Beatrice, Petrarch's
love for Laura, the poet's eye in fine frenzy rolling, Spinoza's
intellectual love of God, and everything that the eighteenth
century, the century educated by Locke and Pope, viewed
askance and stigmatized as enthusiasm.

An exhaustive anatomy of Platonic love would be as
horrible a monument of pedantry as Burton's *Anatomy of
Melancholy*. The topic will recur for a paragraph in the
chapters on French and English literature. We may, at
once, dismiss with contempt the meaning of the term most
familiar to the man in the street and to silly sex novels, and
the theme of cynical comment and ribald jest from Montaigne to Carew, and from Carew to Byron. Most of the
passages are collected in Harrison's *Platonism in English
Poetry*, which, however, strangely overlooks the very passages which I have cited as expressing the true doctrine of
Platonic love.[15] *Hudibras* (III ll. 277 f.) speaks of:

> In raptures of Platonic lashing,
> And chaste contemplative bardashing,

and Steele writes in the *Spectator*:"Though a tolerable good philosopher, I have but a low opinion of Platonic love, and avoid the company of virtuous women." But some think too much of this. As far back as Porphyry's *Life of Plotinus* we read that the Master was often pained and humiliated by the turn which discourses of Platonic love took in his classroom.[16]

The emotional exaltations denoted by this all-embracing term are indeed liable to the same degenerations and exposed to the same censure that moved Plato to distrust all emotional poetry. When the matter is judged in the light of a sober psychology, there appears an affiliation that gives us pause between the ecstasies of hysteric nuns and the eloquent flights of the Platonic Eros. Both are in danger of doing what John Oliver Hobbes, herself a woman, said all women do—mistake their bodies for their souls. The most decadent poets experience ecstasies and give voice to vague and ineffable yearnings for the ideal, which, in sober or matter-of-fact minds, cast a shade on the similar language of Michelangelo, Spenser, and Shelley. What is Baudelaire's hymn "to the thrice fair, the infinite goddess of his idolatry," but a decadent version of Platonic love?[17] Yet no protest against degenerate and aberrant expressions of the feeling can check the human instinct to symbolize, idealize, transfigure, or, as the word now is, sublimate, so tremendous a fact as love. And since Plato, outsoaring ancient poetry and anticipating modern poetry, Platonic love, though it is only one corner of Plato's mind and one tributary of the mighty stream of Platonic influence, will remain a perpetual theme of philosophic and poetical idealism in European literature. We shall thus meet it again in our survey of French and English literature, but may conclude this slight introduction to the subject with Swinburne's beautiful rondel *Eros*. It is fitting that the philosophy of Platonic love should be summed up in the words of a poet whose own spiritual development, from the crude erotics of *Laus Veneris* to the graver patriotic and philosophical inspiration of his later Muse, is itself a noble exemplification of the Platonic gospel.

> Eros, from rest in isles far-famed,
> With rising Anthesterion rose
> And all Hellenic heights acclaimed
>   Eros.
>
> The sea one pearl, the shore one rose,
> All round him all the flower-month flamed
> And lightened, laughing off repose.
> Earth's heart, sublime and unashamed,
> Knew, even perchance as man's heart knows,
> The thirst of all men's nature named
>   Eros.
>
> .   .   .   .
>
> Eros, with shafts by thousands aimed
> At laughing lovers round in rows,
> Fades from their sight whose tongues proclaimed
>   Eros.
>
> But higher than transient shapes or shows
> The light of love in life inflamed
> Springs towards no goal that these disclose.
>
> Above those heavens which passion claimed
> Shines, veiled by change that ebbs and flows,
> The soul in all things born or framed.
>   Eros.

"The soul in all things born or framed"—to that we shall return in speaking of Platonism as the fountainhead of idealism in French and English poetry. But now we have to note the fact that the Plato who gave this poetic gospel to the Renaissance and Modern Europe is also the Plato who crowned Homer with flowers and banished him from the *Republic*.

The paradox that Plato, most poetic of philosophers, exiled the poets, while Aristotle, the dry-as-dust father of all the Leibnitzes and Herbert Spencers of the world, took up the gauntlet in their defense, has always been a problem for the lovers of Plato and a theme of triumph for his enemies. "The two primal discoverers of moral truth, Homer and Plato, are partly at issue," says Ruskin regretfully. "For," he continues,"Plato's logical power quenched his imagination." Schopenhauer says that Plato's banishment of the poets was that tribute to error which every finite mortal spirit must pay. A recent critic has compared Plato's censure and banishment of Homer from his *Republic* with the atrophy of poetic and artistic feeling that overtook Darwin in his later life."Plato's austere intellectualism," he says, repeating Ruskin,"destroyed the capacity for such feeling." Nothing could be farther from the truth. It was Plato's sensitiveness to the stimulus, the excitement, the beauty of art that made him fear for the guardians of his state the potency of the Circean brew which divorces the feeling from her mate, the deed. He could have said far more truly than Calvin, who also banished the drama, says, "By nature I have a strong inclination for poetry." A story in Naomi Mitchison's collection of Greek stories entitled *Black Sparta* prettily sentimentalizes the old anecdote that Plato burned his own plays and youthful poems after conversing with Socrates.

However that may be, Plato is only too susceptible to the fascination of the honeyed Muse, as the fond and frequent citations of Greek poetry, latent and explicit, scattered over his pages prove.[18]"We are very conscious of her charm,and thou too, dear friend, art thou not thyself beguiled by her,

when thou dost contemplate her through Homer? But great
is the prize for which we are striving, and what shall it profit a
man if he gain the whole world of poetry and art, and lose
his own soul?"[19] Symbolic here are Spenser's lines on the
iconoclasm of his puritan hero:

> But all those pleasant bowers and palace brave
> Guyon broke down with rigour pitiless;
> Ne aught their goodly workmanship might save
> Them from the tempest of his wrathfulness.[20]

Or, in Plato's own summary: "and if we admit the honeyed
Muse into our state, pleasure and pain will be the lords of
our city, instead of laws, and the rule that right reason shall
have pronounced to be the best" (*Rep.* 607 A).

The third book of the *Republic* banished imitative poetry
in the person of Homer for two chief reasons: the immorality
of the Homeric mythology, and the incompatibility of un-
restrained mimicry and the mimetic habit of mind with
gravity and stability of character. The first reason has now
chiefly a historical interest. It interests the historical student not only in its relation to the thought of Plato's own
time, but also as the source for similar arguments in the
Christian Fathers,[21] in the Elizabethan and Restoration
polemic against stage plays, and in Rousseau's letter to
D'Alembert opposing the establishment of a theater in the
Geneva where Calvin had prohibited it. But Plato's distrust of tragedy went deeper. His feeling toward it was akin
to that which Howells used to entertain toward romantic
and sentimental fiction. It falsified life more dangerously
than either epic or the open and hearty indecency of comedy.
In his *Laws*, discussing the still vexed problem whether
pleasure is the ultimate and only test of art, Plato asks
whose pleasure—if you instituted a competition, we older
men would choose a stately recitation of Homer by a good
rhapsodist; the boys would prefer the movies, or a farce of

Aristophanes; while sentimental young men and educated women would cast their vote for tragedy. But life itself is the supreme tragedy, which the citizen of our ideal state must enact aright. And we cannot permit even the art of Homer or Sophocles to relax our temper, unsettle our convictions, and untune us for our parts (*Laws* 658 C-E).

Present-day critics would be either shocked or greatly amused by the half-serious declaration in Plato's *Laws*, "We will require our censors to accept the poems of the braver and better men, even if they are not quite so poetical."[22] But whatever our judgments of this *boutade* as a principle of literary criticism, it is a perfectly natural human sentiment. "Good God!" cries the hero of Masefield's novel *Multitude and Solitude*, "it seems to me that a man should not be permitted to write a play before he has risked his life for another or for the state." The principle would not have worked so badly in Greece if it led to the selection of Aeschylus rather than Euripides.

Returning to the subject in the tenth book of the *Republic*, Plato justifies himself, perhaps against contemporary critics, by two explicit arguments: poetry merely excites feeling, whereas what men need in the crises of life is its discipline and control. Aristotle's purgation of the passions through pity and terror in his famous definition of tragedy (*Poet.* 1449 b 24 ff.) is an attempt to answer this last objection. Poetry, Aristotle seems to say, not merely excites emotion but also purges it. A little common sense and a little knowledge of Greek pinches into pillulous smallness the interminable cobweb of controversy spun about this formula.[23] The purge, or *katharsis*, in Greek as in English, may mean literal evacuation, or may imply the purification of the thing purged. Poets and literary critics always have thought and always will think chiefly of the purification, which they will describe in terms of their own conceptions of the ennobling, fortifying, soothing, calming influence of great art. Hardheaded scholars think to show their critical temper and their superiority to such sentimentality by insisting that Aristotle intended *katharsis* to be taken only in the strict physical and medical sense. The Freudians welcome the idea that we naturally tend to accumulate stores of latent and suppressed feeling which fester within us unless safely discharged. But the English critic Hazlitt, who found Aristotle's idea in Burke, was before them with his wittier version: "Not having [sc. country people] the fictitious distresses and gigantic crimes of poetry to stimulate their imagination and their passions, they vent their whole stock of spleen, malice, and invention, on their friends and next-door neighbors."[24] Such, in brief, is the answer of the defenders of poetry through the ages to the count that poetry, dabbling in the fount of fictive tears, is an unwholesome stimulant of idle emotion.

Plato's other objection was that poetry and art imitate not reality but the shows of things, and things themselves are only copies and adumbrations of the eternal ideas. Poetry, then, is at the third remove from reality. The technical answer, in Plato's own terminology, would suggest itself at once to any clever disputant. It was only needful to affirm that the poet by virtue of his gift of divination contemplated the idea, and copied that, not the material object. "Art," says Plotinus (*Enn.* V 8. 1-2), "does not merely imitate the visible, but runs up to the seminal reasons from which nature springs. Phidias fashioned his Zeus on no pattern of sense, but showed him as he would and might be if revealed to mortal eye." This sentence links the centuries together. The words, "as he would and might be," in the Greek repeat verbatim Aristotle's statement that poetry is worthier than history (*Poet.* 1451 b 6), for history shows what was and poetry what would and might be. And the whole anticipates and probably suggested Emerson's lines on the same subject:

Not from a vain and shallow thought
His awful Jove young Phidias brought.

The Problem 9-10

If I had sufficient space to indulge what an old author styles a
"paroxysm of quotations," it would be easy to trace this
thought from age to age. "And that the poet hath that idea
is manifest," says Sir Philip Sidney, and all defenders of
poesy have repeated, with Mrs. Browning,"Art is the wit-
ness of what is behind this show." Browning's *Fra Lippo
Lippi* adds the further suggestion that it is through the
artist's eyes that the ordinary man is also enabled to behold
the idea:

For, don't you mark? we're made so that we love
First when we see them painted, things we have passed
Perhaps a hundred times nor cared to see;

and Hartley Coleridge in his beautiful sonnet, "The Vale of
Tempe had in vain been fair," applies the thought to the
Wordsworthian poetic interpretation of nature:

The beauty to perceive of earthly things,
The mounting soul must heavenward prune her wings.

Sonnets xxxiii

Best of all is Schopenhauer's version. The entire philosophy
of art in his *Die Welt als Wille und Vorstellung* is entitled
The Platonic Idea, the Object of Art. The artist, he says, im-
presses on the unyielding marble the types of beauty which
Nature has bungled in a thousand experiments, and, holding them up to Nature's face, triumphantly cries, "That
was what thou didst intend." "Yes, that was it," echoes from
the beholder's soul. Others argued that the banishment of
the poets represented only a temporary puritanic mood and
appealed from Plato sober to Plato drunk; that is, from the
Plato of the *Republic* to the Plato of the *Symposium*, the
Phaedrus, and the *Ion*, and the doctrines of poetic inspiration, poetic madness, and poetic love there set forth.

The inspiration of the poet, says Plato in the *Ion* (533 D), may be compared to the magnet which not only attracts the iron rings but also communicates to them the virtue by which they attract one another. ". . . the Muse, communicating through those whom she has first inspired, to all others capable of sharing in the inspiration, the influence of the first enthusiasm creates a chain and a succession." The souls of the poets, Shelley's translation of the *Ion* continues, "flying like bees from flower to flower . . . return to us laden with the sweetness of melody, and arrayed as they are in the plumes of rapid imagination, they speak truth. For a poet is indeed a thing etherially light, winged and sacred, nor can he compose anything worth calling poetry until he becomes inspired and, as it were, mad, or whilst any reason remains in him."

This doctrine of poetic madness is still better known from the passage of the *Phaedrus* which enumerates the four kinds of divine possession or madness more desirable than any bourgeois or Philistine sobriety—the madness of the prophet, of the hierophant, of the lover, and of the poet. The Sibyl, the lover, and the poet, Plato says in substance long before Shakespeare, are "of imagination all compact" and roll their eyes in fine frenzy, and whosoever unpossessed by this poetic rage knocks at the Muses' portal, his poetry will come to naught in comparison with that of the inspired madman.

Innumerable paraphrases and developments of these passages in the writers of the Italian Renaissance and their French and European successors, which I have no space to quote, provided a telling retort to the arguments of the ascetic and puritanic Platonists who took their texts from the *Republic*. In any case, the defenders of poetry argued, employing the exegesis of some modern commentators on the Sermon on the Mount, the proscription of poetry was intended only for Plato's ideal state and was not to be applied to human life and nature as they are. "It is possible to love Homer and Plato too," wistfully concluded the Platonic lecturer of the second century, Maximus of Tyre.[25]

Passing over antiquity and the Italians, we may illustrate these arguments by typical passages from Sidney and Milton. Sidney, though writing a defense of poesy, will not condemn Plato. "But now, indeed," he begins, "my burthen is great, that Plato's name is laid upon me, whom, I must confess, of all philosophers I have ever esteemed most worthy of reverence." After expanding this idea and permitting himself an unfair jibe at the community of women in the *Republic*, he concludes: "And a man need go no farther than to Plato himself to know his meaning; who, in his dialogue called *Ion*, giveth high, and rightly, divine commendation unto poetry. So as Plato, banishing the abuse, not the thing, not banishing it, but giving due honor to it, shall be our patron, and not our adversary."[26]

The last and most telling shaft of the defenders of poetry, then, is the schoolboy's retort—poet yourself. To the citation of Plato as an advocate of the censorship, Milton indignantly replies in his *Areopagitica*, "But that Plato meant this law peculiarly to that commonwealth which he had imagined, and to no other, is evident. Why was he not else a lawgiver to himself, but a transgressor, and to be expelled by his own magistrates both for the wanton epigrams and dialogues which he made, and his perpetual reading of Sophron Mimus and Aristophanes, books of grossest infamy?"[27] There is a curious recurrence to this argument in the closing lines of Milton's strange Latin poem on the Platonic idea:

> But thou eternal light of Academe,
> If to the schools thou first didst give this theme,
> This figment passing all in song or ditty,
> Recall the poets from exile to thy city,
> Or thou, the greatest fabler of them all,
> By thine own law art banished past recall.

*De idea Platonica, quemadmodum
Aristoteles intellexit*

That Plato was himself a poet is apparent to every reader who does not require poetry to be tagged and labeled with rhyme. It is a commonplace of literature from the earliest Christian Fathers to the latest romantic critics, whether used in Milton's way to refute, or in Shelley's to exalt, Plato. He is quite literally a poet as the author of the most exquisite of Greek epigrams, almost too familiar to quote. He is a poet by virtue of the incredible constructive imagination which framed the plot of those intricate yet always natural discussions where naïve critics fancy that the argument follows whithersoever the wind blows, but the more penetrating perceive, with Schopenhauer, that Plato really holds the threads of his preconceived design in an iron hand. He is a poet in the all-pervading, figurative, imaginative quality of his diction, the vivid realization of the visible and tangible which again surprises the naïve in the philosopher of the pure colorless essence that eye has not seen.

He has the larger invention of the poet. "A poet," he himself says, "must narrate myths or fables and not merely arguments" (*Phaedo* 61 B), and as Phaedrus says to Socrates: "O Socrates, you can easily invent Egyptian tales or any other kind of tales" (*Phaedrus* 275 B). There are entire peoples whose contribution to the mythology and symbolism of the race would not counterbalance that of the myths of Plato as collected by Professor Stewart. He is supremely a poet in the direct, emotional, and imaginative appeal of his climactic passages, which, as some ancient critics caviled, pale as eloquence when placed beside the glowing logic of Demosthenes, but which modern masters of poetic prose instinctively feel and render as poetry.

This is the note which Jowett too often misses but which the kindred genius of Ruskin infallibly discerned even amid the quibbles and jests and fantastic etymologies of the *Cratylus*. "And so also now," he says in *Time and Tide* (Letter XXIV), "this chance word of the daily journal, about the sirens, brought to my mind the divine passage of the *Cratylus* of Plato, about the place of the dead: 'And none of those who dwell there desire to depart thence,—no, not even the Sirens; but even they, the seducers, are there themselves beguiled, and they who lulled all men, themselves laid to rest—they, and all others—such sweet songs doth death know how to sing to them.' " This recalls Keats's

> Darkling I listen; and, for many a time
> I have been half in love with easeful Death,
> Call'd him soft names in many a mused rhyme,
> To take into the air my quiet breath.
>
> *Ode to a Nightingale* vi

That is no Greek note; you will search classical Greek poetry for it in vain. Only the prophetic soul of Plato, dreaming on things to be, anticipates the Christian, modern, romantic sentiment of St. Francis: "Praised be our Lord for our sister, the death of the body,"—of Henry Vaughan's "Dear beauteous death, the jewel of the just,"—of Keats's, and of Walt Whitman's, "Praise, praise, praise for the sure and winding arms of cool enfolding death." If this were a study of Plato the poet, instead of the history of Platonism, it would be interesting to collect other anticipations by him of images and subtleties of thought and feeling not discoverable in the Greek classical poets, and which, but for him, we might think alien to the Greek mind. But to consider the matter so curiously would take us too far. Yet it was necessary to say something about it. For it is this authentic, poetic inspiration in Plato himself which makes him the magnet of his own symbolism in the *Ion*; a magnet which not only attracts kindred souls, but also communicates its own virtue to the dependent rings of the chain of poetic idealism in the literature of France and England, to which the last two chapters will be devoted.

CHAPTER VI

PLATONISM AND FRENCH LITERATURE

IT MAY BE THOUGHT that if I have space for only two modern literatures, it would have been better to take German literature as the companion of English in the History of Platonism rather than French. The French language is clearness itself, and French literature is the incarnation of good sense—a somewhat prosaic good sense, some of its critics would say—whereas Platonism is by the French themselves supposed to be a dreamy, mystic, cloudy philosophy. It is at Alexandria, they would say, at Florence, in the Germany of the philosophies of nature, in the England of the Spensers and the Shelleys, in the America of Emerson and Alcott and the Concord School of Philosophy that we are to look for the history of Platonism, and not in the France of the *fabliaux*, of the *esprit gaulois*, of Molière, of Voltaire, of Béranger, of Zola, and of Anatole France. There is an element of truth in these objections. But the study of Platonism in German literature would soon transform itself into a study of Platonism in German philology, which, however suitable for a monograph, would not do here.

French literature is the only European literature comparable with English in the length and the continuity of its tradition. There is more than one side to French literature, and more than one aspect of the French mind; and though I cannot maintain that the spirit of French literature as a whole is essentially Platonic, my difficulty will not be to find material for a chapter, but to select from the embarrassment of riches that confronts me.

We need not recur to the Middle Ages further than to add one example of medieval confusion of thought and of the way in which the *Timaeus* of Plato exalted their imaginations and confounded their ideas. Plato says in the *Timaeus*

[146]

that all human discourses partake of the nature of their subject, and that since the knowledge of material things is uncertain and conjectural, our statements on that subject will always be more or less probable suppositions. That is true; and it was especially true for the science of Plato's time, as it was, indeed, for the science that Fontenelle, perpetual secretary of the Académie, explains with such smiling assurance to his *belle marquise*;—and perhaps (who knows?) it remains true even today for our hypotheses about the electrons, the aetherons, the biophores, the chromosomes, the cells, and the micelles.

In the *Roman de la Rose* this passage of the *Timaeus* is cited to justify the use of coarse words when the subject is gross (vv. 7099-7105). From there this interpretation passed to the English poet Chaucer, who, in apology for the obscene words employed in his *Canterbury Tales*, says in his *Prologue* 741-742:

> Eke Plato saith, whoso can him rede
> The wordes moste ben cousin to the dede.

We have not, of course, to repeat the story of the Italian Renaissance of Platonism, and I must ask you to take for granted also the chapter in every history of French literature which explains how the Renaissance came into France in the train of the armies of Charles VIII and Louis XII and under the patronage of Francis I and Margaret of Navarre. The Italians transmitted to the French Renaissance the two chief themes of literary, belletristic Platonism: Platonic love, and poetic enthusiasm—*la fureur poétique*, as they called it,—and it is with these themes that Platonism in French literature begins.

"Parler de l'amour, c'est une manière d'en faire" ("to talk about love is one form of philandering"), says the cynical La Rochefoucauld. That is one aspect of Platonic love, and perhaps the chief one in the French Renaissance. The other aspect, at which we have glanced, and to which we shall return later, is idealism in love, and love as the symbol of all idealism. It is Dante and Petrarch, though they did not know Plato, and the sonnet of Michelangelo, who did, at least through Ficino:

La forza d'un bel viso al ciel mi sprona ... [1]

The courts of love of the Middle Ages refined endlessly on the precise shade of tender sentiment which the young squire might properly feel for the lady of his lord. We, being more intelligent, write doctor's dissertations on the differences between ancient and medieval love, between Provençal love and the love of Dante, between Petrarchan love and the Platonizing love of Ficino and Pico della Mirandola, and the *trattati di amore* of the cinquecento, and the *canzone* of Girolamo Benivieni and the *Asolani* of Bembo and the *Cortegiano* of Castiglione and the treatise of Leo Hebraeus on love human and divine.

At the court of Margaret of Navarre, and in the literary coteries of Lyons, which was the center for the early Renaissance in France, they read these Italian writers and the *Symposium* and *Phaedrus* of Plato, and his *Lysis* or dialogue on Friendship, which Bonaventure Despériers, the secretary of Margaret, had just translated; and they discoursed interminably on the question whether true love is necessarily reciprocated, whether a kiss is a union of souls or of bodies, and whether it is possible for a man and a woman to love passionately and yet spiritually. The echo of these discussions may still be heard in the *Heptaméron* of Marguerite de Navarre (cf., e.g., the epilogue to the eighth story). "Dagoucin," said Hircan, "you fall into the error of supposing that we ought to love women without being loved." "Hircan," said Dagoucin, "what I mean is, that if our love is founded on the beauty, the grace, the love, and the favors of our lady, and our object is pleasure, pride, or profit, our love cannot long endure. For if the thing on which it is

---

[1] Superior figures refer to notes which will be found on p. 247.

based fails us, away flies our love." This, of course, is just
Thomas Carew's *Disdain Returned*:

> He that loves a rosy cheek,
> Or a coral lip admires,
> Or from star-like eyes doth seek
> Fuel to maintain his fires;
> As old Time makes these decay,
> So his flames must waste away.[2]

These discussions gave rise to what is called *la querelle des
amis*, a subject hardly less prolific in doctors' dissertations
and professorial lectures than the quarrel of the Ancients
and Moderns a century later, and the quarrel of the Platonists and Aristotelians a century earlier. I am myself responsible for at least two such doctoral dissertations. But
owing to the nature of the present sketch I do not think it
advisable to enter upon a lengthy discussion of these quarrels which are amply and learnedly described in the super-
abundant literature to which they have given rise.

I have a notebook filled with extracts from the *Parfaicte
Amye* of Antoine Héroët, the *Amye de court* of La Borderie,
the *Contr'Amye de court* of Charles Fontaine, the *Délie* of
Maurice Scève, the *Olive* of Du Bellay, the *Erreurs amour-
euses* of Pontus de Tyard, but I cannot keep them apart in
my memory, and they do not interest me in the least except as precursors or friends of a real poet, Ronsard. It is
apropos of this Platonic literature that Du Bellay compliments Héroët for having erected the Academy on the sum-
mit of the double mount:

> Qui sur le hault du double mont
> As érigé l'Académie.[3]

An erudite French scholar discovered in that verse a hill
with two peaks and an Académie at Lyons. But in fact the
double mount is simply Parnassus,[4] and the Academy is
Platonism, which Héroët was complimented on having in-

troduced into poetry, that is, having interpreted as a poet.
For the rest, I doubt if the courtiers of Margaret of Navarre and the wits of Lyons took all this quite as seriously
as do the young Americans who write doctors' dissertations
about it. It was merely a game, like humanism or tech-
nocracy today, "something doing" in literature. French
good sense and the *esprit gaulois* have always been a little
of Byron's opinion about this ethereal love. Montaigne already says: "My page makes love, and understands it; but
read to him Leo Hebraeus and Ficinus, where they speak
of love, its thoughts and actions, he understands it not,"[5]
and you will never make him believe that it has anything
to do with his own experience. We shall speak of another
aspect of the French mind later.

The second idea that the Renaissance of Platonism introduced into French literature is that of the so-called *fureur
poétique* which, it is true, had become a convention in the
Latin poets. Pontus de Tyard, in his *Dialogue de la fureur
poétique*, expounds it thus: "En quatre sortes peut l'homme
estre epris de divines fureurs. La première est par la fureur
poëtique procedant du don des Muses: la seconde est par
l'intelligence des mysteres et secrets des religions souz
Bacchus: la troisiesme par ravissement de prophetie, vaticination ou divination sous Apollon: et la quatriesme par la
violence de l'amoureuse affection souz Amour et Venus"[6]
("In four manners may man be possessed by madness divine: the first is by poetic fury proceding from the gift of
the Muses; the second is by cognizance of the mysteries
and secrets of religion under the influence of Bacchus; the
third by the transport of prophecy, vaticination, or divination under the influence of Apollo; and the fourth by the
violence of amorous affection under the dominion of Amour
and Venus"). In his *Etudes de littérature européenne*, the professor of comparative literature, Joseph Texte, finds here[7]
an example of the Italian influence and the Italian spirit

that he was trying to define. It is Italian only in the sense that Pontus de Tyard is here practically translating either Plato or Ficino, or somebody who copied them.

As I have already said, there will be something to add at the end of this chapter on Platonic idealism in French literature. But what I have said is a sufficient introduction to Rabelais and Montaigne, who sum up all the general ideas of the sixteenth century and, one might almost say, of French literature. The Platonism of either Rabelais or Montaigne would supply material for a chapter; and yet, many histories of French literature do not mention Plato in this connection. Rabelais read Plato as the scholars of the Renaissance did—in Macaulay's words, "with his feet on the fender." He admires him as a Greek author and the prince of philosophers. But Rabelais had not a Platonic soul, and he made more than Lucianic mockery of Platonic idealism, Platonic love, Platonic dialectic, and Platonic mysticism. But as we have repeatedly said, there are many Platos, and Rabelais found his in Plato the reformer of society and education and author of the *Symposium*, in which Socrates drinking deep put to rout Agathon and Aristophanes (223 CD).

In going through, rather hurriedly, a text of Rabelais I have collected more than forty citations from Plato. I cannot recite them here, but two or three are of special interest. Edmund Gosse in his *Modern English Literature* writes: "A French critic compared Sterne, most felicitously, to one of the little bronze satyrs of antiquity in whose hollow bodies exquisite odours were stored."[8] But Voltaire took this from Rabelais's *Prologue*, and Rabelais took it from the praise of Socrates by Alcibiades in the *Symposium* (215 D ff.), or perhaps from the *Adagia* of Erasmus, where Burton and Sterne may have found it. It is in Plato also, in the *Republic*,[9] that Rabelais found that quaint fancy that your dog is your true philosopher: "C'est comme dict Platon [Lib. II de Rep.], la beste du monde plus philosophe" (*Prologue*). But the development that Rabelais gives to this Platonic fancy is all his own. Rabelais's dog has studied Galen, and knows that the marrow is a nutriment elaborated to the perfection of nature."Mais veistes vous oncques chien rencontrant quelque os medulaire? . . . vous avez peu noter de quelle devotion il le guette, de que soing il le guarde, de quel ferveur il le tient, de quelle prudence il l'entomme, de quelle affection il le brise, et de quelle diligence il le sugce" (*Prologue*) ("Did you ever see a dog negotiating a medullary bone? You may have marked with what devotion he observes it, with what precaution he guards it, with what fervor he clasps it, with what prudence he assails it, with what tenderness he crushes it, and with what diligence he sucks it"). Plato says that the best Republic is that where the will of each is the will of all.[10] Rabelais parodies the sentiment in this fashion: "Si quelqu'un ou quelqu'une disoit 'beuvons,' tous buvoient" (I ch. lvii) ("If any one man or any one girl said 'Let's drink', all drank").

Montaigne regards himself as rather an Epicurean than a Platonist. But he adores the Socrates of Plato, and quotes Plato a hundred and fifty or two hundred times. I have already spoken of his interpretation of Plato in a skeptical sense. The first edition of the *Essays* dates from 1580; the Plutarch of Amyot from 1572, and the *Six livres de la République* of Bodin from 1576. Both the latter are stuffed with citations of Plato. Montaigne had also read Cicero, Erasmus, Justus Lipsius, and he was the friend of the learned Turnebus, all of whom quote Plato abundantly. He says of himself that he does not know Greek well enough to appreciate the beauties of Plato's style.[11] He apparently read Plato in the Latin translation of Ficino, as did Rousseau and all Europe for two hundred years; and he found many Platonic phrases and sayings in the meaty introductions of Ficino. But it is neither possible nor necessary to seek out the sources of all his Platonic quotations. It is enough that Montaigne, who is regarded as the antithesis of Plato, is one of the chief sources of the diffusion of Platonic ideas and sentiments in French literature.

Like Rabelais, Montaigne is not interested in the mystic and poetic Plato, and is distrustful of Platonic ecstasy. "Between ourselves," he says, "I have ever observed supercelestial opinions and subterranean manners to be of singular accord. . . . Instead of transforming themselves into angels, they transform themselves into beasts."[12] Pascal repeats this sentiment in his *Pensées* (§ 427 [358]): "L'homme n'est ni angel ni bête et le malheur veut que qui veut faire l'ange fait la bête," and Flaubert rediscovers it in one of his letters: "Je suis convaincu," he says, "que les appétits matériels les plus furieux se formulent insciemment par des élans de l'idéalisme" ("I am convinced that the fiercest material appetites are unconsciously shaped, formed, awakened by expansions of idealism"). You see again that the history of Platonism anticipates the Freudians at every turn.

Montaigne, like Renan, rightly doubts whether Plato had a system, and he quotes by preference his sensible observations on politics and morals and his cautious ironies about the popular religion. In a word, it is Plato the biographer of Socrates, Plato the satirist and skeptic and ironical man of the world, that Montaigne introduces to French literature.

In an exhaustive study I would, at this point, divide the subject into three branches, and treat of Plato in French literature, French philosophy, and French scholarship. While keeping in mind this distinction, we must confine ourselves mainly to the literature, of which we can take only a bird's-eye view.

The classicism of French literature in the seventeenth and eighteenth centuries was Latin rather than Greek. I will not inquire too curiously into the causes. It is, if you please, the natural affinity of the French language and the Latin genius for the order, the lucidity, the good sense of classical Latin. Or it is, if you prefer, the poetics of Scaliger, who places Vergil above Homer, and the reform of Malherbe, who came at last to prune the exuberance of the Hellenism of the Ronsards and the Rabelaises. Or again, it is Boileau, the legislator of Parnassus, who knew Greek as well as any man in France, who in the quarrel of the Ancients and the Moderns defended the Platos, the Pindars, and the Demostheneses against the outrages of Perrault, but who, at bottom, preferred to the Greeks the Vergil, the Horace, the Juvenal, that he knew by heart. The two chief Platonists of seventeenth-century literature were not Bossuet or Fénelon or Descartes or Malebranche or Boileau. They were simply the simple La Fontaine and that tender and elegant Racine whom Joubert calls the "Vergil of the ignorant." It was only they who really loved Plato, read him in the text, and spoke of him with intelligence.

It is possible that by rereading Racine for the purpose we might find two or three reminiscences of Plato in the tragedies. I shall not hunt for them. Racine was not a pedant; and he was too good a scholar to be tempted to display all his reading on all occasions. He had been well trained at Port Royal, and we have in his handwriting marginal notes on several Greek authors of whom there is no trace in his tragedies. As Epictetus says (*Ench.* 46. 2), "Sheep eat grass, but they grow not grass but wool on their backs." Racine inherited from his father a fine old edition of Plato of the year 1536, the margins of which, annotated by his hand, prove that he had really read and understood a large number of the dialogues. We cannot, here, study these notes, which fill twenty pages of the "édition des grands écrivains." Some of them are quite interesting. For example, he cites from the *Apology* the sentence, "But those are the most dangerous who take your sons from infancy and per-

suade them of the truth of their doctrines." As a good dis-
ciple of Port Royal, Racine adds "nota bene: Jésuites."
Emerson, you remember, tells of a Yankee farmer who bor-
rowed a volume of Plato from him and in returning it said,
"That man has a good many of my idees." I suspect that
La Fontaine would have said the same. In the quarrel of the
Ancients and the Moderns he was an Ancient. He read the
classics, and Plato was one of his enthusiasms. He an-
nounced his discovery of Plato as he discovered the prophet
Baruch, and wished all his friends to discover him.

Taine says, after Olivet, the historian of the Académie,
that La Fontaine had annotated nearly every page of Plato
and of Plutarch, and that most of his notes are maxims that
can be found in the fables.[13] I have been able to find there
only four or five insignificant allusions. Taine, in his doctor's
thesis, discovered the whole court of Louis Quatorze in La
Fontaine; and I presume that a critic of Taine's resources
might find there the dialogues of Plato, his satire, his dialectic, and the Socratic irony. I abandon the subject to
some future doctor and will limit myself to a few analogies,
some of which are indicated by Taine.

There are, to begin with, the variations, the modulations
of La Fontaine's style, the happy combination of art and
nature. Like Plato, he does not write a sententious, dignified, monotonous, stiff style, which wearies by never vary-
ing the tone. There is a mixture of irony and familiarity, of
grace and enthusiasm, which the French critic thinks is
rarely found elsewhere than in Plato and La Fontaine. His
ingenious inventions and charming reveries often recall the
myths of Plato; and in his poetic discourse of reception at
the Académie on May 2, 1684, La Fontaine alludes to Plato's
description of the poet as a sacred, winged thing (*Ion* 534
B), and calls himself:

> Papillon du Parnasse, et semblable aux abeilles
> À qui le bon Platon compare nos merveilles.[14]

(Butterfly of Parnassus, and like to the bee
To whom Plato compares the sweets of poesie).

Taine cites the passage of the *Ion* to which La Fontaine alludes, and adds the description of poetic madness in the
Phaedrus.[15]

But La Fontaine was something more than a "butterfly
of Parnassus." He once wrote a little introduction in prose
to a literary anthology which Bayle commended in the
Nouelles de la République des lettres, and which, indeed, appears to me to be the most reasonable thing said about Plato
in France before Emile Faguet's book *Pour qu'on lise Platon.*
La Fontaine endeavors to meet the objections that the ordinary reader will raise against Plato. They are chiefly two.
To begin with, the dialogues are inconclusive; they decide
nothing. La Fontaine, who was something of a skeptic himself, replies that Plato did not wish, and was unable, to conclude anything because we cannot and ought not to dog-
matize on the great ultimate questions. He thinks that Plato
and Socrates did well to leave these questions open to the
metaphysicians of the future. It is essentially the interpretation of the New Academy and Cicero. It will be, pretty
nearly, the opinion of Renan, who is pleading not less for
himself than for Plato, when he writes: "Plato is an incom-
parable philosopher. I only regret the wrong that has been
done him in exposing him to the rather pedantic admiration
of young disciples who have undertaken to discover a fixed
and systematic body of doctrine in the delightful philosophic fantasies that this rare mind has left us."

The second objection is that Plato is a poor reasoner and
that the dialogues are filled with sophistries, which, as we
shall soon see, was the opinion of Voltaire and the eighteenth
century. La Fontaine explains patiently that the rules of
logic had not yet been codified by Aristotle, that the tone
of conversation about Socrates in the Athenian gymnasium
was not that of a Parisian *salon,* and that many of his dia-

FRENCH LITERATURE 157

logues are dramatic and realistic imitations of such conversations, veritable comedies or even, like the *Euthydemus*, farces. He whom the French call "le bonhomme La Fontaine" here shows himself very intelligent, very discriminating, very well informed.

It is perhaps because of Perrault and the quarrel of the Ancients and Moderns that La Fontaine undertook to explain and defend Plato rather than merely to praise him. Perrault had said in the alleged poem that he read before the Academy, in opening the quarrel:

> That Plato whom men called divine heretofore
> In these modern days is considered a bore.
> In vain his translator, who admires the antique,
> Tries to keep all the grace and the salt of the Greek.
> The most resolute reader can't pierce through the fog,
> Or read to the end a single dialogue.[16]

(Having once got started on this false gallop of verse it is hard to stop.)

> These verses are bad, but I'd fain have you know
> They're not half so bad as the French of Perrault.

La Fontaine is refuting "ces jugements saugrenus." Here too he coincides with Renan, who says in the preface to *Le Prêtre de Némi*, "J'aurais bien mauvaise grâce à me plaindre d'une méthode de critique dont Platon a été victime" ("It would be unbecoming in me to complain of the application to myself of a method of criticism of which Plato was the victim"). Perrault's name today is Flexner or Brisbane, but at least they do not write in verse.

The other writers of the Grand Siècle would yield little to our gleaning. One will not look for Platonism in La Rochefoucauld, the Cardinal de Retz, Madame de Sévigné, and Saint-Simon. One will not find much in Boileau, who derives from the Latin poets and the poetics of Aristotle and from Longinus. There might be a word to say of that Academy of Plato to which Molière alludes in *Les Femmes savan-tes* vv. 846, 909, and of the famous passage on the little lan-guage of lovers which Gassendi is supposed to have shown to Molière in the Latin poet Lucretius, of which the original is found in the *Republic* of Plato,[17] and which Ferdinand Brunetière has dug up in a scribbler of the seventeenth cen-tury, where he maintains that Molière found his goods and took them.

We might visit La Bruyère and find him "penché sur le livre de Platon qui traite de la spiritualité de l'âme"; we might recall and recommend to some dignified British edi-tors Pascal's saying: "On ne s'imagine Platon et Aristote qu'avec de grandes robes de pédants. C'étaient des gens honnêtes et comme les autres, riant avec leurs amis: et quand ils se sont divertis à faire leurs *Lois* et leur *Politique*, ils l'ont fait en se jouant" ("Plato and Aristotle didn't al-ways wear their grand academic robes. They were good, honest fellows, like another, who laughed with their friends, and were only half in earnest when they amused themselves with laying down their laws and expounding their political theories").[18] A letter of Taine,[19] by the way, commenting on the smooth and polished translation of Cousin, goes still further. Taine says that the real, the colloquial Plato would shock such persons if he were rightly translated. We might further recite yet again the cadence of the beautiful phrase that so flattered the ear of Bossuet that he repeats it him-self, the sentence that Matthew Arnold loves to cite as an example of the beauty of French prose. Bossuet says of St. Paul: "Il ira, cet ignorant dans l'art de bien dire, avec cette locution rude, avec cette phrase qui sent l'étranger, il ira en cette Grèce polie, la mère des philosophes et des orateurs; et malgré la résistance du monde, il y établira plus d'Eglises que Platon n'y a gagné de disciples par cette éloquence qu'on a crue divine."[20] Lastly, we might study in Fénelon's *Traité sur l'existence de Dieu* the mixture, already in the style of Victor Cousin, of Cartesianism and Platonism. But our airplane flight hurries us on.

The eighteenth century was perhaps the least Platonic century of French literature. The philosophers expected anything from science, and they thought the spirit of Platonism was the antithesis of science. If they admired Plato it was as a poet, a moralist, a reformer. For Montesquieu, the four greatest poets are Plato, Malebranche, Shaftesbury, and Montaigne[21]—all but Montaigne Platonists, and he, as we have seen, quotes Plato hundreds of times. In any case, with the exception of Rousseau, they did not read him much. But without reading him they could obtain some notion from Brucker's history of philosophy, which on the whole is rather hostile than sympathetic to Plato and the Platonists.[22]

We may begin our necessarily rapid survey of the eighteenth century with a few words about the precursors, Bayle and Fontenelle. M. Faguet refers lightly to the article of Bayle on Plato. But it happens, strangely enough, that there is no article on Plato in that repertory of anecdotage, biography, and skeptical thought, Bayle's *Dictionnaire historique et critique*. There are only a few apocryphal anecdotes scattered through other articles. Bayle occasionally ridicules the dreams of the Platonists and repeats some of the calumnies collected by Athenaeus. That is about all. He belongs, then, mainly to the history of anti-Platonic prejudice.

Fontenelle has heard of Plato and speaks of him and of classical studies in the style of our modern orators of science, the H. G. Wellses and the Ostwalds. "Plato and Pythagoras," he says, "believed that Phaethon, in the opera, soars aloft because he is composed of certain numbers that make him rise." But Fontenelle himself, being an enlightened scientist, knows very well that Phaethon rises because he is drawn by ropes. I need hardly point out that this is the ancient confusion between Plato and Pythagoras, and also the modern scientist's hostility to what he supposes to be the antimechanistic and therefore antiscientific philosophy of Plato. There is nothing new under the sun. Fontenelle's paragraph is precisely on the level of this which I culled from a recent utterance of the highest paid and most widely read journalist in America. "William MacAndrew, who was superintendent of Chicago schools, leaves for Athens to spend a year studying Socrates' methods of teaching. His plan, may heaven thwart it, is to revive the Socrates method in modern schools. Socrates, if Plato describes his method accurately, touched a new peak in boredom. Instead of saying what he had to say, he went around Robin Hood's barn with questions and answers tiresome beyond measure. . . . What modern education needs is moving pictures, . . . not Socratic vogues."[23]

In Fontenelle's *Dialogues des morts*, which have very little likeness to the dialogues of Plato, Anacreon proves to Aristotle that he is the better philosopher, and Socrates proves to Montaigne that the world has not degenerated. In his *Histoire des oracles* (ch. iii) Fontenelle expounds the doctrine of the Platonists about daemons. But he is of the opinion that Plato himself, perhaps, did not seriously believe it.

To turn now to the philosophers, Montesquieu, Buffon, Diderot, Rousseau, D'Alembert, and Voltaire. Montesquieu, as a conscientious Hellenist, cites the *Laws* of Plato throughout his *De l'esprit des lois*, which may have been the source from which the authors and expounders of the American Constitution were led to consult Plato. Montesquieu himself probably read the *Laws* in Ficino, but, as we have seen, he could have found hundreds of quotations from them in Montaigne, Justus Lipsius, and Bodin, to look no further.

"The Laws of Minos, Lycurgus, and Plato," says Montesquieu, "assume that all the citizens exercise a singular observation on one another."[24] It was perhaps for this reason that under the Revolution a delegate of the Convention called for the laws of Minos at the Bibliothèque Nationale and was very indignant when informed that the library did not possess them. For Montesquieu, as we have seen, Plato was a poet, and he does not take his philosophy seriously. He, of course, had no real understanding of it, and merely accepted the prejudices of his time.

The article on Plato of Diderot in the *Encyclopédie* is not half bad.[25] He took his facts, naturally, from Brucker. But he kindles into a fine enthusiasm for the moral teaching of Plato,"who," he says, a little naïvely, "strove all his life to make youth instructed and virtuous."[26] To prove that Plato professes the double doctrine in religion, he mistranslates again the famous sentence of the *Timaeus* which is quoted by nearly every Christian Father and likewise misrepresented by some. Diderot's version is: "It is difficult to rise to the author of this universe, and it would be dangerous to publish what one might discover about him."[27] Diderot is, obviously, thinking of the persecution of the philosophers in France, as some Christian Fathers were thinking of the persecution of the Christians when they, likewise, substituted "dangerous" for Plato's "impossible."

The Platonism of Rousseau is a much larger topic. He really read, apparently in Ficino, the *Republic*, the *Laws*, and some other dialogues, and further steeped himself in Platonism by reading Plutarch, not to speak of the quotations in Montaigne. We have already referred to his statement that the *Republic* is the best existing book on education (*Emile* I *in init.*)[28] Elsewhere Rousseau appeals to Plato for his fundamental educational principle. "Plato," he says, "in the *Republic*, which is deemed so austere, educates the children only through festivals, sports, and jolly pastimes. We might almost say that he regards it as the sole task of education to teach them to have a good time." We cannot here undertake a complete concordance of Rousseau and Plato on education. But in turning the pages of *Emile*, I note among many other explicit Platonic reminiscences the disparagement of the printed page in comparison with the living voice, the method of instruction by parables and ingeniously devised stories, the reiteration of the conservative principle repeated by Ruskin and Carlyle, that entire ignorance and inexperience is far less dangerous than the impudent self-confidence encouraged by false conceit of knowledge—or, as Arnold puts it, after Goethe, all that merely frees our spirits without giving us self-control is deleterious,—the insistance on simple music and the harmfulness of all complicated and emotional forms of art, the distrust of medicine and the recommendation in its stead of hygiene and a hardening regime.

Rousseau supports this last idea by an amusing application of a supersubtle Platonic abstract distinction. Plato had said in another connection that every art and science in the abstract is infallible. It is only the human practitioner that errs. The pure art and science of medicine may be infallible, says Rousseau; bring it on, then, without the physician, and we will welcome it.[29] When I was last in Paris, this jest was making the Parisians laugh every night in Jules Romains's comedy *Knock ou le triomphe de la médecine*.

Plato the bachelor and Rousseau the irresponsible father both begin education at birth or earlier; and both prescribe minutely for the nursing and care of babies. As my own forty years' experience, like Plato's, has been limited to the college and the graduate seminar, I will glide lightly over this thin ice. Both Plato and Rousseau are much concerned about the character and the speech of the nurse. Both concur in the precept that you should never explain your reasons to a nurse or a servant, but merely give them explicit orders. Both disapprove of allowing babies to cry, because it may spoil their tempers for life. President Stanley Hall, on the contrary, I believe, maintained that crying is a wholesome and lung-developing exercise. I have already disclaimed competence in these high matters; and as Plato elsewhere puts it, the argument must hasten on, veiling her face (*Rep.* 503 A).

Hardly less was the influence on Rousseau's political ideas of his reading of the *Republic* and the *Politicus*. But leaving the details and the comparison of Rousseau's *Social Compact* with Plato's to the future historian of the science of politics, I will confine myself here to one main point. For Rousseau Plato is essentially a reformer, a Utopian. The question whether Plato really was a radical or a conservative is as pretty a topic for discussion as that recently debated by the Australian and the University of California teams: "Resolved, that the rule of convention should be deplored." Professor Murray brackets Plato and Euripides as both children of a great tradition and both rebels against it. That is to me as if one should couple Matthew Arnold and Bernard Shaw as equally rebellious to British tradition. Plato was too great a thinker to be a blind irrational partisan. But in relation to the radicalism of his own time or ours, he was of essentially conservative temper. He was a conservative in ethics, religion, and literature. And the idealistic reforms which he dreamed of in education and politics were based on the conservative ideals of discipline and aristocracy in the true and etymological sense of the words.

Plato, then, as Emile Faguet clearly shows, is fundamentally conservative. But just as Plato, though himself free from superstition, has been one of the fountainheads of superstition in European literature, so, though he is essentially conservative, his influence has fostered the radical temper in hasty and prepossessed readers. He encourages them, to begin with, in the fatal belief in the omnipotence of education and environment and in the complete plasticity of human nature to reformatory legislation. His writings are like Ruskin's—too exciting for Utopian minds. They are a veritable poison for chimerical and revolutionary spirits who overlook the qualifications and limitations and pay no attention to the dialectic. History repeats itself; and as through Rousseau Plato stimulated the revolutionary spirit in France, so today through Ruskin he is one of the chief sources and inspirations of visionary political economy and Utopian rhetoric in England and America. This consideration would take us too far.

It is not easy to distinguish the petulances of Voltaire from his genuine opinions. It is not necessary. As Chateaubriand says in his *Genius of Christianity*,"Voltaire, having sustained alternately the pro and the contra, and having continually varied in his sentiments, his opinions in morals and philosophy and religion do not greatly signify." Voltaire might have been expected to admire in Plato the artist, the satirist, and the man of the world. But he transfers to Plato his detestation of the Platonists. He is the *enfant terrible* of criticism; and it amuses him to besplatter the greatest names—Homer, Dante, Shakespeare, Plato. Here is his explanation of Aristotle's reasons for writing a logic: "Il fallait des règles sûres pour démêler cet épouvantable galimatias par lequel la réputation de Platon fascinait les esprits" ("There was need of fixed rules to clear up the horrible galimatias by which the reputation of Plato cast a spell upon men's minds").[30] He knows very little of Plato and is unable to distinguish Platonism and Neo-Platonism, but he mentions Plato several times in his philosophical dictionary and almost always with a sarcasm. One of his disciples annotates these utterances thus: "M. de Voltaire has attacked Plato several times, whose galimatias has done more harm to the human race than is generally believed."

Voltaire often says that Plato wrote better than he reasoned. That is not true. But I did not undertake to refute it when I lectured on Plato to French audiences, for it is the received opinion in French literature. Nisard, for example, the classical historian of French literature, was fond of contrasting the reason of Descartes and of Pascal and the errors —errors, he condescendingly adds, honorable to the human mind—of Plato. I despair of telling you how excruciatingly funny to a serious student of Plato's methods is the idea that Descartes and Pascal are better reasoners than Plato. Montesquieu says, in a much quoted passage: "The dialogues in which Plato reproduces the arguments of Socrates, these dialogues so admired by the ancients, are today insupportable. All those ratiocinations no longer signify anything." Joseph de Maistre, who did not love the Greeks any more than Brunetière did, calls Plato in a word a sophist. Stendhal in his *Racine et Shakespeare* styles Plato "écrivain de premier ordre et raisonneur puéril."[31] Plato, says Ferdinand Brunetière, in the speeches which he has well named *Combative Discourses*, Plato thinks like a child and reasons like a sophist.[32] "Plato," says Joubert, in a passage on which Matthew Arnold has set the seal of his approval,[33] "teaches us nothing. But he clarifies our vision for the perception of the highest truths."[34] I could multiply these examples indefinitely and supplement them by utterances of French-minded critics in the English literature of the eighteenth and nineteenth centuries and orators of science in the twentieth. But enough is enough; and though this is the characteristic and typical view of Plato, it is by no means the only one.

At last Chateaubriand came. Chateaubriand is absolutely lacking in the critical sense, not from any deficiency of intelligence, but because, like some of the most popular of twentieth-century scholars and statesmen, he felt that criticism would cramp his style and interfere with his main business, which was rhetoric. He defends his practice by a quotation from Montesquieu: "There is no genius which is not narrowed by being enveloped in millions of vain scruples," which, by the way, is an interesting anticipation of the delightful aphorism of President Stanley Hall—"Accuracy atrophies." Chateaubriand pretends to believe, after Madame Dacier and on the faith of an apocryphal epistle, that Plato knew the Trinity. He copies Ficino's demonstration that Plato had borrowed that doctrine from the Italian school and from Pythagoras. He confounds or falsifies the unverified reminiscences of his own readings of the *Republic* and *Laws* of Plato to round out an eloquent period.

All that is of no importance. All that we need remember is that it was probably in Chateaubriand, perhaps supplemented by the *Voyage of the Young Anacharsis*, that Lamartine found the conception of Platonism which inspired him for some of the most beautiful verses in modern French poetry. Lamartine's Plato is the Plato who revealed the truths of natural religion, the Plato who anticipated Christianity, the Plato who contemplated God in the order of the stars and in the design manifested in the structure of the human body; finally it is the chaste old man without wife and without family seated at the foot of a temple at the extremity of a wave-beaten cape, teaching to his disciples the existence of God.[35]

This invites a digression on the difficulty, not to say the impossibility, of a really international and cosmopolitan culture. Chateaubriand is thinking of the *Voyage du jeune Anacharsis* of the abbé Barthélemy, which he recommends somewhere as a guide for the traveler in Greece, and which conveniently and typically sums up the knowledge and the ideas of the eighteenth century about Hellenic things. Barthélemy, in a famous episode of that now forgotten but still useful book, places the aged Plato on Cape Sunium, there to recite his *Timaeus*. When Emile Faguet says of a certain contemporary philosopher, "C'est un idéaliste du cap Sunium," every educated Frenchman catches the allusion at once. But it would be a riddle without a key to an English

or German reader who had not found a second literary fa-
therland in France. On the other hand, what Sunium suggests to an English reader is Byron and the *Ajax* of Sophocles; and it is of them that he thinks when he hears the
words, "Place me on Sunium's marbled steep" (*The Isles of
Greece* 16). But the French reader murmurs after Lamartine:

> Socrate te cherchait aux beaux jours de la Grèce;
> Platon à Sunium te cherchait après lui
>
> (Thee Socrates sought while fair Greece was yet free,
> And at Sunium Plato was still seeking thee).
>
> *La Foi* 106-107

Chateaubriand is the chief source of ideas for the authors
of the first generation of the nineteenth century. With the
renewal of classical studies and the development of the
critical spirit the insufficiency of his knowledge and scholarship has become only too apparent. We cannot examine the
prose literature and the French Platonic scholarship of the
nineteenth century. I should like to speak not so much of
Victor Cousin's well-known book, *Du Vrai, du Beau et du
Bien*, as of the many interpretations of Platonic and still
more of Neo-Platonic philosophy of which he was directly
or indirectly the inspiration; of Taine and Renan, whom I
have occasionally quoted, and both of whom knew and read
Plato; of the youthful work of the philosopher Alfred Fouil-
lée on Plato; and of the book of Emile Faguet, *Pour qu'on
lise Platon*, which is naturally not a work of critical scholarship, but which is in many respects the most sensible account of Plato in recent years. But there is time only for the
promised conclusion on Platonizing idealism in nineteenth-
century French lyric poetry.

I said at the beginning, and our survey has confirmed it,
that the clarity and the good sense which are the master
qualities of French literature do not easily lend themselves
to the ecstasies, the mysteries, the enthusiasms, the dreams

of what is called Platonic idealism. The Frenchman is an idealist, very much of an idealist in his own fashion. He can personify an abstraction and adore l'Humanité, l'Egalité, la Justice, la Liberté, la Beauté, la Femme, if la Femme may be called an abstraction. But his idealism does not usually seek expression in Platonic rhetoric or poetry. And so it will be more natural for an English speaker and English readers to discuss poetic Platonic idealism in the phrases of English poetry. Perhaps it is a natural illusion to believe that it is our own national poetry rather than another that speaks the true language of the heart and the lofty idealism. In any case, there is more than one type of Frenchman and more than one kind of French poet. The *esprit gaulois*, clarity, reason, good sense, and rules of Boileau do not exhaust French literature.

A French poet said that the French language is afraid of poetry. He added, however, that poetry is afraid of the English language.[36] But that is not our present concern. If we confine ourselves to the two centuries that precede the Revolution, I understand the dictum of André Chénier. But if we turn our eyes to the generation of Ronsard and the generation of Lamartine, we get a very different conception. For the rest, it is not the poetry of Platonism that alarms French good sense. It is the sickly ecstasies, the cloudy visions, that are associated, as we have already seen, with a certain type of unwholesome Platonic poetizing. Platonic love may be what the new psychology, after Michelangelo and Emerson, calls the sublimation of instinct, and, so understood, it may lift us to the loftiest heights of idealism. But that kind of idealism, as Rabelais and Montaigne and many cynics after them have said, and as the examples of Verlaine and Oscar Wilde illustrate, is liable to unfortunate slips and lapses. At any rate, before celebrating Platonism as the chief source of poetic idealism it is well to mark off the idealism that is equivocal and unhealthy.

Two French poems typify and mark this distinction. For the false, or at any rate the sickly, idealism we may take the, in the original, very beautiful hymn of Baudelaire:

> To the thrice fair, the infinite
> Goddess of my idolatry
> Who floods my soul with radiant light,
> Greetings in immortality.
>
> Her presence diffused doth penetrate
> My life like airs impregned with balm
> And soothes the heart insatiate
> With foretaste of eternal calm.
>
> A sachet ever fresh that fills
> With faint perfume some loved retreat,
> Forgotten censer that distills
> On the lone night its incense sweet.
>
> Love thrice refined, what words suffice
> To give thee truly as thou art,
> Slight grain of music that hidden lies
> In deep recesses of the heart?
>
> To her most pure, to her most fair,
> My joy, my peace eternally,
> Angel and idol of my prayer—
> Greetings in immortality.[37]

That is beautiful, exquisite, if you will. It has all the allurements of the exotic and of forbidden fruit. But the exoticism of that loved retreat is a little too suggestive of the den of a Chinese opium-smoker; its insalubrious and etiolated beauty is sickly and unwholesome; the fruit is just a little too ripe; and there clings to it a faint odor of degenerescence and decay. There is too much sensation. Too many perfumes make the air heavy. This ideal love speaks a little too fa-

miliarly the language of the alcove. It is not quite the
authentic Platonism of Ficino or Spenser or even of Shelley.
But nowhere in English literature can one find a nobler expression of the true Platonic and poetic idealism than in
that sonnet of Du Bellay which is a translation from the
Italian of Bernardino Daniello.[38]

Si notre vie est moins qu'une journée
En l'éternel, si l'an qui fait le tour
Chasse nos jours sans espoir de retour,
Si périssable est toute chose née,

Que songes-tu, mon âme emprisonnée?
Pourquoi te plaît l'obscur de notre jour,
Si pour voler en un plus clair séjour,
Tu as au dos l'aile bien empennée?

Là est le bien que tout esprit désire,
Là, le repos où tout le monde aspire,
Là est l'amour, là, le plaisir encore;

Là, o mon âme, au plus haut ciel guidée,
Tu y pourras reconnoître l'Idée
De la beauté qu'en ce monde j'adore.[39]

It is in vain that matter-of-fact, positive minds ask us
with D'Alembert, What does that prove? and tell us that it
is vague, cloudy, hollow, and chimerical. The Platonist will
reply to them that this superfluity is, in Voltaire's epigram,
chose très nécessaire; that without that breath of the ideal
the soul stifles, poetry is dead, science becomes an arid no-
menclature, and life is but vanity. "C'est grâce à l'idéal que
l'humanité dure," says Sully-Prudhomme. And the ideal of
which Sully-Prudhomme speaks at times takes possession
even of its mockers. Montesquieu himself, whom we have
cited in the contrary sense, relapses into Platonism and
writes: "Dire qu'il n'y a rien de juste ni d'injuste que ce

qu'ordonnent ou défendent les lois positives, c'est dire qu'avant qu'on eut tracé des cercles, tous les rayons n'étaient pas égaux" ("To say that there is nothing just or unjust in the world except that which positive laws command or forbid, is equivalent to saying that before men drew circles on the blackboard, the lines from center to circumference were not equal").[40]

Take the realist, the disenchanted, the mocking, the positivist Flaubert. Open his correspondance, and what do we find? He writes to a friend: "Dans la précision des assemblages, l'harmonie de l'ensemble, n'y a-t-il pas une vertue intrinsèque, une espèce de force divine, quelque chose d'éternel comme un principe (je parle en platoniste)"[41] . . . "du beau indéfinissable . . . qui est la splendeur du vrai, comme disait Platon"[42] ["In the precision of the assemblage, the harmony of the ensemble, is there not an intrinsic virtue, a kind of divine force, something as eternal as a principle (I am speaking as a Platonist)" . . . and further on he talks of the "undefinable beauty . . . which is the splendor of the true, as Plato said"]. Take Anatole France. He too is a scientific and skeptical mind, if there ever was one, who loves to ridicule the subtleties of Platonists about the soul. But when he makes a return upon himself and delivers to us his most intimate thought, he is transformed into a Platonic idealist. "They have no Vergil," he says, "and they are called happy because they have elevators." And again: "The real serves us to construct for better or worse a little of the ideal. That is perhaps its chief utility." You see, all those who, to speak with Margaret of Navarre, have felt "l'ennui commun à toute créature bien née," cannot endure life without this form of Platonism.

Ferdinand Brunetière, as we have seen, never lets slip an opportunity to condemn Plato as a sophist. But when he quoted Du Bellay at Ancenis (on September 2, 1894), it befell him to add: "The critic must say and repeat it, that

from the time when verse was first written in our language,
no one had ever before written verses like those; and since
Du Bellay, Lamartine alone has written even more beautiful lines on the same theme and of the same inspiration."[43]
The learned critic, apparently, had no suspicion that the
reason is that before Du Bellay no French poet was steeped
in the Platonism of the Renaissance, none sought his inspiration, not merely in the thoughts of Plato, but in the very
turns of phrase of the *Phaedrus* and the *Symposium*.

We have to await the second Renaissance of idealism, of
Platonism, of lyrism in France to find again "ces accents in-
connus à la terre" without which rhythm turns to discords,
hearts to dust and ashes, and all the loveliness of life vanishes
as a mirage, lost in hard, unseeing eyes (ὀμμάτων δ' ἐν ἀχηνίαις
ἔρρει πᾶσ' Ἀφροδίτα, Aesch. *Agam.* 418). We meet them again,
these accents, this breath from the beyond, this shuddering
delight, sometimes in André Chénier, almost everywhere in
Lamartine—in *La Mort de Socrate*, in *L'Homme*, in *Le Déses-
poir*, *L'Immortalité*, in *La Foi*, *Le Vallon*, *La Semaine sainte*
—, often in De Vigny and in Sully-Prudhomme, from time
to time in Leconte de Lisle, and even sometimes blended
with the rhetoric of Victor Hugo.

> Vers ce grand ciel clément où sont tous les dictames,
> Les aimés, les absents, les êtres purs et doux,
> Les baisers de l'esprit et les regards de l'âme,
> Quand nous en irons-nous, quand nous en irons-nous?

And yet again:

> Dans vos cieux au delà de la sphère des nues,
> Au fond de cet azur immobile et dormant,
> Peut-être faites-vous des choses inconnues
> Où la douleur de l'homme entre comme élément

(In yon heavens that our eyes through the clouds cannot scan,
In the depths of that blue vault so tranquilly sleeping,
Ye are weaving perhaps some mysterious plan
That has need of our sorrow, our anguish, our weeping).

It matters little, and time does not suffer me to distinguish among these poets the few who learned Greek and read Plato in the text from those who received the inspiration indirectly from Chateaubriand and Victor Cousin, the Italian and English poets, and German scholars. We have the right to associate the name of Plato with all those lovely things because Plato was the initiator of them for European civilization and literature, and has remained to this day their supreme exemplar and principal source. Whenever, indeed, the soul with her desires constructs for herself an asylum "où l'on puise à jamais la science et l'amour"; whenever she dreams of summers that never fade and kisses that endure, of the loftiest star of all in unascended heaven; whenever she sees in this so real and solid globe only the adumbration, the image, of the perfection that she strains to conceive "and abandons herself to the fruitful illusion of taking flight to the very portals of being"; whenever from the depths of the exile of this life she overhears the harmonies of the world for which she yearns

> (partout où du fond de l'exil de la vie
> elle entend les concerts d'un monde qu'elle envie);

whenever, hovering on the verge of futurity, she distinguishes more clearly those far, faint notes; whenever our feeble reason is baffled and confounded to see

> La valeur sans les dieux décidant les batailles,
> Un Caton libre encore déchirant ses entrailles
> Sur la foi de Platon

> (Force victorious in wars where the gods have no part,
> And a Cato still free plunge the sword in his heart
> In his Platonic faith);

whenever she seeks in vain a refuge where the last waves of sound from the world die away and breathes for a few moments "some foretaste of the calm of eternity's peace,"

> La calme avant-coureur de l'éternelle paix;

whenever man "borné dans sa nature, infini dans ses vœux" ("bounded in his nature but infinite in his desires") trails after him the unassuageable yearning for some far-off paradise; whenever the poet and artist wander in quest of that implacable beauty that eludes their grasp and cradle themselves in the illusion that they have found it in the imitation of forms, themselves copies of the ideas

> Qui brillent plus pure encore
> Au paradis profond de l'Art
> Où Platon pense et les adore
>
> (Of the ideas that shine apart
> In the pure paradise of art
> Worshiped by Plato's mind and heart);

whenever hope and love murmur to our souls, "Hope, sister, and a little faith"—

> Espère o ma sœur, crois un peu,
> C'est à force d'aimer qu'on trouve;

whenever, in answer to the mechanists of dissection who discover

> Dans un coin de cerveau nouvellement décrit
> Voit penser la matière et végéter l'esprit
>
> (In some corner of brain that their scalpels reveal
> That matter can think and vegetation feel)

they cast down the gauntlet of defiance,

> Vous n'avez pas sondé tout l'océan de l'âme
>
> (You have not yet plumbed the abyss of the soul);

there the so lucid, the intelligent, the witty, the cynical, the rational literature of France abandons itself gloriously to the Platonic inspiration, and to that Bacchic madness of idealistic philosophy which Alcibiades said all disciples of Socrates would understand (*Symp.* 218 B).

CHAPTER VII

PLATONISM AND ENGLISH LITERATURE

A PRELIMINARY enumeration of what would be the chief topics and periods of a history of Platonism in English literature may help us not to miss the wood for the trees. After a perfunctory glance at Chaucer and the Middle Ages we should come to the English Renaissance of Colet, Grocyn, Elyot, Ascham, More, and their associates, mainly dependent, of course, on the writers of the Italian and French Renaissance. This leads directly on to the great names of Spenser, Shakespeare, Bacon, and Milton. From these we would pass to the seventeenth-century scholars, preachers, and theologians,[1] the Burtons, the Sir Thomas Brownes, and the so-called Cambridge Platonists, with whom are associated on the one hand the later preachers and theologians, such as Jeremy Taylor and the Deists, and on the other hand the metaphysical and minor poets who versified some fancy of the *Timaeus* or the Neo-Platonists, or touched on Platonic love. The Platonism of the latter half of the seventeenth and of the eighteenth centuries does not differ greatly in tone from that of contemporary France. But Shaftesbury, Berkeley, Pope, Mandeville, Tucker, and perhaps Burke for different reasons would deserve special consideration. The Romantic movement and nineteenth-century scholarship brought a revival of Platonism comparable to the Renaissance. In the index to Sandys's *History of Classical Scholarship* the references to Plato for the four centuries from 1350 to 1750 occupy a quarter of a column; for the century and a half from 1750 to 1900 they fill a column and a quarter.

The first great English poet, Chaucer, knew Plato as he knew the classics generally, mainly from Boethius and from

---

[1] Superior figures refer to notes which will be found on pp. 248-249.

such Italian and French sources as Petrarch, Boccaccio, Guido delle Colonne, and the *Roman de la Rose*. The amusing misapplication, already quoted,[2] of the phrase of the *Timaeus* about the kinship of word and deed is in the *Roman de la Rose* (7099-7105), and was a commonplace in the Middle Ages. Chaucer repeats it in the *Manciple's Tale* (18088-18089). The *Canon's Yeoman's Tale* attributes to Plato and a disciple a dialogue attributed to Salomon in a medieval treatise on alchemy. The passage could be used to illustrate the deplorable association of Platonism with superstition and with mystic secret doctrines through the ages.[3] The expression in the *Knight's Tale*, "Out of the foule prison of this life" (*vers.* 3061), is not, of course, taken from the famous passage of the *Phaedo* (82-83), but from Boethius. In the same tale a notable idea of the *Symposium* (208 B) is clearly expressed:

> And therefore of his wise purveyance
> He hath so wel beset his ordinance,
> That speces of thinges and progressions
> Shullen enduren by successions,
> And not eterne, withouten any lie.

> *Knight's Tale* 3011 ff.

But that could come from Aristotle directly or indirectly, or perhaps from the Pythagorean discourse in Ovid which inspired Spenser's *Canto on Immutability*.

The *Philobiblon* of Richard de Bury,[4] a contemporary of Petrarch, contains some coincidences with Platonic thought, possibly derived from Boethius. His complaint that men fitted for the liberal arts and the Church ". . . by a kind of apostasy . . . return to the mechanical arts solely to gain a livelihood" (pp. 3-4) recalls Plato's description in the *Republic* of the backsliders from philosophy. And another closer parallel makes it probable that he had read this part of the *Republic* in some translation or extract: "While nowadays our contemporaries," he laments, "carelessly spread

a few years of hot youth and ... they soon become involved
in worldly affairs and retire, bidding farewell to the schools
of philosophy" (p. 66). He quotes from Boethius (*Consol.
Phil.* I 4) the sentence that either philosophers must be
kings (*Rep.* 473 C-D), or kings philosophers, and from the
Phaedo (65 C ff.) the statement that the philosopher sepa-
rates soul from body more than other men. But this he
could have found in the Christian Fathers and elsewhere
(p. 92). Very quaint are his references to Plato's ideas. In
one place he speaks of the "tyrannies of demons described,
such as neither the ideas of Plato transcend ..." (p. 9). In
the lament for the destruction of ancient books he apostro-
phizes the iniquitous power of darkness,"which does not fear
to undo the approved divinity of Plato, who alone was worthy to submit to the view of the Creator, before he assuaged the strife of warring chaos, and before form had put
on its garb of matter, the ideal types, in order to demonstrate the archetypal universe to its author, so that the
world of sense might be modelled after the supernal pattern" (p. 47).

There is a useful German dissertation by Kurt Schroeder[5]
on Platonism in the English Renaissance, which records
names and dates and the more obvious direct allusions to
Plato in Colet, Grocyn, Lupton, Linacre, Lyly, Sir Thomas
More, and others. My notebooks contain many more from
Mulcaster, Ascham, and Elyot. They alone would swamp
this chapter, and the only points we need to remember are,
first, that while some of these writers doubtless read Plato
in the original or in Ficino, they say very little that they
could not have got from Ficino's *Introductions*, from Pico
and Erasmus and obvious French sources. Sir Thomas
More's *Utopia*, for example, while it will always hold its
place in the long line of imitations of Plato's *Republic*, ex-
hibits no more acquaintance with the *Republic* than could
be got by turning over its pages for an hour or two, or from

a conversation with Erasmus. Secondly, we may note that before and aside from Spenser, there is little reference to Platonic love. That came in later. The Platonism of the early English Renaissance is mainly concerned with liberal theology, education, politics, and perhaps a little mysticism. Lastly, we may observe that there need be no mystery about any suggestions of Platonism that we may discover in Shakespeare. He could have found them, without looking further, in Elyot, Mulcaster, Plutarch, and Montaigne.

We have already quoted Spenser for the noblest expression of the true gospel of Platonic love.[6] Of his *Foure Hymnes* only the first two express Renaissance Platonism. The two hymns on *Heavenly Love* and *Heavenly Beautie* belong rather to the tradition of Christian mysticism, colored, of course, by Platonism. In these, Spenser affects repentance for the wantonness of his earlier love poems:

> Many lewd layes (ah, woe is me the more!)
> In praise of that mad fit which fooles call love,
> I have in th' heat of youth made heretofore,
> That in light wits did loose affection move:
> But all those follies now I do reprove,
> And turned have the tenor of my string,
> The heavenly prayses of true love to sing.
>
> *Hymne of Heavenly Love* 8 ff.

But this is a regular convention of writers on divine love, and, in fact, the hymn to earthly beauty rises to heights of Platonic idealism quite as spiritual as anything in the *Hymne of Heavenly Beautie*. Spenser's precise sources in these hymns have been the theme of several special studies, none of which I would trust without verification. For parallel passages are slippery things.[7] I am tempted myself to add another to these studies. In Cardinal Bembo's much overrated dialogue *Gli Asolani*, one speaker praises love and another dispraises it and describes its tortures. I think it could be argued that this is the source of Spenser's development of the same theme:

> The gnawing envie, the hart-fretting feare,
> The vaine surmizes, the distrustfull showes,
> The false reports that flying tales doe beare,
> The doubts, the daungers, the delayes, the woes,
> The fayned friends, the unassured foes,
> With thousands more then any tongue can tell,
> Doe make a lovers life a wretches hell.
>
> *A Hymne in Honour of Love* 259 ff.

There are several other Platonic thoughts for which verses of Spenser supply the aptest crystallization before Shelley —for example, the beautiful line, "For soule is forme and doth the bodie make" (*Hymne in Honour of Beautie* 133).

The hunt for parallels and sources for Shakespeare is hampered by the reflection that any idea which could occur to any man, Shakespeare would independently think of and express better. The late Churton Collins' list of parallels between Shakespeare and the Greek drama is a warning.[8] Still, it is known that Shakespeare borrowed freely from the books that he did read. There are many coincidences in thought or imagery between Shakespeare and Plato. Some of them may be mere coincidences. Others may be derived from secondary sources, such as Cicero, Plutarch, Montaigne, Erasmus, Elyot's *Governour*, Mulcaster, Ascham, the conversation of Ben Jonson, Spenser's *Faerie Queene*, the first seven books of Chapman's *Iliad*, etc. For others we need look no further than the general atmosphere of the Renaissance in which Shakespeare lived and moved and had his being. Lastly, in a few cases there is a possibility that Shakespeare did look into some reprint of a part of Ficino or into some French version. Whatever the explanation, the examples are not without interest.

The sonnets ring the changes on the idea of the *Symposium* that a man's offspring or his books are his immortality (*Symp.* 208-209), and they contain touches of what may be loosely styled Platonic idealism. The Pythagorean and Platonic music of the spheres is the theme of the lovely passage in the moonlight scene of the *Merchant of Venice*, possibly derived from Du Bellay. Several passages seem to reflect the parallelism and harmony of the parts of a citizenship or social organism and the parts of the soul in the *Republic*, and the question of the unity or plurality of such an organism. More frequently noted are the lines from *Henry V* I. 2. 178-183:

> While that the armed hand doth fight abroad
> The advised head defends itself at home.
> For government, through high and low and lower,
> Put into parts, doth keep in one concent,
> Congreeing in a full and natural close,
> Like music.

(Cf. Rep. 434 C-E.) Here belong also *Julius Caesar* II. 1. 67-69:

> ... and the state of man
> Like to a little kingdom, suffers then
> The nature of an insurrection.

And *Coriolanus* I. 1. 114: "The kingly-crowned head"; and *Othello* III. 4. 144: "For let our finger ache"; and *The Tempest* V. 1. 26-27:

> Yet with my nobler reason 'gainst my fury
> Do I take part.

These and similar passages are quite as close parallels to the text of Plato as many on which far-reaching conclusions are based in doctoral dissertations. Similarly, the immoralist utterances of ethical nihilists in Shakespeare, whether thence derived or not, are excellent summaries of the teaching of Callicles in the *Gorgias*, and of Thrasymachus in the first book of the *Republic*. Most notable in this kind is:

> Conscience is but a word that cowards use,
> Devised at first to keep the strong in awe.
>
> *King Richard III* V. 3. 309-310

Much has been made of the agreement of Shakespeare and Plato in the application of the thought that

> ... the eye sees not itself but by reflection,
> By some other things,

as it is put in *Julius Caesar* (I. 2. 52-53). It is thus developed in *Troilus and Cressida* III. 3. 105 ff.:

> Nor doth the eye itself,
> That most pure spirit of sense, behold itself,
> Not going from itself; but eye to eye oppos'd
> Salutes each other with each other's form.
> For speculation turns not to itself
> Till it hath travell'd and is mirrored there
> Where it may see itself. This is not strange at all.

In the *First Alcibiades* (132 D) we read that the eye sees itself only in another eye, and in the best part of the eye, the pupil. But Ulysses himself replies in Shakespeare,

> I do not strain at the position,
> It is familiar.
>
> *Troilus and Cressida* III. 3. 112-113

The idea is found in St. Augustine, who took it from Cicero, who found it in Plato. The *First Alcibiades* was reprinted from Ficino at Basle in 1551 and Paris in 1560 under the subtitle *vel De Natura Hominis*, and Shakespeare might have seen it. There is another parallel between *Measure for Measure* and the spurious little dialogue, the *Axiochus*, which I think quite plausible. In both, a man about to die is consoled by reflections on the worthlessness of human life. The words of Shakespeare (*Meas. for Meas.* III. 1. 6-11) are familiar:

> Reason thus with life:—
> If I do lose thee, I do lose a thing
> That none but fools would keep: a breath thou art,
> Servile to all the skyey influences
> That dost this habitation where thou keep'st,
> Hourly afflict: Merely, thou art death's fool.[9]

Socrates in the *Axiochus* (370 C-E) says much the same.

These are commonplaces, it is true, and Shakespeare, if he needed the hint, might have found it in Cicero's *Tusculans* I. 31. 76: "In your consolation you have sufficiently deplored the evils of life. When I read it, there is nothing I desire more than to leave such a world." But both in Shakespeare and in the *Axiochus* the auditor is suddenly and completely convinced. In Shakespeare's comedy Claudio says:

> I humbly thank you.
> To sue to live, I find I seek to die.
> And seeking death find life; let it come on.
>
> *Measure for Measure* III. 1. 42-44

And in Plato Axiochus says: "Your argument has brought me around to the opposite. Death is no longer a terror, but a thing to desire." These examples sufficiently illustrate the possibilities of such inquiries.

Bacon's reaction to Plato and Platonism was what the psychoanalysts have taught us to call ambivalent. The positivism of the Italian scientific philosophers to whom Bacon was so greatly indebted drew him into opposition. Plato was mystic, speculative, religious, poetical, unscientific. He was devoted to those barren daughters, final causes, and corrupted physics with natural theology, as Aristotle corrupted it with logic. But Bacon, the elegant classical scholar, the literary artist and orator of science, was irresistibly attracted to Plato. He read him and discovered what is true, that Plato's dramatization of the Socratic method is a striking anticipation and still the best illustration of the Baconian logic of induction as a process of scientific investigation. Plato's guesses at truth have a strange facility in accommodating themselves to translation into the language of advancing science. And the Baconian forms turn out, like Mr. Santayana's essences, to be the Platonic ideas in a new guise. Apart from this essential point, Bacon's not infrequent citations of Plato are of the nature of literary allusion and quotation or sporadic and incidental illustrations of fact.

Macaulay's *Essay on Bacon* set the still prevailing fashion of opposing the Baconian to the Platonic philosophy. As a matter of fact, Bacon always spoke respectfully of Plato and was deeply indebted to him. Not only does he quote and apply to the illustration of his own thought many of Plato's most famous or most interesting sentences, but indeed three or four of his fundamental ideas seem to be derived directly from Plato. The method of induction, he himself says, is excellently practiced by Plato in the investigation of Socratic definitions. Bacon proposes to transfer it to the investigation of nature, and there are many parallels in detail between his method and the procedure in the Platonic dialogues.

The Baconian doctrine of forms presents this analogy in another way. The Baconian form is the Platonic idea conceived as the as yet unknown law of a quality or effect to be investigated. Bacon is himself aware of this resemblance also. Finally, the chief error which Bacon attributes to the unguided human intellect, and the one on which Macaulay and Mill and other Baconians chiefly dwell, is derived from Plato. The human mind, says Bacon, is impatient of the slow processes of graded thought, and leaps at once from the particulars of sense to the highest generalizations, where it seeks repose, neglecting those intermediate propositions which constitute the main part of our real knowledge.[10] This at once reminds a Platonist of the notable passage near the beginning of the *Philebus* where Plato sets forth the same doctrine. And the conjecture is confirmed by the fact that Bacon elsewhere explicitly quotes this passage of the *Philebus* with approval.

Milton,[11] as one of England's most learned poets, had of course read Plato. He was not by choice or temperament especially a Platonist. The references to Plato in his poems

are mostly commonplaces. *Il Penseroso* (87-90) associates
Plato with Hermes Trismegistus and the tradition of mysticism and superstition:

> Where I may oft outwatch the Bear
> With thrice-great Hermes or unsphere
> The spirit of Plato, to unfold
> What worlds or what vast regions hold.

(Cf. *An tenebras Orci visat vastasque lacunas*, Lucretius I
115.) And again:

> The immortal mind, that hath forsook
> Her mansion in this fleshly nook:.
> And of those Daemons that are found
> In fire, air, flood, or under ground.
>
> *Il Penseroso* 91 ff.

The *Arcades* (63 ff.) describes the music of the spheres in the
words of the tenth book of the *Republic* (617 C). To the
tenth book of the *Republic* also might be referred the description of Lethe in Book II:

> Lethe, the river of oblivion, rolls
> Her wat'ry labyrinth; whereof who drinks
> Forthwith his former state and being forgets.
>
> *P. L.* II 583 ff.

The punishment of the damned may be a reminiscence of
the *Phaedo* and the *Republic*:

> Thither by harpy-footed Furies hal'd,
> At certain revolutions all the damn'd
> Are brought.
>
> *P. L.* II 596 ff.

Milton's apology for his anthropomorphism is Platonic
in spirit: and what surmounts the reach

> Of human sense, I shall delineate so,
> By lik'ning spiritual to corporal forms,
> As may express them best; though what if earth
> Be but the shadow of Heav'n; and things therein
> Each to other like, more than on earth is thought?
>
> *P. L.* V 571 ff.

In the same passage there is a suggestion of the *Timaeus* in the comparison of time and eternity:

> For time, though in eternity, appli'd
> To motion, measures all things durable
> By present, past and future.   *Ibid.* 580 ff.

"Heaven's great year" (*ibid.* 583), in the same context, is a reference to the Platonic year. The familiar line, "Thrones, Dominations, Princedoms, Virtues, Powers" (*ibid.* 601), is the classification of the Platonist Dionysius the Areopagite.

The picture of heaven recalls, though I presume unintentionally, Plato's satirical description in the second book of the *Republic* (363 C-D) of the Orphic and Hesiodic heaven as an everlasting picnic:

> Tables are set, and on a sudden piled
> With angels' food; and rubied nectar flows
>
> . . . .
>
> On flow'rs reposed, and with fresh flow'rets crowned,
> They eat, they drink, and in communion sweet
> Quaff immortality and joy.   *P. L.* V 632 ff.

A famous passage of the *Phaedo* is always illustrated by the virtual translation of it in *Comus* (463 ff.):

> ... but when lust,
> By unchaste looks, loose gestures, and foul talk,
> But most by lewd and lavish act of sin,
> Lets in defilement to the inward parts;
> The soul grows clotted by contagion,
> Imbodies and imbrutes, till she quite lose
> The divine property of her first being.
> Such are those thick and gloomy shadows damp,
> Oft seen in charnel vaults, and sepulchres
> Lingering and sitting by a new-made grave,
> As loath to leave the body that it loved.

(Cf. *Phaedo* 81 C-D.) The following description of "divine philosophy. . . But musical as is Apollo's lute" (*ibid.* 476-478) is a blend of another phrase of the *Phaedo* (60E-61A) which calls philosophy the supreme music and a phrase from Shakespeare's *Love's Labour's Lost* (IV. 3. 339), "As bright Apollo's lute strung with his hair." The refrain at the end of *Comus* (1018-1019),

> Mortals that would follow me,
> Love Virtue, she alone is free,

is from the same concluding myth of the *Republic* (617 E ἀρετὴ δὲ ἀδέσποτον) to which we have found two other allusions. The famous story of Cleombrotus, who killed himself after reading the *Phaedo*, is glanced at in the words of *P. L.* III 473 ff.:

> and he who to enjoy
> Plato's Elysium, leap'd into the sea,
> Cleombrotus.

(Cf. Cicero, *Tusculans* I 84, and the epigram of Callimachus, *Anth. pal.* VII 471.) The stairs of Jacob's ladder owe something also to the myth in the tenth *Republic*. The heavenly orbs that,

> as they move
> Their starry dance in numbers that compute
> Days, months, and years,
>
>   *P. L.* III 579-581

repeat a thought of the *Timaeus* (39 B-C).

More specific and perhaps more significant are the references to Plato in Milton's prose. We have already spoken of his answer in the *Areopagitica* to Plato's censorship of poetry and seen that it involved no serious disparagement of Plato himself.[12] The *Tractate on a Free Commonwealth* transmits many ideas from the *Republic* and the *Laws* of Plato to America and some of them to the Constitution of the United States: Patrick Henry's return to a state of nature when the ruler breaks the covenant; the necessity of a ruler's neglecting his own affairs[13] (Vol. II 116); the requirement that the general council be always in session (II 122) (cf.

Laws 758), because the ship of state is always under sail
(II 122); partial rotation in the senate, a third part going
out according to the precedence of their election (*ibid.*); the
need of maintaining a balance against the dangers of "a licentious and unlimited democracy" (II 124-125); ingenious
devices to qualify and refine election (II 125-126); the idea
that wisely chosen legislators will not be distrusted but will
be "the true keepers of our liberty"[14] (II 126); local self-
government and locally controlled schools.

Like Socrates, he affirms that there is no political science
separable from ethics: "There is no art that hath been
more cankered in her principles, more soiled and slubbered
with aphorising pedantry than the art of policy; and that
most, where a man would think should least be, in Christian Commonwealths. They teach not, that to govern well,
is to train up a nation in true wisdom and virtue. . . . Other
things follow as the shadow does the substance: to teach
thus were mere pulpitry to them.[15] A Commonwealth ought
to be . . . one mighty growth and stature of an honest man."[16]
He praises a just monarchy almost in the terms of Plato
and remarks after Plato that the Tyrant fears good men
(*Eikonoklastes* I 428). He thinks England the best example
of the mixed government which Cicero and Polybius approved in Rome and Plato's *Laws* in Sparta (*Of Reformation in England* II 408). He approves Plato's prefacing of
the *Laws* with a persuasive proemium instead of a threat,
and quotes Plato against the immoralists' opposition of
nature and law.

His *Tractate on Education* illustrates again that dependence
on Plato of the Renaissance ideal of education to which I
have already referred. As he himself says in his program,
"The course of study hitherto briefly described is, what I
can guess by reading, likest to those ancient and famous
schools of Pythagoras, Plato, Isocrates, Aristotle and such
others, out of which were bred such a number of renowned

philosophers, orators, historians, poets and princes. . . ."
(III 474); he stresses exercise and music as Plato does (III
468; 475); he would have the elements of geometry taught
in play, as Plato would in the *Laws*; he objects, as Plato
and John of Salisbury do, to beginning education with the
most "intellective abstractions" (III 466) (cf. *Rep*. 498);
and deplores, as they do, the desertion of philosophy and
culture for affairs by promising youth.

Other incidental Platonisms are his explicit quotation of
Plato's illustration in the *Euthyphro* of the principle of elementary logic that you cannot directly convert a universal
affirmative: "for where shame is, there is fear; but where
fear is, there is not presently shame";[17] his citation of Plato
and the Stoics and Cicero for the idea that God cannot
punish man more, nor make him more miserable, than by
making him still more sinful (cf. Plato, *Theaetet*. 176 D;
177 A; *Laws* 728 B-C; 904 C ff.). An amusing example of the
logic of the harmonization of Christianity and Platonism
in Renaissance literature is his parallelism of the *Symposium* and Moses: "Hence it is that Plato, in his festival discourse, brings in Socrates relating what he feigned to have
learned from the prophetess Diotima, how Love was the
son of Penury, begot of Plenty in the garden of Jupiter.
Which divinely sorts with that which in effect Moses tells
us, that Love was the son of Loneliness, begot in Paradise
by that sociable and helpful aptitude which God implanted
between man and woman towards each other."[18]

One would not look to Burton's *Anatomy of Melancholy*
for a systematic and exhaustive study of anything, least of all
the philosophy of Plato. Burton is good reading for those who
like rambling, miscellaneous erudition, and by no means as irrational or quaint as Taine and recent English essayists conceive him to be. He interests the student of literary influences
as the mine from which many generations of writers, including Emerson himself, dug their quotations. Here we have

only to note the number and quality of his references to
Plato.[19] He quotes the *Republic* twice: for the principle that
"many laws, many lawsuits, many lawyers and many phy-
sicians" are the "manifest sign of a distempered, melancholy state" (p. 54); and, without warning, in Ficino's Latin
for the statement that old age frees us from the fierce
domination of the passions. He compares Plato's ideal state
with modern imitations in Campanella and Bacon and objects to Plato's community that it "in many things is impious, absurd and ridiculous, it takes away all splendor and
magnificence" (pp. 64-65). He cites Bodin for Plato's comparison of the political and economic body. He refers to the
Republic,[20] the *Laws* (625 D; 704-705; 747 D), and Bodin
for the idea, now generally associated with Buckle, that
laws and institutions and the character of men may be determined by climate (pp. 453 ff.). And he also, of course,
knows the philosopher kings and the many-headed beast
(*Rep.* 588 C), and the myth of immortality reported by Er
the son of Armenius (*Rep.* 614 B ff.), the "diapason and
sweet harmony" (*Rep.* 432 A) that makes a unity of a state
(p. 596; 66); and like Plato (*Laws* 742 C) he would limit
and regulate dowries in the ideal state (pp. 477-478).

The *Symposium*, as was to be expected, receives the
most attention. It is freely quoted with the comments of
Ficino and Leo Hebraeus in the introduction to the third
partition, that treats of love-melancholy. He answers those
who "carp at Plato's majesty" that they reprove Plato
without cause, as Ficinus pleads, "for all love is honest and
good, and they are worthy to be loved that speak well of
love," and quotes Maximus Tyrius, "a great Platonist himself," who is amazed that Plato and Socrates should expel
Homer from their city because "he writ of such light and
wanton subjects" in view of the love scenes in Plato's own
writings. He further quotes the *Symposium* (pp. 155-156)
for the anecdote of Socrates (220 C) standing fixed in medi-

tation all day and through the night to the amazement of the soldiers; for the birth of love from poverty and plenty (*Symp.* 203 B ff.) with the remark,"The moral of this is in Ficinus" (p. 443); for the two kinds of love, the heavenly and the earthly (*Symp.* 180 C-D); for the speech of Aristophanes (*Symp.* 189 A ff.) about the original four-limbed man-woman, where he adds again, naming his source,"Many such tales you shall find in Leon Hebraeus *Dial. III* and their moral to them." To the *Symposium* also he attributes Socrates' words that the eye of the mind brightens as the eye of the body grows more dim (p. 345). And from the *Symposium* (195 D) is derived the reference to Ate walking softly on men's heads, which Emerson quotes without acknowledgment in Burton's English rendering. To these items we may add the temptation of Socrates by Alcibiades (215 A ff.) and the sentiment, "My words are my children" (p. 530), and the Sileni of Alcibiades, which, however, all Renaissance scholars knew from the *Adagia* of Erasmus.

Next in frequency, perhaps, are the references to the *Phaedo*. He quotes it for metempsychosis and reminiscence (pp. 104-105), adding,"I rejourn all such atheistical spirits" to the proofs of immortality there (p. 105). He twists into an apology for suicide Socrates' doubtful allowance of it in the *Phaedo*[21] in extreme cases (p. 262). He mentions Socrates' dismissal of the women (60 A) that he may die in tranquillity (p. 371). He develops from the *Symposium* (178 D-E) the idea dear to Tennyson and Coventry Patmore that love makes cowards brave (p. 516). He quaintly renders Plato's statement that love is not a god, but a great daemon in the form (*Symp.* 202 D-E): "Plato calls it the great devil, for its vehemency" (p. 426). And while on the subject of love, he expands into a riotous page of unsavory synonyms for female uncomeliness the commonplace which Lucretius and Molière borrowed from the *Republic*[22] that to the lover even blemishes seem beautiful (507). He mistakenly refers to the *Phaedo* the theory of vision of the *Timaeus* (p. 101) and is probably thinking of the *Phaedo* when he says, "Plato will have all to be innate" (p. 106), and likewise quotes Socrates' answer to Crito's question (115 B) "How shall you bury me?" for the idea which he crystallizes in the Latin, *"facilis iactura sepulchri"* (p. 371).

To the *Timaeus* he refers the idea that the earth is an animal (p. 297), the influence of climate on character again (p. 293), and from it are probably derived, though he does not say so, the phrases "waking dream" (p. 640) and, with Neo-Platonic coloring,"the nature of good is to be communicated" (p. 655). Of the proverbial obscurity of the *Timaeus* he says (p. 424),"A far greater part had rather read Apuleius than Plato: Tully himself confesseth he could not understand Plato's *Timaeus*, and therefore cared less for it." From the *Phaedrus* (pp. 244-245) he cites the doctrine of prophetic madness (p. 523), the veiling of Socrates' face (237 A) when he spoke of love (p. 425), "that pleasant tale of Socrates [229 A ff.], which he told fair Phaedrus under a plane-tree at the banks of the river Iseus [*sic*], about noon when it was hot, and the grasshoppers made a noise, he took that sweet occasion to tell him a tale, how grasshoppers were once scholars, musicians, poets, etc., before the Muses were born, and lived without meat and drink, and for that cause were turned by Jupiter into grasshoppers" (p. 191). To the *Phaedrus* also belongs the baffling allusion to "that Theutus in Plato" (274 C), one of the "inventors of all mischief" (p. 119).

The few references to the *Laws* on politics (p. 208), education, the value of music (p. 336), and the prohibition of beggars (*Laws* 936 B-C) in a well-ordered state (p. 60) are hardly to be distinguished from similar ideas in the *Republic*. But he quotes explicitly from the *Laws* (853 C) the famous limitation of Utopianism,"We are legislating for men, not gods" (p. 68), as a justification for tolerating some kind of usury for the hardness of men's hearts.

He confirms the still persisting association of Platonism with mysticism and superstition in many places: Epicures and atheists may deny the existence of spirits and devils, "because they never saw them. But Plato, Plotinus, Porphyrius, Iamblichus, and Proclus, insisting in the steps of Trismegistus, Pythagoras, and Socrates, make no doubt of it" (p. 115). His list of learned men who were dear to monarchs repeats a motive of the spurious first epistle of Plato (p. 197). He naturally has much to say of the Socratic daimonion: "That which Apuleius, Xenophon and Plato contend of Socrates' Daimonium is most absurd," he says, making no distinction between Plato and the others in this matter (p. 119). But he admits that Plotinus the Platonist "laughs them to scorn, that hold the devil or spirits can cause any such diseases" (p. 126).

A few other random or doubtful or erroneous references may be mentioned. He refers to the *Protagoras* a sentence which is not there (p. 196): "Plato in his *Protagoras* well saith, a good philosopher as much excels other men, as a great king doth the commons of his country." He quotes the *Charmides* (156 B) for the principle that a good physician will not treat the eye without the whole body, nor the body without the mind (p. 332). He repeats in a Latin version of Callimachus' epigram the story of Cleombrotus (p. 264). He refers to the *Second Alcibiades* with its imitations in Latin poetry for the folly of the prayers of ordinary men (p. 619). He attributes to Plato the designation of man as "the marvel of marvels" (p. 85), and the statement, "No man can so severely punish his adversary as God will such as oppress miserable men," and he lists Plato among the authors of consolation together with "Seneca, Plutarch, Xenophon, Epictetus, Theophrastus, Xenocrates, Crantor, Lucian, Boethius and some of late . . ." (p. 341).

Sir Thomas Browne can hardly be classed as a Platonist either in temperament or in scholarship. Yet the first paragraph of his address to the reader begins with one explicit and two latent quotations from the *Meno*, the *Symposium*, and the *Timaeus*.

Would truth dispense, we could be content with Plato, that knowledge were but remembrance. . . . For (what is worse) knowledge is made by oblivion, and, to purchase a clear and warrantable body of truth, we must forget and part with much we know; . . . like the great and exemplary wheels of heaven, we must observe two circles; that, while we are daily carried about and whirled on by the swing and rapt of the one, we may maintain a natural and proper course in the slow and sober wheel of the other.

(These are the circles to which Emerson so frequently refers.) He is a Late Renascence scholar of the Burton type. We need not look to him for a systematic interpretation of, or new light upon, Plato. But we may find a certain interest in noting the suggestions for his thought or the ornament for his style that he discovers in certain Platonic texts.

There was little occasion for quoting Plato in his chief work, *On Vulgar Errors*. I note the few instances. The query (*Vulg. Er.* I 1) whether the whole relation of Genesis be not allegorical, "that is, whether the temptation of the man by the woman be not the seduction of the rational and higher parts by the inferior and feminine faculties," may contain a reference to the tripartite division of the soul in Plato and his definition of the virtues, to which Browne elsewhere refers. His scorn (*ibid.* I 3) of those who "embrace not virtue for itself, but its reward" may be suggested by a passage of the *Phaedo* of which he elsewhere makes fuller use. His denunciation of "fortune-tellers, jugglers, geomancers and the like incantatory impostors" somewhat resembles the passage in the second book of the *Republic* (364 B; cf. 489 B) about the fortunetellers, and so forth, who go to rich men's doors. Interesting is his remark (*ibid.* I 8), for the history of Platonism, that Athenaeus "was probably a better gram-

marian than philosopher, dealing but hardly with Aristotle
and Plato." His protest against those who deny the providence of God in particulars, on the ground that "he intend-
eth only the care of the species or common natures, but
letteth loose the guard of individuals" (*ibid*. I 10), and
"looks not below the moon, but hath designed the regiment
of sublunary affairs unto inferior deputations," comes ultimately, like most similar arguments, from the theodicy in
the tenth book of the *Laws*. He incidentally refers to Plato's
"opinion of sight by extramission" (*ibid*. III 7).

In the chapter on the belief,"That a Wolf first seeing a man,
begets a dumbness in him" (*ibid*. III 8), while quoting Vergil and Theocritus, he strangely omits the first book of the
Republic. He attributes to Plato the fantasy of the original
man-woman in the speech of Aristophanes in the *Symposium*
(189 C ff.) (*Vulg. Er*. III 17),"Plato, and some of the rab-
bins, proceeded higher, who conceived the first man an
hermaphrodite." In dealing with the error that only man
hath an erect figure, he says, "the ground and occasion of
that conceit was a literal apprehension of a figurative expression in Plato" (*ibid*. IV 1), a warning that interpreters
of Plato might still take to heart. But he himself fails to
heed it when he says that "the philosophy of Plato, and
most of the Platonists, abounds in numeral consideration"
(*ibid*. IV 12). And again, when he writes (*ibid*. IV 12), "For
first, it is implicitly, and upon consequence, denied by Aristotle in his Politicks, in that discourse against Plato, who
measured the vicissitude and mutation of states, by a per-
iodical fatality of number." Plato was no more serious than
Browne is himself, when, in the *Religio Medici* I 12, he
writes, "I have often admired the mystical way of Pythagoras, and the secret magick of numbers."

The moral and religious works, as was to be expected, refer to Plato more frequently. The *Religio Medici*, the *Urn
Burial*, and the *Christian Morals* contain some forty quota-

tions. Many of these are familiar commonplaces, as "to see ourselves again, we need not look for Plato's year . . . the world is now as it was in ages past" (*Rel. Med.* I 6); the references to the music of the spheres (*Rel. Med.* II 9); to the myth that concludes the *Republic*: "Plato's historian of the other world lies twelve days incorrupted, while his soul was viewing the large stations of the dead";[23] to Cato, reading the *Phaedo* on the night of his death (*Urn Burial* 4); to the geometry of God, "for God is like a skilful geometrician" (*Rel. Med.* I 16); to the wild horses of the soul in the *Phaedrus* (248 ff.; cf. *Christian Morals* I 24), and to the wings of the soul (*Urn Burial* 4): "Before Plato could speak, the soul had wings in Homer"; to the many-headed beast which is man (*Rep.* 588 C; *Rel. Med.* I 55); and to the great beast which is the public (*Rep.* 493 A-B; *Rel. Med.* II 1); to the creation of the soul by God, for which he says we have the "flat affirmative of Plato" (*Rel. Med.* I 36); to St. Paul's idea of the war in our members, for which, however, he does not explicitly refer to Plato (*Rel. Med.* I 7); to the metaphysical necessity of evil as the logically inseparable counterpart of good, for which again he does not explicitly refer to the *Lysis* and *Theaetetus* (*Rel. Med.* II 4); to the allegory of the cave in the *Republic* (514 ff.): "Methinks we yet discourse in Plato's den, and are but embryo philosophers" (*Urn Burial* 4); to the immortality through offspring of the *Symposium* (*Rel. Med.* I 41), which seems to him "a mere fallacy, unworthy the desires of a man." Sometimes he errs or quotes carelessly (*Rel. Med.* II 9): "I will not say, with Plato, the soul is an harmony"—an opinion which Plato puts forward in the *Phaedo* only to refute.

Like most writers of these centuries, he confirms the view that Platonism inclines not only to religion, but also to mysticism and superstition (*Rel. Med.* I 32).

Now, besides these particular and divided spirits [i.e., witches and so forth, in which Browne believes], there may be (for aught

I know) a universal and common spirit to the whole world. It was the opinion of Plato, and it is yet of the hermetical philosophers. And again (*Rel. Med.* I 33), speaking of demons and tutelary and guardian angels, he says, "It is not a new opinion of the Church of Rome, but an old one of Pythagoras and Plato." He himself holds one opinion which is found in Aeschylus and Pindar and other Greek poets, which is current today, and which, though rejected by Plato, is often attributed to him (*Rel. Med.* II 11): "We are somewhat more than ourselves in our sleeps; and the slumber of the body seems to be but the waking of the soul. It is the ligation of sense, but the liberty of reason." Plato himself held precisely the opposite, not to say the Freudian view, that in sleep the censorship of the reason is suspended and the lawless part of the soul is released from its control (*Rep.* 571 C ff.).[24]

Shrewd and happy observations are not lacking: "I am now content to understand a mystery, without a rigid definition, in an easy and Platonic description. That allegorical description of Hermes pleaseth me beyond all the metaphysical definitions of divines" (*Rel. Med.* I 10) (he is referring to the famous *sphaera cujus centrum ubique, circumferentia nullibi*); "Aristotle doth but instruct us as Plato did him, that is, to confute himself" (*Rel. Med.* II 8); "Aristotle, whilst he labours to refute the *ideas* of Plato, falls upon one himself: for his *summum bonum* is a chimaera; and there is no such thing as his felicity" (*Rel. Med.* II 14); "Nothing can be said hyperbolically of God, nor will his attributes admit of expressions above their own exuberances. Trismegistus's circle, whose center is everywhere and circumference nowhere, was no hyperbole" (*Chr. Mor.* III 2).[25]

Slight or possible allusions to passages in Plato are: the warning against the rhetoric of Satan, where he may have had in mind the first ten pages of the second book of the *Republic* (*Rel. Med.* I 19); the deploring of the corruption of these times ". . . everyone having a liberty to amass and

heap up riches" (*Rel. Med.* II 1); the censure of the sump-
tuary law in Plato's *Laws*: "But Plato seemed too frugally
politick, who allowed no larger monument than would contain four heroick verses," which he might have found in the
Christian Fathers (*Urn Burial* 3); the dry humor of "whether
Plato died in a dream, as some deliver, he must rise again
to inform us"; the image, "but be thou what thou virtu-
ously art, and let not the ocean wash away thy tincture,"
which may have come from Marcus Aurelius or Epictetus
rather than the *Republic* (*Chr. Mor.* I 9); the admonition,
"If you cannot imitate Job, yet come not short of Socrates"
(*Chr. Mor.* I 14); the reference (*Chr. Mor.* I 17) to Adraste,
which may be Plato's Adrasteia (*Rep.* 451 A); the true use
of wealth: "if they be but rich enough to be honest, and to
give every man his due" (*Chr. Mor.* I 26); the statement,
perhaps from the *Timaeus*: "Figures of most angles do
nearest approach unto circles which have no angles at all"
(*Chr. Mor.* II 6); the principle of punishment: "the mercy
of God hath singled out but few to be the signals of his justice, leaving the generality of mankind to the pedagogy of
example" (*Chr. Mor.* II 11), which recalls, if not derived
from, the *Gorgias*; the pronouncement, "He honours God,
who imitates him," which, whether taken from Plato or not,
exactly repeats his language (*Chr. Mor.* III 2); the denial
"that there is any servitude in virtue" (*Chr. Mor.* III 3),
which parallels a phrase of Milton and of the tenth book of
the *Republic*; the archetypal sun in the city of the new Jerusalem, and the sentence quoted by Pater: "Things are really
true as they correspond unto God's conception; and have so
much verity as they hold of conformity unto that intellect,
in whose idea they had their first determination."[26]

An instructive warning may be found in the dealings of
modern essayists with a notable sentence of the *Religio
Medici* I 16: "In brief, all things are artificial; for nature is
the art of God." The second clause is almost verbatim from

Plato's *Sophist* 265 E. Pater[27] quotes this in support of the criticism that Browne "seems to have no true sense of natural law, as Bacon understood it; nor even of that immanent reason in the natural world, which the Platonic tradition supposes." Texte, in his *Etudes de littérature européenne*,[28] likewise criticizes the passage with no awareness of its origin.

The so-called Cambridge Platonists have been studied so fully in German dissertations and British and American monographs and reprints that I can be brief.[29] They were a group of liberal Christian scholars and preachers who lived at Cambridge through the middle of the seventeenth century and drew their moral and sometimes their intellectual inspiration from a not very critical study of Plato and Plotinus. So far as they had any philosophical aim beyond edification, they endeavored to adjust and relate their Platonic or Neo-Platonic ideas to the then new philosophies of Bacon and Descartes, and above all to use them in refutation of the materialistic psychology and positivist ethics of Hobbes, as great a bugaboo in fundamentalist circles then as Darwin is today.

Cudworth is the only one that interests me. But I will enumerate them rapidly. Benjamin Whichcote (1609-1683) was an eloquent and popular preacher. He was assailed by a fundamentalist named Tuckney for "having studied other authors more than the Scriptures, Plato and his scholars above others."[30] I do not find much specific reference to Plato in him.

John Smith's (1616-1652) *Select Discourses* were recommended by Matthew Arnold as the most salutary reading for young clergymen. That defines his place in the tradition of liberal Platonic Christianity for those who know Arnold. He, too, uses Plato chiefly for illustration and edification.

Nathanial Culverwel (1618-1651), among other topics, preached on the Light of Nature, a favorite idea with the eighteenth-century Deists and one that the historians of ideas have traced back through many Renaissance, medieval, and postclassical writers, to Cicero.

Henry More (1614-1687) is to many the most interesting and the most spiritual of the Cambridge Platonists. His *Psychozoia Platonica* or *A Platonical Song of the Soul* is especially curious. He quotes Plato and the Neo-Platonists frequently, but not so learnedly or systematically as Cudworth. He allows his speculation free play in many fancies which he does not affirm to be true. He has much to say of Hermes Trismegistus and Pythagoras and the Chaldees; and sometimes seems to confirm the association of Platonism with the belief in witchcraft and other superstitions. Fashions change in books as in bonnets. The learned Cudworth hoped that his philology might sweeten the severity of his philosophy; but largely because of this erudition modern critics dismiss him as a tiresome pedant. There are, perhaps, other more creditable reasons than hatred of scholarship why some readers of today may be more attracted by the wistful vagueness of Henry More, or the edifying, rational, moral temper of Whichcote and Smith.

Ralph Cudworth (1617-1688) is the scholar and, I think, the philosopher of the group. His huge work, *The True Intellectual System of the Universe*, edited later with notes and translated into Latin by the German scholar Mosheim,[31] is used by many modern writers on the Cambridge Platonists as an illustration of the futility of old-fashioned pedantic footnote erudition. I take the opposite view of it for two reasons: first, its enormous stores of quotations from Plato and other ancient philosophers have been a sourcebook for all subsequent English literature; second, despite his many uncritical fancies, he elaborates against Hobbes the conclusive refutation of psychological materialism in Plato's *Theaetetus* in a fashion by which the materialists of today might well, but will not, profit.[32]

Cudworth is for the historian far the most significant of

the Cambridge Platonists. He quotes and interprets Plato
extensively and, for his age, critically, and his quotations
have been the repertory and secondary source of much later
Platonism in English literature. Many of his observations
on the *Theaetetus* and the tenth book of the *Laws* are still
instructive, and their value is not seriously impaired by the
occasional oversights of his scholarship or by the uncritical
character of his main thesis—as, for example, the Mosaical
origin of the atomic philosophy, the monotheism of all the
deeper thinkers of antiquity, the resemblance of a Platonic
to the Christian Trinity. Cudworth holds that the earlier
Mosaical atomic philosophy was transmitted through the
Phoenician Mochus or Moschus to Pythagoras and other
early Greek philosophers, who accepted it as the most intelligible explanation of material phenomena but thought it
consistent with and held it subject to the independence and
priority of mind.

It was the school of Democritus that identified atomism
with materialism, and it was Plato's reaction of disgust
against this Democritean atheism and, by anticipation,
against the "sottish corporeality" of Epicurus, that made
him mistakenly reject the atomic philosophy and incline
to more fanciful hypotheses that later gave rise to the Aristotelian substantial forms. Cudworth, then, does not perceive that the construction of the elements in the *Timaeus*
is a virtual atomism. But he is entirely right in stressing
hostility to materialism as one of the main impulses of
Plato's philosophy. Cudworth identifies the new philosophy
of Hobbes with the philosophies of materialism, atheism,
relativity, and immoralism combated by Plato and he
makes effective use against Hobbes of the arguments of the
Theaetetus and the *Laws*. His occasional misinterpretations
of the *Theaetetus* do not affect the validity of the arguments
which he drew from it for this purpose and which have been
repeated by subsequent English Platonists all the way down

to Martineau and after. Cudworth enlisted Plato also in his attack on another fashionable philosophy of the day. Taking the provisional skepticism of Descartes as an encouragement to a universal skepticism, he invokes against it Plato's profound faith in the reality of truth and the possibility of knowledge.

Another fundamental Platonic trait in Cudworth is his insistence on the sovereignty of ethics and the autonomy of the moral law. Against many medieval and Renaissance thinkers he reaffirms in substance the principle of the *Euthyphro* (10 A ff.) that right is right not because God loves it or wills it but God wills it because it is right, and the whole of his *Immutable Morality* and many passages of his *True Intellectual System of the Universe* are in effect reiterations of Plato's faith that morality is of the nature of things, and his assurance that the moral law is as certain as the existence of the island of Crete (*Laws* 662 B). In this connection he takes note of Plato's distinction between the Idea of Justice and the Idea of Good. The immoralists, he says, affirm that Justice is only what the ruling power chances to decree. But no one ventures to say that of Good. Many other recurrent topics in the history of Platonism find ample illustration in Cudworth's voluminous treatises —for example, the association of Platonism with superstition in many minds, and the relation of Platonism to Christianity and to Christian theology in its varied forms. But the detail of Cudworth's citations of Plato would fill a volume, and here, as throughout this sketch, I can only endeavor to keep the perspective true and illustrate the real course of the Platonic tradition and the true connections of ideas by a selection of the best typical examples. Any other method would swell this book to several volumes.

Jeremy Taylor is ranked by Coleridge with Shakespeare, Bacon, and Milton as a master of English style. He is well read in the classics and makes constant use of them in explicit and latent quotations. The majority of these quotations, as happens often even with professional Hellenists, are from the Latin poets. He was not a thinker and would not be interested in dialectics or in the deeper things of Platonic philosophy. He would borrow Platonic images to illumine his style and combine with Christian precepts Platonic ethics, often at second hand from his favorite guide Epictetus, as when, in *Holy Living*, his faith affirms, "But when a man suffers in a good cause, or is afflicted, and yet walks not perversely with his God, then, Anytus and Melitus [*sic*] may kill me, but they cannot hurt me."[33] He alludes to the story that Plato was sold into slavery by Dionysius, adding the motive, "for disputing better than he did" (III 96). There may be a reminiscence of the *Phaedo* in the image at the end of the fine sentence in the *Liberty of Prophesying*: "or else we must lie safe in a mutual toleration and private liberty of persuasion, unless some other anchor can be thought upon where we may fasten our floating vessels and ride safely" (V 483). He quaintly commends the Christian virtue of humility by

the method of the Platonists, who reduce all the causes and arguments for humility, which we can take from ourselves, to these seven heads: the spirit of a man is light and troublesome; his body is brutish and sickly; he is constant in his folly and error, and inconstant in his manners and good purposes; his labours are vain, intricate, and endless; his fortune is changeable, but seldom pleasing, never perfect; his wisdom comes not till he be ready to die, that is, till he be past using it; his death is certain, always ready at the door, but never far off. Upon these or the like meditations if we dwell or frequently retire to them, we shall see nothing more reasonable than to be humble, and nothing more foolish than to be proud.[34]

These are his chief references to Plato. My notes on his Platonic quotations form thirty-three typewritten pages, but, as they contribute nothing new, I pass them by.

The seventeenth-century minor and metaphysical lyric poets are pretty fully, though not always quite critically, treated in Harrison's *Platonism in English Poetry*, and Fletcher's *Religion of Beauty in Women*. As already said, the true gospel of Platonic love is summed up in a few great passages, most of them already quoted, of Spenser, Shelley, Tennyson, and, if you please, Coventry Patmore's *Angel in the House*. These passages, perhaps because they do not mention Plato by name, are strangely overlooked by Harrison and Fletcher. Otherwise, the allusions to Platonic love in minor English poetry alternate between a sniggering Byronism and a somewhat affected and overstrained idealism that doth protest too much. One or two specimens will serve as well as a score. Here, for example, is John Cleveland's vulgarization of the theme:

> 'Twas but an Insurrection
> Of the Carnal Part,
>   For a Quaker in Heart
> Can never lose Perfection.
> For so our Matters teach us,
> The Intent being well directed,
>   Though the Devil trapan
> The Adamical Man,
> The Saints stand uninfected.[35]

And here, a hundred and fifty years later, is Byron's comment:

> Oh, Plato! Plato! you have paved the way,
>   With your confounded fantasies, to more
> Immoral conduct by the fancied sway
>   Your system feigns o'er the controlless core
> Of human hearts, than all the long array
>   Of poets and romancers:—You're a bore,
> A charlatan, a coxcomb—and have been,
>   At best, no better than a go-between.
>   *Don Juan* Canto I cxvi

The idealistic view may be represented by Donne's compliment to the Countess of Bedford:

> Madam
> You have refined me, and to worthiest things.[36]

Or Drummond's:

> Most true it is, for straight at the first Sight
> My mind me told, that in some other place
> It elsewhere saw the idea of that face,
> And lov'd a love of heavenly pure delight;
> No wonder now I feel so fair a flame,
> Sith I her lov'd ere on this earth she came.

Poems Pt. I. Son. vii

Or More's:

> But yet, my Muse, still take a higher flight,
> Sing of Platonick Faith in the first Good,
> That Faith that doth our souls to God unite.

III. iv. 14

More interesting to me are the occasional Neo-Platonic fancies, or versifications of the *Timaeus*; as for example, Vaughan's:

> I saw Eternity the other night
> Like a great Ring of pure and endless light,
>   All calm, as it was bright,
> And round beneath it, Time in hours, days, years
>   Driv'n by the spheres
> Like a vast shadow mov'd. In which the world
>   And all her train were hurl'd;[37]

or Cowley's:

> Before the Branchy head of Numbers Tree
> Sprang from the Trunk of One.[38]

Or Phineas Fletcher's paraphrase in *The Purple Island* of Plato's description of the human body.

The polished, formal, Latinized classicism of English literature from Milton to Shelley seems to us now to lack the deeper appreciation of the Hellenic genius which returned with romanticism and the new German renascence of scholarship. The Platonic tradition flowed on, but in a shallower channel. Plato was still read or, when not read, could be quoted at second hand from Plutarch, Montaigne, Bodin, Heinzius, Ficino's *Introductions*, Burton, Sir Thomas Browne, Cudworth, and Jeremy Taylor. Platonism and Platonists remained convenient synonyms for idealism, mysticism, enthusiasm, natural religion, and teleology. Platonic love remained an easy theme of sentimentality, cynicism, and satire. Berkeley, Shaftesbury, and Tucker, though they contribute little to the critical interpretation of Plato, cannot themselves be understood apart from him. The analogies between Platonic dialectic and psychology and the thought of Locke and Hume would repay study, whether they are the coincidences of great minds grappling with the same problems, or indicate more acquaintance with Plato's writings than is generally attributed to these philosophers. These and similar topics would not be without interest if developed in a critical and exhaustive study. But in this sketch the Platonism of the so-called Age of Reason may without much loss be treated merely as a transition to the more interesting Platonism of romanticism and the nineteenth century, and we may be content to sample it in a few typical examples.

On a superficial view Locke is a link in the Bacon-Mill empiric philosophy which is the antithesis of Platonism. But he is one of the half-dozen philosophers who, like Plato, thinks over the whole ground—and his thought, like Mill's, will parallel or translate back into Platonism more readily than that of the pseudo Platonists. I do not know how far the many analogies I have observed are due to firsthand knowledge of Plato, perhaps derived from Shaftesbury, and how far to Locke's university study of Aristotle at the time when Oxford was a battleground for the debate between the Platonizing Ramists and the anti-Ramists. He rarely, if ever, quotes Plato in terms. Locke's assault on innate ideas is directed probably against neither Descartes nor Plato, but the Platonists Herbert of Cherbury, Cudworth, and the rest. For that hopeless tangle of equivocation I must refer you to Professor Dewey's *Leibniz*.[39] Plato, on my interpretation, is not involved. For he made all ideas innate, and Locke himself says, "they must all be innate or all adventitious."[40] What I mean by saying that Locke easily translates into the logic if not into the metaphysic of Platonism appears from the two following sentences: "Each abstract idea with a name to it, makes a distinct species" (II 66); "Why Plato's 'animal implume bipes latis unguibus' should not be a good definition of the name man, standing for that sort of creatures, will not be easy to show" (II 123). One way of explaining this is to say that extremes meet. But I think there is more in it.

Locke's dialectic, his running fight against equivocation, his divisions and dichotomies, his conception of method, his comparison of the mind to soft or hard wax—much that he says about power, pleasure and pain, the observation that the mind like the eye sees not itself, the comparison of intellectual inquiry to hunting, the observation that smells have not species, and several other touches, are Platonic. I think that in a monograph I could make it probable that Locke had read the *Theaetetus* and *Philebus* and the *Symposium*, from which last probably comes his favorite thought of the incessant mutability not only of our bodies but also of our minds. For the mystic *a priori* Platonism of his day he could have no sympathy. He remarks slyly in one place, "And whether that which we call 'ecstasy' be not dreaming with the eyes open, I leave to be examined."[41] The objective relation of his epistemology to Plato we have already spoken of. It is incredible that Höffding[42] should say that the distinction between primary and secondary qualities originates in Galilei, Hobbes, and Descartes. It is a commonplace of

ancient atomism recognized by Plato, as Berkeley says in
Siris, and was accessible to Locke and everybody else in
Lucretius or his interpreter Gassendi.

Locke's pupil Shaftesbury defended Platonism against
him in respect of enthusiasm and the autonomy of absolute
ethics in relation to religion revealed and dogmatic. Here,
as often, the Platonist is at bottom more rational than the
so-called experience philosopher. The deplorable affectations of Shaftesbury's style have impaired his credit with
modern English critics. The Germans were less sensitive
and his influence on German literature was very great. He
is a clear thinker and a well-informed and sound Platonist
in two directions: natural religion, and aesthetics. In the
first, he professes a latitudinarian theology of the Schleiermacher and Matthew Arnold type—"morality touched with
emotion." Indeed, it has been said that without Shaftesbury English literature would have had neither Matthew
Arnold nor Ruskin. In his aesthetics, not of course to be
sharply distinguished from his ethical religions, he coquets
with Platonic love and the doctrine of poetic and enthusiastic madness. His essay on *Enthusiasm* contains many
such characteristic passages.[43]

A serious study of the relation of Berkeleian idealism to
Platonic idealism would plunge us into abysmal depths of
epistemology and metaphysics. I must keep to the surface
of English literature. Berkeley's earlier writings are apparently at the opposite pole from Platonism. They teach an
extreme nominalism and deny the existence of abstract
ideas even in our own minds. Later, he became much interested in Plato and the Platonists, whom he quotes abundantly and wistfully in that quaintly entitled work, *Siris, or
a Chain of Philosophical Reflexions and Inquiries Concerning
the Virtues of Tar-Water and Divers Other Subjects*.[44] How
far he really altered his metaphysical opinions is a question
for a seminar in philosophy. But the historian of Platonism

may note with amusement that he said "No, I still maintain that we have no abstract general ideas—but we do have notions." The conjunction of Platonism with tar water as a panacea greatly entertained the contemporary wits and minor poets. One of them wrote:

> Here battered rakes for taint or gout
> A sure balsamic find;
> Here sophs may learn what Plato thought
> Of the eternal mind.
>
> Henceforth let none the lawn decry,
> If Berkeley's pious care
> Teach wits to own a Trinity
> And beaux to relish tar.

Pope's classical culture was derived from the French critics and the Latin poets. He was, of course, not a Platonist nor a scholar. Such reminiscences of Platonic phrases and thought as we may discover were picked up in his multifarious readings of French and English literature, or were given to him by Bolingbroke, or acquired in the studies preparatory to the *Essay on Man*. The theodicy of the *Essay*, its vindication of the ways of God to man, like all theodicies, runs back through Leibnitz, the Schoolmen, Raymond de Sebonde, and the Stoics to the tenth book of Plato's *Laws*. We cannot judge the designs of God because we see only a part:

> has thy pervading soul
> Look'd through? or can a part contain the whole?
>
> *Essay* I 31-32
>
> whatever wrong we call,
> May, must be right, as relative to all.
>
> *Essay* I 51-52
>
> God sends not ill, if rightly understood;
> Or partial ill is universal good.
>
> *Essay* IV 113-114

Nearly all the parallels with Plato which a specialist notes may have come to Pope from secondary sources, many, for example, from Boethius. The "music of the spheres" is a commonplace (*Essay* I 202). The distribution of powers to the animals might, but need not, come from the *Protagoras* (320 D ff.):

> Nature to these, without profusion, kind,
> The proper organs, proper powers assigned,
> Each seeming want compensated, of course,
> Here with degrees of swiftness, there of force.

The lines   *Essay* I 179 ff.

> Its proper power to hurt, each creature feels;
> Bulls aim their horns, and Asses lift their heels[45]

are as likely to come from Anacreon as from the *Protagoras*. It is as idle to ask whether he took "the people are a many-headed beast" (*Im. of Hor.* Bk. I Ep. I. 121) from the *Republic* (588 D) as it is to ask whether Hamilton in turn found it in Pope or elsewhere. Pope repeats it in the form "the many-headed Monster of the Pit" (*Im. of Hor.* Bk. VI Ep. I. 305). The passage in *An Essay on Criticism* (245-246):

> 'Tis not a lip, or eye, we beauty call
> But the joint force and full result of all,

need not have gone to Plato's *Phaedrus* (268 D) for the principle of organic unity in a work of art. The lines in *Eloisa to Abelard* (227-228),

> Then conscience sleeps, and leaving nature free,
> All my loose soul unbounded springs to thee,

anticipate Freud, but need not have been consciously taken from the still fuller anticipation at the beginning of the ninth book of the *Republic*. A trivial reference is:

> For Attic phrase in Plato let them seek,
> I poach in Suidas for unlicensed Greek.
>
> *Dunciad* IV 227-228

> Where beams of warm imagination play,
> The memory's soft figures melt away
>
> *Essay on Criticism* I 58-59

suggests the image of the wax tablets in the *Theaetetus* (191 C-D), but need not come from it any more than the image of a light-armed combatant in the *Dunciad* I 306.The goodness of God in the universal prayer may come from Boethius or Ausonius as well as from Plato.

> What Plato thought, and godlike Cato was,

in the prologue to Addison's *Cato* (18), could have been written by anybody, as could the reference to the "sacred rage" of poesy in *Windsor Forest*. Pope himself attributes to the language of the Platonists his Ariel's words in *The Rape of the Lock* (I 107 ff.):

> Late, as I ranged the crystal wilds of air,
> In the clear mirror of thy ruling star
> I saw, alas! some dread event impend,

and says that the "bright image" in the *Dunciad* (IV 487) was the title given by the later Platonists to that vision of nature which they had formed out of their own fancy (αὔτοπτον ἄγαλμα). His most notable characterization of Plato and Platonism is the line in the Second Epistle of the *Essay on Man* (II 23 ff.):

> Go, soar with Plato to the empyreal sphere,
> To the first Good, first Perfect and first Fair;
> Or tread the mazy round his followers trod,
> And quitting sense call imitating God.[46]

We have already twice quoted this last line, which is perhaps derived from St. Augustine's definition of ecstasy as *alienatio mentis a sensibus*.

Pope's chief significance for the history of Platonism is that all educated Americans of the eighteenth century knew the *Essay on Man* by heart, and before we seek any other literary source for their ideas we should look there.

Of other eighteenth-century poets I need speak only of Gray and Akenside, though Edward Young's *Night Thoughts* contain some Platonism. Gray was one of the most learned of English poets, as the *Marginalia* of his editions of the classics show. Among his many unfulfilled plans was an edition of Plato, full notes for which Mason found among his papers. In a letter to Walpole, November 9, 1735, he writes: "Plato improves every day; so does my friendship with him." We may, if we please, attribute the superiority of his poetry in part to this inspiration. But amid all its classical reminiscences there is nothing that distinctly suggests a text of Plato.[47]

Akenside was an assiduous reader of the classics and delighted to imitate them in the eighteenth-century manner. He greatly admired Plato but regards him rather as a poet, a theologian, and a moralist than as a thinker, and, being himself a man of science and a poet, it is his ambition

> To paint the story of the soul,
> And Plato's visions to control
> By Verulamian laws.
>
> *Ode* 16 stanza 5

He also would

> . . . entwine a wreath
> Of Plato's olive with the Mantuan bay.
>
> *The Pleasures of Imagination* I 404-405

He repeats the apostrophe and the commonplace of the Platonic theodicy with explicit quotation of Plato in his notes:

> Vain are thy thoughts, O child of mortal birth!
> And impotent thy tongue. Is thy short span
> Capacious of this universal frame?
>
> . . . .
>
> Dost thou aspire to judge between the Lord
> Of Nature and his works?
>
> *Pleasures of Imag.* II 242 ff.

He understands chaos as the unformed, undigested mass of
Moses and Plato which Milton called "the womb of Nature" (*Par. Lost* II 911). He conceives creation as so many
before and after him by the Neo-Platonic interpretation of
the *Timaeus*:

> Then lived the Almighty One; then, deep retired
> In his unfathom'd essence, view'd the forms,
> The forms eternal of created things.
>
> *Pleasures of Imag.* I 64 ff.

(Cf. Tennyson's remark,"What an imagination God has!").
And it was "by immense benignity inclined" that he passed
from contemplation to act, and brought into being

> Answering the mighty model he had chosen,
> The best and fairest of unnumber'd worlds,
> That lay from everlasting in the store
> Of his divine conceptions.
>
> *Pleasures of Imag.* II 334 ff.

He uncritically quotes in a note on this passage the forged
Timaeus Locrus for the antiquity of this opinion. The creator is δαμιουργὸς τῶ βελτίονος.[48] (Cf. Ovid's *mundi melioris
origo, Met.* I 79.) He pictures himself now tasting "the
Ionian song," now bending

> . . . to Plato's godlike tongue
> Resounding through the olive shade.
>
> *Ode* II stanza 7

He anticipates the rhetoric of the famous book of Cousin,
On the Good, the True, the Beautiful, in the lines:

> Thus was Beauty sent from heaven,
> The lovely ministress of Truth and Good
> In this dark world: for Truth and Good are one,
> And Beauty dwells in them and they in her,
> With like participation. Wherefore then,
> O sons of earth! would you dissolve the tie?
>
> *Pleasures of Imag.* I 372 ff.

On his own image

As flame ascends,

. . . .

So all things that have life aspire to God.

Ibid. II 350 ff.

He comments: "This opinion, though not held by Plato, . . . is yet a very natural consequence of his principles." He refers to the story of Atlantis (*ibid.* III 405 ff.) and is so good as to give us the name of the Egyptian priests who had taught it to Solon, "the venerable Sonchis" (*ibid.* III 393) and "that great Psenophis" (*ibid.* III 405).

As Cudworth was a Platonist largely in order to refute Hobbes, so Mandeville is anti-Platonist in his disgust with Shaftesbury's sentimental Platonic moralizing and absolutism. But Mandeville professes great admiration for Plato, quotes him frequently, and uses the example of Socrates in Plato to justify his own employment of plain, homely, undignified images, as Tucker and Emerson did later. Mandeville was the eighteenth-century Nietzsche[49] and Bernard Shaw[50] and Westermarck.[51]

His *Fable of the Bees* is a coarse but plausible summary of all that could be deduced against the sovereignty of ethics from the writings of such skeptics and cynics as Machiavelli, La Rochefoucauld, Bayle, Hobbes, and the eighteenth-century French *philosophes*, supplemented by topics from the philosophy of Spinoza, Gassendi, and Locke. It had a success of scandal and was assailed by many defenders of the faith and representatives of the philosophy of eternal and immutable morality. We need not here ask how far he was led to exaggerate his thesis to attract attention ("The true Reason," he says, "why I made use of the Title . . . was to raise Attention," *Fable of the Bees*, p. 412), or by his deep distaste for the mincing elegance of Shaftesbury's preaching of ethical idealism ("The noble Author of that System had a most charitable Opinion of his Species, and extoll'd the Dignity of it in an extraordinary manner," *ibid*. II 51; "I could swagger about Fortitude and the Contempt of Riches as much as Seneca himself, and would undertake to write twice as much in behalf of Poverty as ever he did, for the tenth Part of his Estate: I could teach the way to his 'Summum Bonum' as exactly as I know my way home," *ibid*. p. 152; "The attentive Reader, . . . will soon perceive that two Systems cannot be more opposite than his Lordship's and mine. His Notions I confess, are generous and refined:...What Pity it is that they are not true," *ibid*. I 324).

This thesis, essentially that of the Platonic Thrasymachus and Callicles, classes him with the opponents of Platonism, but he professes a great admiration for Plato and the Platonic writings. He ironically apologizes for his own homely images as Socrates does in Plato, and as Tucker did later.[52] He says that the objection to writing in dialogue is its difficulty, not any inherent defect of that method of exposition, as is proved by Plato's success.

The chief of Plato's Interlocutors was always his Master, Socrates, who everywhere maintains his Character with great Dignity; but it would have been impossible to have made such an extraordinary Person speak like himself on so many Emergencies, if Plato had not been as great a Man as Socrates (*ibid*. II 9).

He misapprehends or perhaps quotes loosely from memory when he says:

The Reason why Plato preferr'd Dialogues to any other manner of Writing, he said, was that Things thereby might look, as if they were acted, rather than told: The same was afterwards given by Cicero in the same Words rendered into his own Language (*ibid*. II 8).

(This seems to be a misunderstanding of the passage in the *Theaetetus*—143 B-C—in which Plato says that he presents the conversation in dramatic form in order to avoid the tediousness of the "said I's" and "said he's.")

His explicit references to Platonic thoughts are rare or doubtful and may be taken from secondary sources. Kaye comments (p. lxxiii), "Shaftesbury said, 'Consider the Whole and the individual will then be cared for'; Mandeville said, 'Study the individual and the Whole will then look after itself.' " Shaftesbury's principle was of course Platonic. The statement (*ibid.* I 345), "There is nothing Good in all the Universe to the best-designing Man, if either through Mistake or Ignorance he commits the least Failing in the Use of it," is an idea that recurs in more than one Platonic dialogue. But its occurrence in Mandeville may be a coincidence.

Abraham Tucker's *Light of Nature Pursued* would supply a text for the vanityof literary fame and the topic of fashion in literature. Published between 1760 and 1770, it appeared in a seventh edition in 1848 from which I quote. Yet it is not mentioned in Edmund Gosse's *English Literature* and is nothing in the lives of twentieth-century readers, though, as a matter of fact, the readers of those seven editions were perhaps more profitably engaged than are the readers today of Wells and Shaw and Dreiser. For these lectures the book would be a convenient illustration of secondary Platonism in the second half of the eighteenth century.

Tucker also exemplifies, as Berkeley and Grote and Mill do, the spell that Plato may cast over minds of a very different temperament and trend of thought. Though not a professional scholar, Tucker was well read in Cicero and the Latin poets including Lucretius, and knew Plato, as he says, from some direct reading of the dialogues and through Cudworth and other Cambridge Platonists. ("So I shall content myself with setting down such conception of the Platonic opinions as remains with me from what little reading I have had in his dialogues and Cudworth's intellectual system," *Light of Nature*, Vol. II, p. 188.) He thinks that Plato had a "clearer head than our modern philosophers" (*ibid.* II 189). His comments are sensible and sometimes surprisingly judicious, though, as writers who should know better still do, he confounds Plato with Neo-Platonism,

Accordingly Plato, observing that we must have a motive or disposition of mind to set our understanding at work, and a volition or power to make it take effect, before we can execute what we know, ascribed three similar principles to the divine nature: the first he called To Agathon or Goodness, the second Nous or Intelligence, and the third Psyche or Activity: and conceiving our knowledge of objects to be a voluntary act of the mind . . . (*ibid.* II 190),

and actually quotes him as using words that do not occur anywhere in his writings:

The Greek word for person was Hypostasis, which being used by Plato in speaking of the Deity, induced many of the ancient Christians to adopt his notions into their system, the more readily because their zeal made them desirous of showing that the Trinity was so rational a doctrine as to have been discovered by the human reason of Plato. Cudworth will not allow him the discoverer, but to have learned it from Pythagoras, and that it had probably been taught before by Orpheus: but when we reflect how apt Plato was to put things into the mouth even of his master Socrates which never were in his head, and how natural it is for each new philosopher to improve largely upon the hints afforded him by his predecessors, we cannot depend upon the hypostatic doctrine being older than Plato himself (*ibid.* II 188).

Note also (*ibid.* I 372): "And Plato, with some others, carried this notion so far as to say, that if any single event had happened otherwise than it did, the whole universe would have been damaged thereby."

He is especially attracted by the liveliness of Plato's style and his freedom in the use of homely and trivial images to illustrate his thought.

There seems to be no likelier method of answering this purpose than that of Plato, if one could be so happy as to copy him: I mean, in his art of illustrating and exemplifying abstruse notions by the most familiar instances taken from common life, though sometimes of the lowest and basest kind. We find him indeed rebuked, particularly in the Hippias, or Dialogue upon Beauty, for introducing earthen crocks and pitchers into discourses upon philosophy: and if the plainness of ancient times could not endure such vulgar images, what quarter can we expect for them in this nice and refined age? (*ibid.* I 8).

He is not greatly troubled by the transcendence of the Platonic ideas, which he is willing to translate into the necessity for abstractions and ideals that common sense must admit. In a *Dialogue of the Dead* he even represents Plato as thanking Locke for "the honour you have done my Ideas by bringing them into greater repute in the Tin Islands than ever I could do in Athens" (*ibid.* I 453). The paradox that philosophers must become kings he immediately explains and softens by saying (which is true) that Plato meant "that the world would never go well ... until both sciences of political and moral wisdom centered in the same persons" (*ibid.* I 258).

His liberal theology is, like Arnold's, essentially Platonist in that he rejects atheistic materialism but would conform to the rites of his country and not disturb popular doctrines when they were not immoral.

Worship the immortal Gods according to the rites of thy country: let this be thy general rule, nor admit thou exceptions without urgent cause. Rites are indifferent in themselves, and may be turned as well to good as bad purposes: popular doctrines are for the most part figurative, and may by proper interpretation be accommodated to sound reason (*ibid.* I 467).

And

Then if we regard the interest of Philosophy, and the interest of mankind, there is no cause to fear they should receive damage by joining Religion to co-operate with reason. The best-policied

PLATONISM ANCIENT AND MODERN

and most flourishing states have been remarkable for the attachment to the forms of belief and modes of worship established among them, and in proportion as these lost their credit, they fell into confusion and decay. This we may learn from historians, particularly Polybius, one of the most judicious and clearest from superstition among them, who attributes the then disjointed condition of the Greeks to their contempt for the sacredness of an oath: and Cicero, in his treatise upon the laws, ascribes the vigour of the Roman commonwealth to their veneration for auguries, and other public or family ceremonies received from their ancestors. If we would take examples from the Philosophers, we shall find that Pythagoras, Socrates, and others of the soundest, were no ridiculers of established doctrines or forms of worship, but strove to turn them to profitable uses, and lead men by popular opinions into such sentiments of philosophy as they were capable of receiving: and often endeavoured by Mythology to allegorize the Gods into the powers of Nature, affections of the mind, and moral virtues; of which we have given specimens in Eros and Eris, the Thalassian and Uranian Venus (*ibid*. II 337).

He has evidently read, directly or indirectly, the theodicy in the tenth book of Plato's *Laws* and uses one of its arguments almost verbatim against the Stoics.

Shall we then say with the Stoics, that God cares for great things but neglects the small? that his providence is over the human race? over empires or nations, but not over single persons? We do not say this of an earthly politician, if we believe him a righteous one (*ibid*. II 348).

His ethics are, in general, Ciceronian and Platonic in tone and sometimes in detail. He states the true doctrine of punishment almost in the words of the *Protagoras* (324 A-B).

Why this is the very thing I have been contending for all along, that the true ground of punishment is not the mischief done, or the crime committed, but the prevention of future enormities, productive of future mischiefs, and this object I think may fairly rank under the class of utility (*ibid*. I 572).

And his sober ideal of practicable happiness is that of Plato's
Laws.

Therefore the true art of pleasure lies in bringing the mind to take
it in as many things as we can, more careful to be always pleased
than highly pleased, to have many desires but no wants; for then
we shall be indifferent to all our pleasures, but tasteless to none
(*ibid*. II 554).

With all this common sense he is like Berkeley in his old age
and, with or after Henry More, willing to dally and flirt
with the fancies or superstitions of the later Platonists. To
one of them in particular he recurs with apparent serious-
ness—the doctrine of the material vehicle, or ὄχημα,[53] which
conveys the soul when it leaves the body.

Therefore, by virtue of the privilege constantly claimed in making an hypothesis, I may fairly assume, what nobody can dis-
prove, that the spirit, upon quitting her present mansion, does
not go out naked, nor entirely disengaged from matter, but car-
ries away with her an integument from among those wherewith
she was before invested (*ibid*. I 384).

Then if we consider the finer and smaller composition of a vehicu-
lar or spiritual body, bearing a nearer proportion to the sphere of
the spirit's presence than our present gross bodies, which we
move by long strings of complicated engines, wherein are many
mechanical motions interfering with our voluntary, and not to be
corrected by them without much labour and practice; it will appear probable they are much more manageable, and that the force
of example with our endeavours to apply it, may operate more
strongly to work new habits; especially if there should be such a
sentient language as suggested in the Vision, whereby the very
ideas passing in our Pattern might be conveyed more exactly and
fully than can be done here through any of our senses (*ibid*. II
219-220).

He says, however:

It was lucky I happened to escape the notion of pre-existence; for
though I have shown upon several occasions how that whimsy
may be turned to excellent advantages, yet it might have set

some fanciful people a-dreaming, that they conversed with the unborn in their sleep, or had scenes renewed of occurrences passing with them in a former state, or perhaps they might have given in to the only foible remaining upon the record of Socrates, who imagined that when a man, after poring over a mathematical demonstration, happens at once to discern the force of it, this was a reminiscence or recollection of a truth familiarly known to him a hundred years before (*ibid*. II 683).

Burke's classicism was, of course, mostly Latin, derived from Cicero and the Latin poets. But he read Greek and presents a few explicit references to Plato as well as some coincidences in thought and expression due to the fact that both were poets and political thinkers and conservative moralists in ages of "enlightenment." The title page of his speech *On the Nabob of Arcot's Debts*[54] quotes in the Greek a passage from the seventeenth epistle of the Emperor Julian in which the philosophical emperor asks how a disciple of Plato and Aristotle should deal with corruption in high places. A sentiment of the *Letter to the Sheriffs of Bristol* expresses an idea of the *Republic* (409 C) which may have occurred to Burke independently: "They who raise suspicions on the good on account of the behavior of ill men, are of the party of the latter" (*The Works of Edmund Burke* II 38). Platonic in principle also is the remark in the *Speech at Bristol*, "I could hardly serve you as I have done, and court you too" (*ibid*. II 132). In the *Reflections on the Revolution* the statement that "equality in geometry is the most unequal of all measures in the distribution of men" (*ibid*. II 444) expresses a Platonic[55] thought unplatonically. Plato opposes geometrical (proportion) to arithmetical equality. But Burke here uses geometrical for mathematical. The distinction in the *Thoughts and Details on Scarcity*: "Philosophical happiness is, to want little. Civil or vulgar happiness is, to want much and, to enjoy much" (*ibid*. V 85), exactly expresses the opposition of Socrates and Callicles in

the *Gorgias* (492 A). In a letter to a member of the National
Assembly the description of the fear of God as the "only
sort of fear which generates true courage" (*ibid*. II 542)
is Platonic in substance if not precisely in terms. The admonition "that he should approach to the faults of the state
as to the wounds of a father, with pious awe and trembling
solicitude" (*ibid*. II 368) recalls a favorite idea of Plato implied in the *Euthyphro* (4 B-C) and distinctly stated by
Socrates in the *Crito* (50 E ff.). *The Vindication of Natural
Society* contains an explicit reminiscence of the *Republic*
(557 D): "A republic, as an ancient philosopher has observed, is no one species of government, but a magazine of
every species" (*The Works of Edmund Burke* I 30).

The Platonist's conception of liberal religion which we
have met frequently and shall meet again in Arnold and
Schleiermacher, appears in the *Reflections on the Revolution
in France* (*ibid*. II 429-430):

Superstition is the religion of feeble minds; and they must be
tolerated in an intermixture of it, in some trifling or some enthusiastic shape or other, else you will deprive weak minds of a
resource found necessary to the strongest.

The real meaning of Plato's number,[56] as distinguished from
the mere mathematical puzzle, is aptly illustrated by a sentence from the *Letters on a Regicide Peace* (*ibid*. V 153), "I
doubt whether the history of mankind is yet complete enough,
if it ever can be so, to furnish grounds for a sure theory on
the internal causes which necessarily affect the fortune of a
state." A psychological observation of the *Gorgias* seems to
be repeated in the *Essay on the Sublime and Beautiful* (*ibid*.
I 52): "For if there were not some principle of judgment as
well as of sentiment common to all mankind, no hold could
possibly be taken either on their reason or their passions,
sufficient to maintain the ordinary correspondence of life."
The statement, "Plans must be made for men" (*Letter to a*

Member of the National Assembly, ibid. II 549), repeats, whether consciously or not, one of the most famous sentences of the *Laws* (853 C). Quite in the spirit of both the *Laws* and the *Republic* is the declaration in a letter to a noble (*ibid.* V 122): "I have ever abhorred, . . . all the operations of opinion, fancy, inclination and will, in the affairs of government, where only a sovereign reason, paramount to all forms of legislation and administration, should dictate." The quaint sentence (*Sublime and Beautiful, ibid.* I 160), "Beauty acts by relaxing the solids of the whole system," is equally pertinent as an illustration of the jargon of modern physiological psychology and of a dithyrambic sentence of the *Phaedrus* (251 C-E).

Other psychological parallels, perhaps accidental, are Burke's affirmation of a state of indifference between pleasure and pain (*Sublime and Beautiful, ibid.* I 69) and the suggestion that pain is the sign of an unnatural process or condition (*ibid.* I 145). The idea summed up in Shakespeare's

> And by my body's action teach my mind
> A most inherent baseness
>
> *Coriolanus* III. 2. 122-123

is elaborated in the *Republic* (395 C-D), and developed by Burke (*Sublime and Beautiful, ibid.* I 55-56). Interesting is the observation (*Sublime and Beautiful, ibid.* I 99): "Before the Christian religion had, as it were, humanized the idea of Divinity, . . . there was very little said of the love of God. The followers of Plato have something of it, and only something." Other sentences, whether taken from Plato or not, aptly illustrate some of his utterances. "Bodies which are rough and angular rouse and vellicate the organ of feeling" (*Sublime and Beautiful, ibid.* I 161) is somewhat nearer to the account of sensation in Plato's *Timaeus* than it is to the atomism of Lucretius, with which Burke was doubtless more familiar. Many misapprehensions of the meaning of imitation in Plato and Aristotle would be done away with by a passage in the *Sublime and Beautiful* (*ibid.* I. 177):

Hence we may observe that poetry, taken in its most general sense, cannot with strict propriety be called an art of imitation. It is indeed an imitation so far as it describes the manners and passions of men which their words can express; where *animi motus effert interprete lingua.*

Many of Burke's conservative warnings that it is not safe "to encourage every individual to let the imagination loose upon all subjects"[57] could be used to illustrate the warning in the *Republic* against premature and unsettling dialectics (*Rep.* 537 D-E ff.). Burke's complete success in imitating the style of Bolingbroke in his *Vindication of Natural Society* may be used to confirm the argument that the speeches of Lysias in the *Phaedrus* and of Protagoras in the dialogue that bears his name could have been composed by Plato.

Romanticism, the reawakening of wonder, predisposed the poetic mind to sympathy with the revival of Platonism in scholarship and criticism. And this thought might serve as a transition to Coleridge, Shelley, and Wordsworth. Or we might find a transition in the sources of Emerson's knowledge or inspiration—in the Germans, in Victor Cousin, in Degérando's history of philosophy,[58] in old Thomas Taylor, in the mysticisms and symbolisms of Swedenborg and Blake, and, qualifying them all, in the sober sense of Sir James Mackintosh's *Dissertation on the Progress of Ethical Philosophy*, which was the best textbook of the subject Harvard ever had, and which left its impress deep on the mind of Emerson and Margaret Fuller and a whole generation of Harvard students. But we have no time for transitions, and must turn at once to Coleridge and Shelley and Wordsworth.

Through Mill's essay on Coleridge, Coleridge has come to be regarded as the founder or representative of English nineteenth-century conservative historical and religious philosophy. It is a curious sign of the times that the latest edition of the *Encyclopaedia Britannica* (14th) makes no allusion to this essay of Mill which the 9th edition dwells upon. Mill's statement of Coleridge's philosophy is perhaps colored by Mill's own Platonism. Mill says that Coleridge's method is to study any institution not as an irrational survival, but in the light of its idea, that is, its intended purpose and historical function—the good it was meant to accomplish. This, though Mill is not distinctly aware of it, is the application to historical criticism of Plato's much misapprehended doctrine of the Idea of Good.

Coleridge himself says: "I have read most of the works of Plato several times with profound attention, but not all his writings. In fact, I soon found that I had read Plato by anticipation. He was a consummate genius" (*Table Talk*, April 30, 1830). We are thus forewarned of the character of Coleridge's exegesis. "After I had gotten my principles," he says, "I pretty generally left the facts to take care of themselves" (*Table Talk*, July 13, 1832). He often took both facts and principles from Schelling and mixed them in his notebooks. Like some brilliant modern professional scholars who have less excuse, he is capable of quoting as from the Platonic text tags of Neo-Platonism. In *Aids to Reflexion* (*Aphorism*, XXXI, note) he actually attributes to Plato the word θεοπαράδοτος σοφία, wisdom delivered from God. We expect from Coleridge, then, only suggestions, points of view, illuminating sentences, and *aperçus*. Mixed with the truth is much mischievous and persistent error. "Plato's works," Coleridge says, "are preparatory exercises for the mind" (*Table Talk*, April 30, 1830). And he continues: "He leads you to see, that propositions involving in themselves a contradiction in terms, are nevertheless true; and which, therefore, must belong to a higher logic—that of ideas in the Aristotelian logic, which is the instrument of the understanding." This Coleridgian poison has been widely diffused by Jowett, who attributes to Plato a Hegelian logic of the future—which is the polar antithesis of the true Platonic dialectic.

"Lucidity is the good faith of philosophers," said a wise Frenchman. The higher logic is to philosophy what the higher law is to a criminal court—an evasion of responsibility. Coleridge probably took it from Schelling together with the distinctions between ideas and concepts, the reason and the understanding. The first condition of understanding Plato's *philosophy* at all is to perceive that he does not distinguish concepts and ideas, but is ready at any time to make an *idea* of any *concept*.And neither the Kantian distinction between the understanding and the reason nor any of its fifty-seven post-Kantian varieties can be adapted for any useful purpose to any of Plato's psychological classification and terminology. It is at the best a convenient literary but utterly confusing device for translating νοῦς and διάνοια. The moral of contradiction in Plato is: Define your terms more carefully; not,Take an appeal to the higher logic. Another aspect of Coleridge's Platonism is that despite his nominal orthodoxy and his recantation of Unitarianism he prepares the way for Matthew Arnold and nineteenth-century latitudinarianism by allegorizing dogma. Carlyle speaks of Coleridge's device for believing with the reason what was incredible to the understanding, and talks of certain clergymen who saved themselves into a Colerridgian shovel-hattedness, but Mill points out that the rising generation of Tories and High-churchmen were likely to find him vastly too liberal.

Shelley illustrates again that compatibility of Platonic enthusiasm with an essentially Lucretian or eighteenth-century philosophy which we meet in Giordano Bruno, in Berkeley, and in John Stuart Mill. In his quality of poet Shelley is a Platonist who realized abstractions. We call this Platonic—we might call it Aeschylean or Aristophanic; it is

Greek—perhaps Aryan, whatever that may mean. Specifically Platonic is Shelley's renewal of the poetic philosophy
of Platonic idealism whose catchwords are Form, Soul,
Beauty, and Platonic Love. Unlike many Platonists he was
a student of the text of Plato. Like Giordano Bruno he felt
no incompatibility between the *De rerum natura* of Lucretius and the *Timaeus*. Like Sidney and other Platonists of
the Renaissance he could love Plato and Homer too. In fact,
he hardly deigns to go out of his way as Sidney does to use
the passionate Plato of the *Symposium* and the *Phaedrus*
against the puritanic Plato of the *Republic* and the *Laws*.
He scorns the whole difficulty. He often translates, paraphrases, or alludes to Plato's very words.

Almost too familiar for quotation by anybody but the
present shameless lecturer is his version of Plato's lovely
Greek epigram:

> Thou wert the Morning Star among the living
>   Ere thy fair light had fled.
> Now having died, thou art as Hesperus giving
>   New splendour to the dead.

(The Greek original of this epigram written by the spirits on
a closed slate was once brought to me after a lecture by a
lady who thought herself a Platonist.) There are frequent
allusions in Shelley's poem to this and the great passages of
the *Ion* and *Symposium* which he translated—and to the
form of idealism to which we shall recur, which makes an
unsubstantial pageant of all the solid globe and all that it
inherits. This last idea is combined with Platonic love and
the conception of art as no copy but the direct embodiment
of the idea—in the obscure lines of the *Prometheus* III 3
49 ff.:

> And lovely apparitions, dim at first,
> Then radiant, as the mind, arising bright
> From the embrace of beauty (whence the Forms

> Of which these are the phantoms), casts on them
> The gathered rays which are reality,
> Shall visit us, the progeny immortal
> Of Painting, Sculpture and Rapt Poesy.

The Platonism here is better than the syntax.

Exquisite is the well-known verbatim quotation of the *Symposium* in a stanza of *The Sensitive Plant* (I 75 ff.)— which is Platonic throughout:

> For the Sensitive Plant has no bright flower;
> Radiance and odour are not its dower;
> It loves, even like Love, its deep heart is full,
> It desires what it hath not, the Beautiful.

To compare and contrast the *Hymn of Intellectual Beauty* with Spenser's *Hymne* would take us too far.

I will conclude with an admonition which will discredit me with uncompromising Shelleyans. The Platonic love of *Alastor* and *Epipsychidion* is not the genuine gospel—even of the Renaissance. "The might of *one* fair face sublimes my love," says Michelangelo. But Shelley was not content with one. And what he describes in *Alastor* and *Epipsychidion* as the quest of the ideal is merely an etherealized Don Juan-like pursuit of the successive incarnations in which a very earthly susceptibility led him to imagine that he saw the embodiment of the ideal. I have sometimes imagined that it was his Puritanic distaste for this bastard Shelleyan form of Platonic love that closed Matthew Arnold's mind to this aspect of Platonism. Though a close student and frequent quoter of Plato, Arnold rarely alludes to the *Symposium* or the *Phaedrus*.

Wordsworth was not, like Shelley and Coleridge, a student of Plato's text, or indeed a student of any books. Professor Stewart's essay on *Platonism in English Poetry*[59] sees in the *Prelude* the classic authority on Platonism in poetry (p. 35). But that is because Professor Stewart has intentionally adopted a definition of personal Platonism which owes no account of itself to history or fact. I find in the *Prelude* Pope's and Wordsworth's own pantheistic nature worship and exaltation of childhood—but little Platonism except a few allusions to Coleridgean Platonism and the vague ecstasies and spiritualisms which we may call Platonism if we will. But yet there is one Platonic thought—and it is precisely the one which Professor Stewart neglects to mention,—the formative power of beautiful surroundings in youth, ultimately derived from the great sentence in the *Republic* almost too often quoted to quote again:

Not only in painting and sculpture, but in all the arts and crafts, in weaving, embroidering, and every kind of manufacture—in all these there is grace or the absence of grace—and grace and harmony are the twin sisters of goodness and virtue, and bear their likeness. Let our artists be those who are gifted to discern the true nature of beauty and of grace. Then will our youth dwell in a land of health and fair sights and sounds, and receive the good in everything. And beauty, the effluence of fair works, shall flow into the eye and ear like a health-giving breeze from a purer region, and insensibly draw the soul from earliest years into likeness and sympathy with the beauty of reason.[60]

The *Ode on Intimations of Immortality* deals with the obviously Platonic themes of preëxistence and reminiscence. But its dominant emphasis on childhood is un-Platonic and un-Greek. The ancients had little romantic sentiment about infancy. Youth was for them a promise, not a fulfillment. No child can be really happy, says Aristotle's *Ethics* in effect. And if we speak of children as happy they are called so because of our hopes (*Ethics* 1100 A 2-4). Plato, it is true, speaks of the apprehension of the ideas as the recovery by reminiscence of the beatific prenatal vision. But we win to the recovered vision only through years of laborious thought, and it is the eye of maturity or old age that sees them best. In Plato, Heaven does not lie about us in our infancy.

Every soul, he says, is drunk and crazed when first plunged into the vortex of a body subject to perpetual influx and efflux. And it is only as the tumult and turmoil of undisciplined sense abates that it quiets down to sobriety and clear consciousness, so that the purged eye of the mind can discern and hold fast to the eternal values.

There is more of the true spirit of Plato in one line of *Laodamia* (74-75) than in the entire ode:

> for the Gods approve
> The depth, and not the tumult, of the soul.

The Wordsworthian sentimentality, however, is found in the late Neo-Platonist Olympiodorus, from whom Mrs. Browning took the suggestion of

> those murmurs of the outer infinite
> That unweaned babies smile at in their sleep.

Better than either Mrs. Browning or Wordsworth is Vaughan's anticipation:

> Happy those days, when I
> Shin'd in my angel-infancy!
> Before I understood this place
> Appointed for my second race,
> Or taught my soul to fancy ought
> But a white, celestial thought
> When yet I had not walk'd above
> A mile or two from my first love,
> And looking back—at that short space—
> Could see a glimpse of His bright face. [61]

Arnold's influence is, in fact, still growing—though the Germans have never understood a word of him, and the "young lions" of the press after first learning to quote him as they used to quote Macaulay have already begun to patronize him as a superseded Victorian. Like Shelley, Arnold really knew his Plato in the text. His Platonism has obvious limits. Platonic love and the mystic Plato, as we have seen, are repugnant to him. And he affects perhaps rather than really feels a distaste for the logical and metaphysical Plato—for what he with singular infelicity stigmatizes as "the barren logomachies of the *Theaetetus*"—the greatest or at any rate the most original psychological treatise in the world.

Arnold's Plato is the literary artist—the conservative satirist preaching Spartan discipline to the lax democracy of Athens, or German thoroughness to the muddling middle-class Englishmen—the conservative religious reformer who seeks to save the spirit by throwing overboard the dogma. To this Plato he pays the tribute not only of frequent quotation but also of constant unavowed imitation. Two of the *Discourses in America* are preachments from Platonic texts and all three quote Plato repeatedly. *Culture and Anarchy* with its dozen or more allusions to Plato is in its serious argument a development and application of Plato's warning against mistaking the machinery of government for its true end and aim, and confounding the things *of* the self with the real self. In its literary art it is an ingenious transposition and adaptation to the England of the 'sixties of Plato's satire on the excesses of the spirit of democratic liberty at Athens. Platonic is Arnold's trick of classifying by nicknames—Barbarians—Philistines—Populace,—and the witty satire on doing as one likes is one of many modern imitations of the inimitable passages of the eighth book of the *Republic*[62] on the same theme. Plato says that the very slaves and dogs and asses on the streets of Athens are so chockful of democratic liberty that they butt into you as you walk along. Arnold puts it thus: The English rough "is just asserting his personal liberty a little, going where he likes—bawling as he likes, hustling as he likes . . . and if he is stopped from making Hyde Park a bear-garden or the streets impassable he says he is being butchered by the aristocracy."[63] The peculiar serenity of the aristocracy, says

Arnold, is due not to their having made order among their ideas—but to "their never having had any ideas to trouble them."[64] This is an attempt to render Plato's delicious coinage and compound ὑποαμουσότερον (*Rep.* 548 E) applied to the Spartanizing aristocracy of the timocratic state—a little below par in *mousike*—and a little above par in *gymnastike*.

We glanced at the large topic of Arnold's Platonizing liberal theology in an earlier chapter. It differs from the theodicy of Plato's *Laws* there discussed in being a solely ethical religion and caring nothing for natural theology, which Arnold disdainfully abandons to Martineau and the Unitarians. But even there we saw that when confronted with a Clifford, Arnold instinctively turns about and adopts a Platonic attitude.

I could easily substantiate my statement which called forth indignant protest a few years ago that Mill is perhaps the greatest of nineteenth-century Platonists. His three essays on religion are in some respects more Platonic than Matthew Arnold. The volume on representative government is in its different way almost as Platonic in thought and specific allusion as Ruskin's *Munera Pulveris* or *Fors*. The essay on *The Subjection of Women* adopts Plato's argument[65] that you might as well exclude all red-headed men from politics as all women.

The *Utilitarianism* differs from the pure Benthamite gospel of the word mainly by qualifying concessions due to the study of Plato and Coleridge, and it finds the ultimate ethical sanction in the direct adoption of the argument of the *Republic* (582 A ff.) that the *virtuous philosopher* has experienced both the higher and the lower pleasures while the hedonist knows only the lower. The more than mere analogies between the *Examination of the Philosophy of Sir William Hamilton* and the *Theaetetus* would take us into the forbidden domain of metaphysics. Mill's father made him read the *Theaetetus* at the age of eight. But my seminar smiled a sickly smile when I quoted to them Mill's later modest admission that he did not think he understood quite all of it then. In addition to these precocious studies Mill reread the entire Greek text of Plato in preparation for his review of Grote. And Mill's affirmation that he had read a book means more than a similar statement from Coleridge or Landor. The review itself remains to this day the best available general introduction to the study of Plato.

If Mill's spirit and temper appear to the casual reader the reverse of Platonic, it is because, in Coleridge's phrase, we habitually confound Platonist with Plotinist, and also because we think only of Plato the poet, the artist, the preacher, and not of Plato the dialectician and social reformer. But as John Morley, a disciple of Mill and also a student of Plato, says, "Not every one who cries Plato Plato is admitted to that intellectual kingdom." So far from being anti-Platonic in temper, Mill is a typical Platonist in his combination of severe logic with a passion for reforming the world. That he did not add to these qualities the unction of the mystic Plato and the genius of Plato the poet and artist, is no abatement of his claim to the title of Platonist. That was a synthesis unique in the history of the human mind.

I have quoted Emerson throughout these lectures. An exhaustive study of Emerson's Platonism would be a commentary on his writings. He was not a critical scholar, and was capable of gorgeous howlers when he mixed his notes or his memory failed him. But if we are forewarned, that does not greatly matter. He interprets Plato not systematically, but in single illuminating sentences, which, as so often happens with Emerson, if I may mix the metaphor, hit the nail exactly on the head. John Morley says that "there are pages [sc. in Emerson] that to the present writer, at least, ... remain mere abracadabra." "For much of this in Emerson," he adds, "the influence of Plato is mainly responsible, and it may be noted in passing that his account of Plato (*Rep. Men*) is one of his most unsatisfactory performances."[66] This is a complete misunderstanding. There are some obscure sentences in Emerson, but no obscure pages; only loose or abrupt transitions, much hyperbolical rhetoric, and some colossal blunders. With fair allowance for these Emersonianisms, the essay on Plato is one of Emerson's most satisfactory performances. It contains more essential truth about Plato than any equal number of pages known to me in the literature of either scholarship or criticism. Uncritically read, however, it is, like much of Emerson, pure poison to rhapsodical or confused minds. It needs a corrective and a stabilizer.

The same may be said of two other books on Plato, which, with this restriction, I would cordially recommend: Emile Faguet's *Pour qu'on lise Platon*, which is especially good for Plato's relation to the politics and social life of his time; and Walter Pater's *Plato and Platonism*, which is the best account I know of certain aspects of Plato's literary style and artistic genius. The stabilizer that these three books need exists. It is, as I have said, John Stuart Mill's elaborate review of Grote's *Plato*. The reader who will take that as his guide will not be harmed by Emerson, Pater, Faguet, and the many eloquent and random observations on Plato diffused through Ruskin's writings.

We have from time to time glanced at the chief causes of distaste for Plato. He is supposed to be undemocratic, aristocratic, bookish, antiscientific, scholastic. Some regard him with suspicion as the covert ally of mysticism and superstition. To many wholesome natures the entire rhetoric of poetical idealism and Platonic love is repugnant. Others are simply tired of hearing Aristides called the Just. They are sickened by the perpetual laudation of the divine Plato with whom Cicero had rather err than be right with plebeian Epicureans.

I have omitted many illustrations of this feeling from Lucian to *Hudibras*, who writes of a contemporary Platonist,

> Th' intelligible world he knew,
> And all men dream on 't to be true,
> That in this world there's not a wart
> That has not there a counterpart.

II. 3. 225 ff.

In the nineteenth century, I suspect that the exaggerations of old Thomas Taylor and the unintelligible Neo-Platonic disquisitions of Coleridge were the chief cause of the boredom or reaction of such typical British minds as Bentham, Hallam, De Quincey, and Macaulay. We discussed Landor's anti-Platonism in connection with Epicurus and again in speaking of the defense of poetry. De Quincey confessed to a sneaking dislike for the whole Platonic crowd; and his account of the *Republic* is the most vulgar of parodies. It is written in the temper of the most vituperative of the Christian Fathers but without their excuse.

Macaulay praises Plato's wit and says that he often bursts out laughing over his old copy of Ficino. He defines a scholar as one who reads Plato with his feet on the fender. He describes eloquently how Lady Jane Grey, while the Court was at the chase, and the hounds in full cry, sat with head bowed over the immortal page (of Plato's *Phaedo*) that tells how sweetly and bravely the first great martyr of intellectual liberty met his end. But he holds the French view of Plato's reasoning powers, and says with characteristic sledgehammer emphasis that the author of the *Soirées de Saint-Pétersbourg* would be ashamed of some of the metaphysical arguments of Plato. His essay on Bacon, which competes with Herbert Spencer's *Education* for the honor of having propagated more error than any other writing of the nineteenth century, has familiarized a million readers with a sophistical contrast between the Platonic and the Baconian method.

I must pass over, as I did the history of technical scholarship in France and Germany, Platonic scholarship in England from Sir William Hamilton and Whewell to Grote, and from Jowett and Campbell to Taylor and Burnet. And I can only remind you by name of a few other writers whose relation to Plato would find place in a fuller treatment: Gilfillan, a forgotten mid-Victorian critic, who protested against Macaulay's *Essay on Bacon* at the time of its appearance; Ruskin, whose sometimes perverse but always eloquent and interesting references to Plato can be found in the great index to the magnificent new forty-volume edition,[67] and whose significance for the history of Platonism lies chiefly in the fact that he has been the transmitter not of Platonic scholarship, but of unrecognized Platonic influence to important schools of modern thought, especially with respect to the relation of art and literature to morals, the relation of ethics to politics and social reform, and the theory of political economy in relation to ethics and psychology; Martineau, whom I might have added to the list of English books on Plato that dispense an English reader from bothering with German; Huxley, who admires and quotes the *Republic*; Chesterton, a paragraph of whose *Heretics*[68] I have repeatedly quoted as the best, if unintended, interpretation of Plato's Idea of Good; H. G. Wells, who says that he was freed from Herbert Spencer by Plato's influence, and whose novel *The Invisible Man* took its motive from a passage of the *Republic*;[69] Bernard Shaw, whose dictum that we must reform society before we need try to reform ourselves is the diametrical opposite of the Platonic principle that you have no business to try to reform society until you first have reformed yourself; and the poet Lionel Johnson, a stanza or two of whose *Plato in London* will be a relief from all this prose, and a return to our main concluding theme, Platonic idealism. [See overleaf for the stanzas here referred to.]

Lean from the window to the air:
Hear London's voice upon the night!
Thou hast held converse with things rare:
Look now upon another sight!
The calm stars, in their living skies:
    And then, these surging cries,
    This restless glare!

. . . .

That starry music, starry fire,
High above all our noise and glare:
The image of our long desire,
The beauty, and the strength are there.
And Plato's thought lives, true and clear,
    In as august a sphere:
    Perchance, far higher.[70]

NOTES

[1] Cf. e.g. J. Lofberg, "The Date of the Athenian 'ephebeia,'" *Class. Phil.* 20 (1925) 330-335 (esp. 332); Alice Brunot, *Recherches sur l'éphébie attique et en particulier sur la date de l'institution*, Paris 1920, pp. 28, 41; Wilamowitz, *Aristoteles und Athen* Vol. I p. 194.

[2] On this topic cf. Ueberweg-Praechter, *Die Philosophie des Altertums* p. 207; Zeller, *Philos. d. Gr.* II I[4] p. 551 n. 2; Budé, *Republic*, Intro. pp. xlix-lii; Adam, *Republic* I pp. 345-355.

[3] Cf. Meineke's index *s.v.* Πλάτων; Diog. Laert. 3, 26 ff.; Athen. 59 C ff., 509 C, 215 C ff., 504 E ff.; H. Alline, *Histoire du texte de Platon*, Paris 1915, p. 7.

[4] Cf. *What Plato Said* pp. 14 ff., 31 ff.

[5] R. Fenk, *Adversarii Platonis quomodo de indole ac moribus eius iudicaverint*, Jena 1913; E. L. Theiss, *Hostility to Plato in Antiquity*, Chicago 1916 (typed). Cf. further Zeller II I[4] pp. 427 ff.; Christ-Schmid, *Gesch. d. gr. Lit.* I[6] p. 664 n. 7.

[6] Cf. *What Plato Said* p. 52 and his *Plato and Lucian*, Boston and New York 1931, pp. 166-167.

[7] Cf. *What Plato Said* pp. 35-37, 450; Ueberweg-Praechter pp. 200, 78*; Zeller II I[4] p. 428 n. 1; Christ-Schmid, *op. cit.* pp. 512-516.

[8] A. Boeckh, *De simultate quae Platoni cum Xen. intercessisse fertur*, Berlin 1811 (= *Kleine Schriften* IV pp. 1 ff.).

[9] G. F. Rettig, "Ueber die λύγξ des Aristophanes in Platons Symposion 185 C ff.," *Progr. Acad. Bern* 1869.

[10] *Phaedrus* 264 D. Cf. *What Plato Said* p. 554.

[11] For the relations between Plato and Isocrates cf. Blass, *Attische Beredsamkeit* II[2] pp. 28-41; Christ-Schmid, *op. cit.* p. 566 n. 4; Ritter, *Platon* I pp. 129 ff.; G. Mathieu, *Les Idées politiques d'Isocrate*, Paris 1925, pp. 177-181; Ueberweg-Praechter pp. 204 ff., 252-253, 66-67*, 91*; *What Plato Said* pp. 32-35, 450.

[12] Cf. *What Plato Said* pp. 167-168, 522, and *Class. Phil.* 17 (1922) 261-262.

[13] Cf. Zeller II I[4] pp. 413-414; E. Meyer, *Gesch. d. Alt.* V[3] (1921) pp. 500 ff.; *What Plato Said* pp. 42 ff.

[14] Cf. Diog. Laert. 3. 46-47, 4. 2; Mekler, *Academ. philos. Index Hercul.* pp. 33 ff.; Croenert, *Kolotes und Menedemos* p. 183; Zeller II I[4] pp. 420 ff.; *What Plato Said* p. 449.

[15] On Aristotle's relation to Plato and his criticism of his teacher's philosophy cf. J. Stenzel, *Zahl und Gestalt bei Plato und Aristoteles*, Leipzig-Berlin 1924; W. Jaeger, *Aristoteles, passim*; Ueberweg-Praechter p. 286 n. 1 and pp. 360 ff., 380 f., 114*, 91*.

[16] *Eth. Nic.* 1096 a 16, in Roger Bacon, *Opus maj.* I cap. VII (ed. Bridges Vol. I p. 16), we read: *amicus est Socrates, magister meus, sed magis est amica veritas.* This is derived from Ammonius' *Aristotelis vita*, ed. Westermann, p. 399: φίλος μὲν Σωκράτης ἀλλὰ φιλτέρα ἡ ἀλήθεια. In Don Quixote Part II ch. 51 we have the form in which the proverb is usually quoted: *amicus Plato, sed magis amica veritas.*

[17] *Met.* 991 a 21-22; Cf. *Anal. post.* 83 a 33: τερετίσματα.

[18] *Frg.* 673 Rose. Cf. W. Jaeger, *Class. Quart.* 21 (1927) 13-17.

[19] Coleridge, *Table Talk*, July 2, 1830.

[20] G. Murray, *The Stoic Philosophy*, New York and London 1915, p. 14.

[21] Cf. in general the following works on the Stoics: P. Barth, *Die Stoa*[4], Stuttgart 1922; E. Bevan, *Stoics and Sceptics*, Oxford 1913; St. George Stock, *Stoicism*, London 1908; E. V. Arnold, *Roman Stoicism*, Cambridge 1911; R. M. Wenley, *Stoicism and Its Influence*, New York 1927; Zeller, *Philos. d. Gr.* III I[4] pp. 27 ff., 572 ff., 706 ff., III 2[4] pp. 254 ff., *Grundriss* (1928) pp. 255 ff.; Ueberweg-Praechter pp. 125-126*.—On the Skeptics: R. Richter, *Der Skeptizismus in der Philosophie*, I, Leipzig 1904; A. Goedeckemeyer, *Die Geschichte des gr. Skeptizismus*, Leipzig 1905; Zeller III I[4] pp. 494 ff., *Grundriss* pp. 296 ff.; Ueberweg-Praechter pp. 140-141*.—On the New Academy: V. Brochard, *Les Sceptiques grecs*, II: *La Nou-*

velle Académie, Paris 1887; L. Credano, *Lo scetticismo degli accademici*, 2 vols.,
Milano 1889-1893; Zeller III 1⁴ pp. 507-546, 609-632, 671-699; Ueberweg-Praechter pp. 141* ff.—On the Epicureans: R. D. Hicks, *Stoic and Epicurean*, New
York 1910; Zeller III 1⁴ pp. 373 ff., *Grundriss* pp. 281 ff.; Ueberweg-Praechter p.
133*.
   [22] Cf. Malalas, ed. Bonn, pp. 449, 451; C. Wachsmuth, *Die Stadt Athen im
Alterthum*, Leipzig 1874, I p. 721; Krumbacher, *Gesch. d. byz. Lit.*² pp. 6, 940;
Gibbon, ed. by Bury, *Decline and Fall of the Roman Empire* IV (1901) pp. 261 ff.
   [23] Cf. C. Jourdain, *Sextus Empiricus et la philosophie scolastique*, Paris 1858
(=*Excursions historiques et philosophiques à travers le moyen âge*, Paris 1888, pp.
199-217).
   [24] G. Murray, *op. cit.* p. 23.
   [25] Cf. P. Friedlaender, *Platon* I p. 69; W. Jaeger, *Platons Stellung im Aufbau der
gr. Bildung* p. 20; Christ-Schmid, *op. cit.* p. 670 n. 5.
   [26] *Phaedrus* 229 C-230 A. Cf. *What Plato Said* pp. 198-199, 550.
   [27] Cf. Loeb *Rep.* I pp. x-xi, 316, 438-439; *What Plato Said* pp. 16, 56, 497;
Unity p. 68.
   [28] Cic. *De rep.* III 6. 9 ff.; Lactant. *Inst. div.* V 14 ff.; Plut. *Cato maj.* 22. 1 ff.;
Gell. VI 14. 8 ff.; Quint. XII 1. 35; Zeller, *Philos. d. Gr.* IV³ p. 525 n. 1.
   [29] Cf. *Am. Jour. Philos.* IX pp. 281, 399; *What Plato Said* p. 515 on *Meno* 86 B;
Loeb *Rep.* I 309, II 220.
   [30] *The Essays of Montaigne*, trans. by George B. Ives, Cambridge 1925.
   [31] *Essays*, Book I ch. xii (ed. Hazlitt, London 1902, Vol. II p. 357).
   [32] *Harvard Studies* 12 (1901) 201-210.
   [33] *The Principles of Ethics*, New York 1893, Vol. I p. 517.
   [34] On the Academy as a school cf. Ueberweg-Praechter pp. 184-185, 67*; Zeller
II 1⁴ pp. 416 ff., III 1³ pp. 491 ff., 588 ff., 802; Natorp in Pauly-Wissowa I 1134-
1137; *What Plato Said* pp. 28 ff., 449.
   [35] Cf. my paper on "Platonism and the History of Science," *Proc. Am. Philos.
Soc.* LXVI (1927) 159-182.
   [36] *Literary Studies and Reviews*, London 1924, pp. 65-76.
   [37] *Imaginary Conversations*, ed. by Charles G. Crump, London 1891, Vol. I p. 195.
   [38] *Plato and Platonism*, London 1910, p. 50.—Cf. in general Stobaeus *Ecl.* I 1.
12; von Arnim, *Stoic. vet. fragm.* I pp. 121-123; Nicola Festa, *I frammenti dei Stoici
antichi*, Vol. II (Bari 1935) pp. 78 ff.; J. U. Powell, *Collectanea Alexandrina*, Oxford 1925, pp. 227 ff.; James Adam, *The Vitality of Platonism*, London 1911, pp.
108-189; Wilamowitz, *Reden und Vortraege* (1926) Vol. I pp. 306 ff.
   [39] Cf. Cicero *Acad. pr.* II 45. 136; Gilfillan, *A Gallery of Literary Portraits*
(Everyman's Library) p. 131 (said of Seneca).
   [40] Cf. my paper "The Origin of the Syllogism," *Class. Phil.* 19 (1924) 1-19, 28
(1933) 199-204.
   [41] *The Works of Edgar Allan Poe*, ed. by E. C. Stedman and G. G. Woodberry,
New York 1914, Vol. IX pp. 166-167.
   [42] *Op. cit.* pp. 38, 36, 39.
   [43] *Op. cit.* pp. 51-52.
   [44] Thomas Henry Billings, *The Platonism of Philo Judaeus*, Chicago 1919.
   [45] W. Dilthey, *Weltanschauung und Analyse des Menschen seit Renaissance und
Reformation*, Vol. II of: *Ges. Schriften*, Leipzig-Berlin 1921.
   [46] Dilthey, *op. cit.* pp. 443 ff.
   [47] *Tusc. Disp.* I 17 (39).
   [48] Cf. A. Engelbrecht, *Wien. St.* 34 (1912) 216-226, and the additional literature in Ueberweg-Praechter p. 147*.
   [49] For Cicero's acquaintance with the Platonic writings cf. F. Gloël, *Ueber
Ciceros Studium des Platon*, Magdeburg 1876, Progr.; F. Saltzmann, *Ueber Ciceros
Kenntnis der plat. Schriften*, Cleve 1885-1886, Progr.; Ueberweg-Praechter pp.
143-144*.
   [50] R. M. Jones, *The Platonism of Plutarch*, 1916; for Billings cf. *supra* n. 44.

NOTES TO CHAPTER II: PLATONISM IN ANTIQUITY—
NEO-PLATONISM

[1] *The Neo-Platonists*, 2d ed., Cambridge 1918.
[2] *Essays*, ed. by Hazlitt (1902), Vol. II p. 142.
[3] Cf. Loeb *Rep.* II pp. xxxviii, 58-59, 220-221, 223 ff.; *What Plato Said* pp. 81, 316, 463.
[4] *Additions to the Catalogue of Pictures*, 1810. *The Prophetic Writings of W. Blake*, ed. by D. J. Sloss and J. P. R. Wallis, Oxford 1926, Vol. II p. 173.
[5] *Adonais* LII 3-4.
[6] *Phaedrus* 247 C. Cf. *What Plato Said* p. 552.
[7] *The Greek Philosophers*, London 1882, Vol. II pp. 338-339.
[8] Cf. *What Plato Said* pp. 586-587.
[9] *Tim.* 42 E. Cf. *supra* p. 13.
[10] Cf. Loeb *Rep.* II pp. 511 ff.; *What Plato Said* p. 529.
[11] Cf. Zeller II 1⁴ pp. 74 ff.; Ueberweg-Praechter p. 59* with literature; *What Plato Said* pp. 456-457, 518, 662.
[12] Cf. Heinze, *Xenokrates* pp. 89 ff.; *What Plato Said* pp. 546-547.
[13] Cf. Loeb *Rep.* II p. xliv.
[14] *Novum organum* I 104.
[15] Cf. *What Plato Said* pp. 320, 607.
[16] *What Plato Said* pp. 206, 555-556.
[17] *Philos. d. Gr.* III 2⁴ pp. 520-687.
[18] *Of Atheism, in init.*
[19] Cf. Loeb *Rep.* II p. 64, I p. 339; *What Plato Said* pp. 467; 641, 647 on the question whether or not there is any superstition in Plato.
[20] Chap. IV of his *Five Stages of Greek Religion*, Oxford 1925.
[21] *Selections from Berkeley*, by A. C. Fraser, Oxford 1891, p. 285.
[22] *Christian Morals* III 2.
[23] 42 E. Cf. Zeller III 2⁴ pp. 551-552; *What Plato Said* p. 615.
[24] *Paradiso* 29. 142-145:

> e la larghezza
> de l'etterno valor, poscia che tanti
> speculi fatti s'ha in che si spezza,
> uno manendo in sè come davanti.

[25] New York 1916, p. 211.
[26] §§ 4-5 ed. Ruelle.
[27] *Essay on Man*, Epistle II 26.
[28] *Science and the Modern World* (Lowell Lectures 1925), New York 1926, p. 102.
[29] *Enn.* V. 1. 2, Vol. IV pp. 2-3.
[30] *Enn.* V. 3. 17, Vol. IV p. 43.
[31] *Sprüche in Reimen*, in *Zahme Xenien* III. Cf. Loeb *Rep.* II p. 101.
[32] *The Dark Angel: Poetical Works of Lionel Johnson*, London 1917, p. 79.
[33] *Infra* p. 170.

Notes to Chapter III: Plato and Christianity

[1] Cf. e.g. Ed. Caird, *The Evolution of Theology in the Greek Philosophers*, Glasgow 1903; Fr. Ch. Bauer, *Drei Abhandlungen zur Gesch. d. alten Philosophie und ihr Verhältniss zum Christentum*, neu hrsg. von E. Zeller, Leipzig 1876; A. Neander, *Wiss. Abhandlungen*, hrsg. von J. L. Jacobi, Berlin 1851, pp. 169 ff.; E. de Faye, *Clément d'Aléxandrie: Etude sur les rapports du christianisme et de la philosophie grecque au IIᵉ siècle*, 2ᵉ éd., Paris 1906 (*Biblioth. de l'Ecole des Hautes Etudes, Sciences relig.* Vol. XII); K. Krogh-Tonning, *Essays*, I: *Plato als Vorläufer des Christentums*, Kempten, 1906.

[2] *Aratra Pentelici* §107.

[3] Inge, *Christian Ethics* p. 409; *What Plato Said* p. 459.

[4] Cf. the analysis of the dialogue in *What Plato Said* pp. 74-80 with the notes on pp. 456-460.

[5] Cf. St. Augustine, *De civ. dei* II 7: omnes enim cultores talium deorum . . . magis intuentur quid Juppiter fecerit quam quid docuerit Plato vel sensuerit Cato. Loeb *Rep.* I pp. 180, 182; *What Plato Said* pp. 218-219, 561.

[6] 364 B ff. Loeb *Rep.* I pp. 132 ff. Plato's words on this topic are a startling anticipation of Luther's denunciation of Tetzel's sale of indulgences. Cf. *Luthers sämtliche Schriften*, ed. by J. G. Walch, 18 (1746) pp. 254 ff.; A. C. McGiffert, *Martin Luther, the Man and His Work*, New York 1914, pp. 76 ff.; James MacKinnon, *Luther and the Reformation*, London 1928, Vol. II pp. 1-36.

[7] 612 B ff. Loeb *Rep.* II lxiv, 484 ff.

[8] *Div. inst.* VII 8: unum est igitur summum bonum, immortalitas.

[9] Cf. e.g. Lactantius *Div. inst.* VII 8 ff.; Ueberweg-Geyer pp. 58-59; H. Doergens, "Eusebius von Cäsarea als Darsteller der gr. Religion," *Forschungen z. christl. Lit. und Dogmengesch.* 14 (1927) Heft 3 pp. 46 ff.

[10] Tayler Lewis, *Plato contra Atheos*, New York 1845.

[11] Oxford 1915.

[12] Cf. his *Mysticism and Logic*, London 1918, p. 1 ff.

[13] This anticipates the medieval heresy that hell is not a place but a state of mind.

[14] Cf. *What Plato Said* p. 645 on *Laws* 913 A.

[15] Cf. Luthardt, *Die antike Ethik* p. 19; Adam's note on *Rep.* 331 E; Loeb *Rep.* I p. 25; *What Plato Said* p. 468.

[16] *The Works of Walter Bagehot*, ed. by F. Morgan, Hartford 1891, Vol. I p. 106.

[17] *Œuvres complètes* de J. J. Rousseau, Paris 1883, Vol. II p. 597 (*Émile*).

[18] Cf. e.g. Euseb. *Praep. ev.* 11, 10, 14; 12, 12; 13, 12, 1 ff.; *Cl. Alex. Strom.* 1, 22, 150, etc.; Renan, *Histoire du peuple d'Israël* Vol. IV p. 248; Ueberweg-Praechter pp. 520, 571, 576-577, 643; Ueberweg-Geyer pp. 103-104.

[19] *Apolog.* I 44. Cf. Loeb *Rep.* II p. 507; *What Plato Said* pp. 578, 644-645, on freedom of the will.

[20] Cf. also Lact. *Div. inst.* I 8. 1; *De ira* II 11; Tertull. *Apol.* 46; Orig. *Adv. Cels.* VII 42; A. Kurfess, "Lactantius und Plato," *Philol.* 78 (1923) 383; John E. B. Mayor, ed. of Tertullian's *Apologeticus*, Cambridge 1917, pp. 440-441; Th. H. Billings, *The Platonism of Philo Judeaus* p. 19 n. 6.

[21] Cf. Zeller II 1⁴ p. 416 n. 2; Loeb *Rep.* II p. 411; *What Plato Said* pp. 29, 449.

[22] Cf. Loeb *Rep.* II pp. 414-415.

[23] Cf. *supra* p. 26.

[24] For λόγος in Greek philosophy and theology cf. Leisegang in Pauly-Wissowa 13 (1927) 1047-1081; A. Aall, *Gesch. d. Logosidee in d. gr. Philosophie*, Leipzig 1896; J. Reville, *La Doctrine de Logos dans le quatrième évangile et dans les œuvres de Philon*, Paris 1881; E. Sachsse, "Die Logosidee bei Philon und bei Johannes," *Neue kirchl. Zeitschr.* 15 (1904) 47-67; L. Cohn, "Zur Lehre von Logos bei Philon," in *Judaica*, Festschr. zu H. Cohens 70 Geb., Berlin 1912, pp. 303-333; Ch. Bigg, *The Christian Platonists of Alexandria*, Oxford 1913, pp. 40 ff., 89 f.; Billings, *The*

Platonism of Philo Judaeus pp. 39 ff. Cf. further Zeller III 2⁴ pp. 417 ff.; Ueberweg-Praechter pp. 182-183*; Ueberweg-Geyer pp. 8 ff. and lit. on pp. 642, 646-647,
650.—On the doctrine of trinity cf. Cudworth, *The True Intell. System of the Universe*, Vol. I, London 1845, pp. xlii-xliv, 41 ff., Vol. II pp. 74-75, 76, 427-428, etc.;
C. C. Webb, *Studies in the History of Natural Theology*, Oxford 1925, pp. 223-225;
A. Stockl, *Gesch. d. Philos. des Mittelalters*, I, Mainz 1864, pp. 247 ff.; Bigg, *op. cit.*
pp. 295-296.

[25] *Epist.* II p. 312 E. Cf. the notes of Novotny pp. 74-79, 136-140; Apelt p.
115; Howald pp. 186-187; Souilhé pp. lxxvii-lxxix; Bigg, *The Christ. Platonists of
Alex.* p. 296 n. 1; *What Plato Said* pp. 46-47. This passage is often quoted by the
Fathers. Cf. Athenagoras *Suppl.* 23; Justin Martyr *Apol.* I 60; Cl. Alex. *Strom.*
5. 14 §104; Euseb. *Praep. ev.* 11. 20 etc.; Fr. Ast, *Platons Leben und Schriften*, Leipzig 1816, p. 510.

[26] Cf. *Rep.* 503 AB, 538 D; *Prot.* 361 AB; *Phaedo* 76 E, 88 E, 89 BC, etc. Loeb
Rep. II 79; *What Plato Said* p. 500.

[27] *The Dialogues of Plato*, 2d ed., Oxford 1875, Vol. III p. 569.

[28] Cf. E. de Faye, *Origène, sa vie, son œuvre, sa pensée* II (Paris 1923) pp. 138 ff.,
162 ff.; Anna Miura-Stange, "Celsus und Origenes: das gemeinsame ihrer Weltanschauung," *Beih. z. Zeitschr. f. d. neut. Wiss. und die Kunde d. älteren Kirche*, hrsg.
von Dr. Hans Lietzmann, Beiheft 4 (Giessen 1926); Ueberweg-Geyer p. 658 (lit.).

[29] Cf. Tertull. *De carne Christi* V 2: certum est quia impossibile est, often
quoted simply as: credo quia impossibile; St. Aug. *Conf.* VI 5 (7): modestius ibi
minimeque sentiebam juberi ut crederetur quod non demonstrabatur ... et postea
tam multa fabulissima et absurdissima, qui demonstrari non poterant, credenda
imperari. This is regularly quoted under the form: credo quia absurdum (est).

[30] Ernest Havet, *Le Christianisme et ses origines*, Paris 1872-1884.

[31] Cf. e.g. Athanasius *Contra gentes* 9; Euseb. *Praep. ev.* XIII. 13. 66; Loeb *Rep.*
I pp. 2-3.

[32] Gregory *Epist.* lib. XI ep. liv *apud* Hauréau, *Histoire de la philosophie scolastique* Vol. I p. 4.

[33] Saint-Ouen, *apud* Hauréau, *op. cit.* I p. 19.

[34] Ernaud, abbé de Bonneval, *apud* Hauréau, *op. cit.* I p. 486.

[35] Pascasius Radbertus, the Mystic, in Matth. lib. VI, *apud* Hauréau, *op. cit.*
I p. 505.

[36] Adam, abbé de Perseigne, *apud* Hauréau, *op. cit.* I pp. 519-520.

[37] *Apud* Hauréau, *op. cit.* I pp. 516-517.

[38] *The Decline and Fall of the Roman Empire* (1902), Vol. VII p. 114.

[39] *Georgii Monachi Chronicon* (Teubner) pp. 83-84.

[40] *Rep.* 493 E-494 A.

[41] Migne (St. Augustine) I p. 747; cf. *Conf.* VII 21 (p. 142. 1 ed. Knöll).

[42] *Inst.* III 25.

[43] *Apol.* II 10.

[1] *Speculum* I (1926) 3.

[2] *Harvard Studies* 28 (1917) p. 81 n. 8.

[3] *Sancti Thomae Aquinatis in metaphysicum Aristotelis commentaria*, cura e studio p. fr. M.-R. Cathala . . . cum tabula analytica p. fr. Chrys. Egan. . . . 2d ed., Taurini 1926.

[4] London 1913.

[5] *Die philos. Mystik d. Mittelalters von ihren antiken Ursprüngen bis zur Renaissance*, München 1922.

[6] *L'Eresia nel Medio Evo*, Firenze 1884.

[7] *Religio Medici* I §10, *Works*, ed. by Wilkin, Vol. II p. 333.

[8] *The Complete Works of R. W. Emerson*, Boston 1903, Vol. III p. 34.

[9] *A Memoir of R. W. Emerson*, by James E. Cabot, Boston 1888, Vol. II pp. 623-624.

[10] Cf. *What Plato Said* pp. 537, 592; Loeb *Rep.* II pp. xxvii, 200.

[11] Cf. *supra* pp. 45 ff.

[12] *Vita Plotini* 23.

[13] The correct form of the name is Eriugena (from Celtic (h)*eriu* = Erin = Ireland). He is never called Erigena. Cf. Ueberweg-Geyer pp. 167, 693.

[14] Cf. Ueberweg-Geyer pp. 164 ff., with the literature on pp. 693 ff.

[15] Cf. *supra* p. 54.

[16] On the question of universals in the Middle Ages cf. Ueberweg-Geyer pp. 205 ff., with the literature on pp. 701 ff.

[17] *Commentaria in Aristotelem graeca* Vol. IV Part I p. 1 ed. Busse. Cf. Hauréau, *op. cit.* I pp. 47-48.

[18] Cf. Hauréau, *op. cit.* I p. 120.

[19] Cf. John of Salisbury quoted *apud* Hauréau, *op. cit.* I p. 52-53.

[20] Cf. Hauréau, *op. cit.* I pp. 243 ff.

[21] Cf. Hauréau, *op. cit.* I pp. 320 ff.

[22] On this question cf. Zeller II 1[4] p. 664; Ueberweg-Praechter pp. 262 ff.; Loeb *Rep.* II xxi; *What Plato Said* p. 585.

[23] Cf. Zeller II 1[4] p. 664 n. 5; Loeb *Rep.* II xx.

[24] *Dictionnaire philosophique, s. v.* Sophiste; Hauréau, *op. cit.* I 85.

[25] *Duns Scotus*, 2 vols., Oxford 1927, Vol. I p. 145.

[26] *The Mediaeval Mind*, London 1911, Vol. II p. 157 n. 1.

[27] *Illustrations of the History of Mediaeval Thought*, 2d ed., London 1920, p. 120.

[28] Cf. J. Gattifossé and Cl. Roux, *Bibliographie de l'Atlantide*, Lyons 1926; A. Bessmertny, *Das Atlantisrätsel: Gesch. und Erklärung der Atlantishypothesen*, Leipzig 1932; *What Plato Said* p. 620.

[29] For a list of ancient commentaries on the *Timaeus* cf. Fabricius, *Bibl. Gr.* III[4] pp. 95 ff.; Martin, *Etudes sur le Timée de Platon*, Vol. II (Paris 1841) pp. 395 ff.; H. Krause, *Studia Neoplatonica*, Leipzig 1904, pp. 46 ff.

[30] *Class. Phil.* 23 (1928) 343-362.

[31] Cf. B. W. Switalski, *Des Chalcidius Kommentar zu Platos Timäus (Beiträge z. Gesch. d. Philos. d. Mittelalters*, hrsg. v. Baeumker und v. Hertling, III 6, München 1902).

[32] On the whole question of the knowledge of Aristotle's works in the Middle Ages cf. Ueberweg-Geyer pp. 343 ff.

[33] Cl. Baeumker, *Der Platonismus im Mittelalter*, München 1916, p. 37 n. 17.

[34] *The Hexaemeral Literature*. Univ. of Chicago diss. 1912.

[35] Not to be identified, as is often done, with Bernard of Chartres. Cf. Manitius, *Gesch. d. lat. Lit. des Mittelalters*, III p. 205; Sandys, *Hermathena* 12. 434 f.

[36] Cf. Loeb *Rep.* II p. 101.

[37] Cf. Ueberweg-Geyer pp. 236-237, 704.

[38] Manitius, *op. cit.* II p. 581.

[39] *The Mediaeval Mind*, Vol. II p. 377.
[40] *Travels of Anacharsis the Younger in Greece, During the Middle of the Fourth Century Before the Christian Era*, by the abbé Barthélemy, trans. from the French, London 1806, Vol. V pp. 40 ff.
[41] Cf. *Platonism and French Literature* p. 25.
[42] *Works and Days: The Complete Works of R. W. Emerson*, Boston and New York 1904, Vol. VII, pp. 169-170.
[43] *Am. Jour. Philol.* 9 (1888) 395-418.
[44] *Proc. Am. Philos. Soc.* 66 (1927) 159-182; cf. *supra* p. 17 (*vide* n. 35, p. 240).
[45] H. Alline, *Histoire du texte de Platon*, Paris 1915, p. 206.
[46] Alline, *op. cit.* pp. 247, 276 ff., 262.
[47] Alline, *op. cit.* pp. 283-284.
[48] Cf. Sandys, *A History of Classical Scholarship*, II pp. 60-61; Symonds, *The Revival of Learning* p. 248.

[1] Cf. J. A. Symonds, *Revival of Learning*, New York 1881, pp. 198 ff.; J. W. Taylor, *Georgius Gemistus Pletho's Criticism of Plato and Aristotle*, Univ. of Chicago diss. 1921.; Schultze, *Die Philosophie der Renaissance* Vol. I: *Georgios Gemistos Plethon und seine reformatorische Bestrebungen*, Jena 1874; Krumbacher, *Gesch. d. byz. Lit.*[2] p. 429 with literature.

[2] Cf. in general: *The Cambridge Mediaeval History*, Vol. I (1902): P. Monnier, *Le Quattrocento: Essai sur l'histoire littéraire du XVe siècle italien*, nouv. éd., Paris 1920; A. A. Tilley, *Studies in the French Renaissance*, Cambridge 1922; F. J. C. Hearnshaw, *The Social and Political Ideas of Some Great Thinkers of the Renaissance and Reformation*, London, 1923.

[3] Arnaldo Della Torre, *Storia dell'Accademia Platonica di Firenze*, Firenze 1902.

[4] *Critical, Historical and Miscellaneous Essays*, New York 1866, Vol I p. 279.

[5] Cf. my *Platonism and the History of Science*, referred to *supra* pp. 17 (*vide* n. 35, p. 240) and 109.

[6] *Ion* 533 D. Cf. *What Plato Said* pp. 475-476.

[7] *De christiana religione*, ch. xxii.

[8] It was translated for the first time from the Greek by William of Moerbeke in 1260. Cf. Ueberweg-Geyer p. 348.

[9] Cf. Loeb *Rep.* I p. 452-453.

[10] Sandys, *A History of Classical Scholarship*, Vol. II pp. 70, 221.

[11] *Rep.* 505 A ff.; 539 E-540 A. Cf. Loeb *Rep.* II xxiii ff.

[12] Cf. e.g. W. Münch, *Gedanken über Fürstenerziehung aus alter und neuer Zeit*, München 1909; L. K. Born, "The Perfect Prince: A Study in Thirteenth- and Fourteenth-century Ideals," *Speculum* 3 (1928) 470-504.

[13] Cf. p. 58 above, p. 210 below.

[14] Thomas Stanley, *The History of Philosophy*, London 1655-1656, Fifth Part pp. 94 ff.

[15] J. S. Harrison, *Platonism in English Poetry of the Sixteenth and Seventeenth Centuries*, New York 1903.

[16] *Vita Plotini* 15.

[17] Cf. *infra* pp. 169-170.

[18] Cf. G. E. Howes, "Homeric Quotations in Plato and Aristotle," *Harvard Studies* 6 (1895) 153-237; Loeb *Rep.* II lxiii; *What Plato Said* pp. 7-9.

[19] *Rep.* 607 CD. Cf. Loeb *Rep.* II lxiii, 466-467.

[20] *Faerie Queene* II xii. 744 ff. Cf. Loeb *Rep.* II lxiii-lxiv.

[21] Cf. e.g. Tertullian, *Ad. nat.* II 7; St. Augustine, *De civ. dei* II 14; Min. Felix *Oct.* 22; Loeb *Rep.* II 419.

[22] *Laws* 829 DE. Cf. *What Plato Said* p. 639.

[23] Cf. *Class. Phil.* 3 (1908) 461-462; *The Nation* 90 (1910) 319; Loeb *Rep.* II lxiii.

[24] *The Complete Works of William Hazlitt*, ed. by P. P. Howe, London 1930, Vol. IV pp. 123-124.

[25] XVII. 3, p. 211. 3-4 ed. Hobein.

[26] *The Defense of Poesy*, ed. by A. S. Cook, Boston 1890, pp. 40, 43.

[27] *The Prose Works of John Milton*, ed. by J. A. St. John, London 1890, Vol. II p. 72.

[1] *Le rime di Michelangelo Buonarroti*, ed. by C. Guasti, Firenze 1863, No. LXXXI p. 250 (in Piccoli's edition, Torino 1930, No. CCXXXIX p. 175).

[2] Cf. Alexis *frg.* 70 (Kock II 320) quoted in *What Plato Said* p. 544.

[3] Vol. I p. 260, ed. Ch. Marty-Laveaux, Paris 1866.

[4] Cf. my note in *Modern Philology*, 19 (1921) 221-222.

[5] *Essays*, ed. by Hazlitt (1892), Vol. II p. 348.

[6] Quoted by J. Texte, *Etudes de littérature européenne*, Paris 1898, p. 45.

[7] *Op. cit.* pp. 46 ff.

[8] London 1923, p. 245.

[9] 376 A. Cf. Loeb *Rep.* I pp. 172-173.

[10] *Rep.* 462 C. Cf. Loeb *Rep.* I pp. 470-471.

[11] Montaigne tells us repeatedly that his knowledge of Greek is deficient. Cf. *Essays* I 203, II 231 (ed. Hazlitt, 1902).

[12] *Essays* II 620, 621 (ed. Hazlitt, 1892).

[13] Pellisson et d'Olivet, *Histoire de l'Académie Française*, Paris 1858, Vol. II p. 306.

[14] *Œuvres de J. de la Fontaine*, ed. by Henri de Regnier, Paris 1892, Vol. 9 p. 186.

[15] 254 A. Cf. *What Plato Said* p. 551.

[16] *Parallèle des Anciens et des Modernes*, par M. Perrault, 2e éd., Paris 1692, Tome 1er, p. 2 of Appendix.

[17] 474 D.

[18] *Pensées*, Art. VI, 52.

[19] *Letter to Guillaume Guizot*, June 7, 1854.

[20] *Œuvres complètes de Bossuet*, Nancy 1862, Vol. I p. 603.

[21] *Pensées diverses*, in *Œuvres complètes de Montesquieu*, Paris 1883, p. 626.

[22] *Historia critica philosophiae*, 4 vols., Lipsiae 1742-1744; 2d ed., 6 vols., 1766-1767. Cf. the English translation by William Enfield, Dublin 1792, especially I pp. 232-233, 248-249, 249-251 on Plato.

[23] Arthur Brisbane, in the *San Francisco Examiner*, November 9, 1928.

[24] *De l'esprit des lois*, IV 7.

[25] Vol. 16 pp. 312-337 (*Œuvres complètes de Diderot*, Paris 1876).

[26] *Ibid.* p. 315.

[27] *Ibid.* p. 316.

[28] Cf. p. 126 above.

[29] *Rep.* 340 D and *Emile* I. Cf. Loeb *Rep.* I p. 55.

[30] *Dictionnaire philosophique*, *s. v.* Aristote.

[31] Paris 1928, p. 345.

[32] Cf. *Discours de combat, Première série*, Paris 1904, p. 262; *Dernière série*, Paris 1907, p. 125.

[33] *Essays on Criticism*, New York 1883, p. 294.

[34] *Pensées*, Paris 1922, p. 344.

[35] Cf. *supra* p. 108.

[36] André Chénier, *Œuvres poétiques*, ed. by Louis Moland, Paris 1883, Vol. II p. 79.

[37] *Œuvres de Baudelaire*, ed. by Y.-G. Le Dantec, Paris 1931, p. 169: *Les Epaves*, X, Hymne.

[38] Cf. Joseph Vianey, "Les Sources italiennes de l'Olive," *Annales internationales d'histoire*, 1900; R. V. Merrill, *The Platonism of Joachim du Bellay*, Univ. of Chicago diss. 1923, pp. 49-50.

[39] *Œuvres françoises de Joachim du Bellay*, ed. by Marty-Laveaux, Paris 1866, Vol. I p. 137, No. CXII.

[40] *De l'esprit des lois*, I 1.

[41] Lettre à George Sand. *Correspondance, Quatrième série*, Paris 1899, p. 227.

[42] Lettre à Mlle Leroyer de Chanterie. *Corresp.*, 3e *sér.*, Paris 1903, p. 80.

[43] *Discours académiques*, 2e éd., Paris 1901, p. 62. He quotes the same sonnet in his *Discours de combat, Première série*, Paris 1904, p. 56.

[1] Ralph Stob, *Platonism in English Educators and Theologians: Educators of the 16th and Theologians of the 16th and 17th Centuries*, Univ. of Chicago diss. 1930.

[2] Cf. *supra* p. 147.

[3] *Canon's Yeoman's Tale* 1452 ff., quoted *supra* pp. 123-124.

[4] *The Love of Books: The Philobiblon of Richard de Bury*, newly translated into English by C. E. Thomas, London 1913.

[5] *Platonismus in der englischen Renaissance vor und bei Lyly nebst Neudruck von Sir Thomas Eliots "Disputicion Platonike" of that knowledge whiche maketh a wise man 1533*, Berlin 1920.

[6] Cf. *supra* p. 129.

[7] Cf. especially R. W. Lee in the *Philological Quarterly* 7 (1928) 65-77 and F. I. Carpenter, *A Reference Guide to Edmund Spenser*, Chicago 1923, pp. 184 ff., for additional literature on the hymns.

[8] J. C. Collins, *Greek Influence on English Poetry*, London 1910.

[9] *What Plato Said* p. 438.

[10] *Novum organum* I 104.

[11] H. Agar, *Milton and Plato*, Princeton 1928; R. B. Levinson, "Milton and Plato," *Mod. Lang. Notes* 46 (1931) 85-91.

[12] Cf. *supra* p. 143.

[13] *The Prose Works of John Milton*, ed. by J. A. St. John.

[14] Cf. the True Guardians in Plato's *Republic* 421 A.

[15] *Of Reformation in England*, II *in init.*; cf. *Gorgias* 507 and 521; *What Plato Said* p. 510.

[16] Cf. Plato, *Rep.* 423 A-B; 551 D; Loeb *Rep.* II 265.

[17] *The Reason of Church Government* II 3; cf. *Euthyphro* 12 B.

[18] *The Doctrine and Discipline of Divorce* I ch. 4.

[19] Ed. of 1868.

[20] 435 E; 436 A; cf. Loeb *Rep.* I 379-80; *What Plato Said* p. 563.

[21] 61 C; cf. *What Plato Said* p. 525.

[22] 474 D; Loeb *Rep.* I 512-513.

[23] *Urn Burial* 3; cf. Loeb *Rep.* II 492.

[24] Cf. my review of Stewart's *Myths of Plato*, in the *Journal of Philosophy* 3 (1906) 495-498; Loeb *Rep.* II 336-337.

[25] Cf. *supra* p. 54; Loeb *Rep.* II 107.

[26] *Appreciations*, London 1915, p. 146.

[27] *Ibid.*

[28] Cf. pp. 51 ff.: La descendance de Montaigne—Sir Thomas Browne.

[29] Ueberweg-Kohler-Moog, p. 662.

[30] F. J. Powicke, *The Cambridge Platonists: A Study*, London and Toronto 1926.

[31] Joh. Laur. Mosheim, *Systema intellectuale huius universi*, mit Anmerkungen, Zusätzen und einer Biographie Cudworths versehen, Jena 1733.

[32] Kurt Jos. Schmitz, *Cudworth und der Platonismus*, Giessen diss. 1919; H. V. Stein, *Sieben Bücher zur Gesch. d. Platonismus*, III 160 ff.

[33] *The Whole Works of the Right Rev. Jeremy Taylor*, ed. by the Right Rev. Reginald Heber, London 1864, Vol. III p. 95.

[34] *Holy Living*, Vol. III pp. 69-70.

[35] *Works*, London 1687, p. 338, quoted by J. B. Fletcher, *The Religion of Beauty in Women*, New York 1911, p. 189 n. 1.

[36] *The Poems of John Donne*, ed. by J. Russell Lowell, New York 1895, Vol. II p. 18.

[37] *The World* 1 ff., *The Works of Henry Vaughan*, ed. by L. C. Martin, Vol. II p. 466.

[38] *Of Solitude*, Abraham Cowley, *The Essays and Other Prose Writings*, ed. by A. B. Gough, Oxford 1915, p. 135.

[39] John Dewey, *Leibniz's New Essays Concerning the Human Understanding*, Chicago 1888.

[40] Bohn's ed., Vol. I p. 137.

[41] *An Essay Concerning Human Understanding*, II. xix. 1.

[42] *A History of Modern Philosophy*, London 1935, Vol. II p. 384.

[43] Cf. *The Moralists: A Rhapsody*, Sect. II; *Characteristics*, Birmingham 1773, Vol. II pp. 400 ff.

[44] London 1744.

[45] *Imitations of Horace, Sat.* I 85-86.

[46] Cf. *supra* pp. 58, 133.

[47] Miss Grace Harriet Macurdy's paper on "The Classical Element in Gray's Poetry," *Classical Weekly* 4 (1910) 58 ff., does not mention Plato's name.

[48] *Plato*, ed. Hermann, IV p. 407.

[49] Cf. *The Fable of the Bees or Private Vices, Publick Benefits*, ed. by F. B. Kaye, Clarendon Press 1924, I p. 333: "That boasted middle way and the calm Virtues recommended in the Characteristicks, are good for nothing but to breed Drones, and might qualify a Man for the stupid Enjoyments of a Monastick Life."

[50] *Ibid.* p. 198: "Honour in its Figurative Sense is a Chimera without Truth or Being, an Invention of Moralists and Politicians, and signifies a certain Principle of Virtue not related to Religion, found in some Men that keeps 'em close to their Duty and Engagements whatever they be."

[51] *Ibid.* p. 343: "What I have endeavour'd hitherto, has been to prove, that the *pulchrum et honestum*, Excellency and real worth of things are most commonly precarious and alterable as Modes and Customs vary."

[52] Cf. Kaye, p. 105 n. 1: "Mandeville several times apologizes for the *lowness* of his similes...." Cf. *Fable* I 354 and II 322.

[53] *Phaedo* 113 D; cf. *What Plato Said* p. 536.

[54] *The Works of Edmund Burke*, Bohn's ed., Vol. III p. 116.

[55] Cf. *Gorg.* 508 A-B; *Rep.* 558 C; *Laws* 757 A-D; 848 B; cf. Loeb *Rep.* II 291; *What Plato Said* p. 634; 508.

[56] *Rep.* 546 B; Loeb *Rep.* II xliv.

[57] J. Morely, *Burke*, in *English Men of Letters*, p. 15.

[58] Joseph-Marie Degérando (1772-1842), *Histoire comparée des systèmes de philosophie relativement aux principes des connaissances humaines*, 3e éd., Paris 1804.

[59] *Ap.* G. S. Gordon, *English Literature and the Classics*, Oxford 1912, pp. 25-48.

[60] 401 A-D.

[61] *The Works of Henry Vaughan*, ed. by L. C. Martin, Oxford 1914, Vol. II p. 419.

[62] 563 C-E; cf. Loeb *Rep.* II 310-311.

[63] *Culture and Anarchy*, New York 1906, pp. 50-51.

[64] *Ibid.* 54-55; cf. Loeb *Rep.* II 254.

[65] Cf. *Rep.* 454 C.

[66] J. Morley, *Critical Miscellanies*, London 1923, pp. 48-49.

[67] *The Works of John Ruskin*, ed. by E. T. Cook and Alexander Wedderburn, 39 vols., London 1903-1912.

[68] London 1905, pp. 33, quoted in Loeb *Rep.* I xl-xli.

[69] 359 E, 360 A (ring of Gyges).

[70] *Poetical Works of Lionel Johnson*, London and New York 1917, p. 8.

INDEX

INDEX

A

Abélard, 10, 85, 98, 102, 209
Absolution, 103, 213
Abstractions, 40, 41, 43, 45, 59, 133, 217, 255
Academy, Platonic, 1, 5, 9, 12, 74
Addams, Jane, 55, 102
Aeschylus, 35, 71, 88, 139, 196
Aesculapius, 80
Agathias Asianus, 66
Akenside, 211 f.
Albertus Magnus, 101, 102
Alcibiades, 90, 151, 174, 190
Anacreon, 160, 209
Anderson, Sherwood, 57, 59
Apology, 21, 24, 103, 154
Apuleius, 89, 119, 120, 191
Aristides, 80, 233
Aristophanes, 1, 139, 151, 190, 194
Aristotelianism, 19, 85, 119
Aristotelians, various quarrels between, and Platonists, 84, 96, 115, 149
Aristotle, 2, 7, 8, 20, 26, 27, 36, 37, 39, 41, 45, 55, 70, 82, 84, 85, 86, 89, 90, 91, 93, 98, 100, 103, 104, 105, 109, 115, 117, 121, 124, 125, 129, 139, 140, 156, 157, 160, 164, 176, 182, 194, 205, 228
Arnobius, 77
Arnold, Matthew, 12, 13, 16, 22, 35, 39, 43, 44, 54, 58, 70, 72, 123, 158, 162, 163, 165, 198, 207, 217, 221, 225, 227, 229, 230, 231
Ascham, 126, 133, 175, 177, 179
Atheism, 13, 65, 68, 69, 86
Athenaeus, 159, 193
Athenagoras, 77, 80, 81

B

Bacon, Francis, 125, 175, 182 f., 198, 201, 234
Bacon, Roger, 90
Bacon-Mill empiric philosophy, 205
Bagehot, 72

Barthélemy, abbé, 108, 166
Basil, 77, 124
Baudelaire, 129, 135, 169
Bayle, 156, 159, 213
Behaviorists, 17, 98, 99
Bembo, Cardinal, 148, 178
Benivieni, Girolamo, 134, 148
Benn, Alfred, 42-43
Bergson, 28, 37, 56
Berkeley, 54, 70, 175, 205, 207, 215, 219, 225
Bernardus Silvestris, 95, 106, 129
Blake, 41, 42, 223
Bodin, 78, 103, 125, 152, 160, 189, 205
Boethius, 24, 88, 89, 91, 97, 106, 111, 112, 119, 175, 176, 177, 209, 210
Boileau, 108, 154, 157, 168
Bossuet, 154, 158
Browne, Sir Thomas, 54, 92, 175, 192-198, 205
Browning, E. B., 141, 229
Browning, Robert, 141
Brucker, 159, 161
Brunetière, Ferdinand, 158, 165, 171
Bruno, Giordano, 30, 31, 93, 107, 111, 225, 226
Burke, 140, 175, 220-223
Burnet, 103, 235
Burton, 134, 151, 175, 188-192, 205
Byron, 134, 150, 167, 203
Byzantium, 83, 84, 114, 115, 116, 117

C

Callicles, 24, 72, 180, 214, 220
Calvin, 78, 137, 138
Cambridge Platonists, 44, 86, 123, 175, 198-215 *passim*
Campanella, 103, 125, 189
Carew, 134, 149
Castiglione, Baldassare, 131, 148
Catholic: Church, 75, 81, 84, 85; reaction, 86; Scholasticism, 102
Cato, 12, 195